THE SHERIFF

Gerry O'Carroll worked on over 80 murder cases in his 33 years in the force. His conviction rate is unprecedented and he has brought to justice some of Ireland's most brutal gangsters.

THE SHERIFF

A DETECTIVE'S STORY

GERRY O'CARROLL

MAINSTREAM
PUBLISHING

EDINBURGH AND LONDON

This edition, 2007

First published in Great Britain in 2006 by
MAINSTREAM PUBLISHING COMPANY
(EDINBURGH) LTD
7 Albany Street
Edinburgh EH1 3UG

ISBN 9781845962647

A catalogue record for this book is available
from the British Library

Typeset in Dirtyhouse and Ellington

Printed in Great Britain by
Cox and Wyman Ltd, Reading

This book is dedicated to the memory of my parents,
James and Mary Ellen O'Carroll, my sister, Gene, and my beautiful
niece, Louise. And to Kathleen's parents, John and Brigid Murphy.

ACKNOWLEDGEMENTS

A special thanks to Mick Sheridan, my friend, for his professional guidance and encouragement, and his insightful comments during the writing of this book.

I would like to express my heartfelt love and gratitude to my dear wife Kathleen, who has supported me in good times and bad down through the long years.

I want to thank my children – Conor, Margaret, Eleanor, Philip and Brian – for their love and understanding, with a special thanks to Margaret for her patience and advice, and the many hours she spent typing up my manuscript.

Thanks to my dear brother and best friend, Louis, whose own gift of ink was a source of great inspiration for me. To Jim O'Callaghan and Kieran O'Connor, who supported me through some tough times and whose professional help was greatly appreciated, and thanks to Anne and Dick Comerford. To Gerry Fanning, of Fanning and Kelly solicitors, Dublin, who has sadly passed away since the writing of this book, and Kieran Kelly, his partner, for their expert advice and invaluable opinions on all legal matters. I am also grateful to the McMahon family for allowing me to reproduce part of the ballad 'My Silver River Feale'.

I wish particularly to thank Deborah Warner, my editor, for her highly professional contribution and her tireless coaxing without which I would still be scribbling away at this book, and Graeme Blaikie, who was a great help. I would like thank my publishers, Bill Campbell and Peter Mackenzie, for their interest and support in this project.

Thanks to my old friend Paul Williams, who always believed there was a book in me and who first christened me 'The Sheriff' – the title of this book. I also wish to thank Stephen Rea, Mick McCaffrey, Cormac Looney, Ian Mallon and Tara McGinn of the *Evening Herald* for their friendship and help. And thanks to Mercier Press, my good neighbour and lifelong friend John Fitzmaurice and Billy Keane, family friend and bestselling author.

A special acknowledgment to my agent, mentor and close personal friend, Robert Kirby, and of course Connie and Maddie.

CONTENTS

PROLOGUE

MONDAY, 27 SEPTEMBER 1976 STARTED OUT AS A ROUTINE DAY IN THE
Central Detective Unit in Dublin. I was still on probation and had been
a little over a year in the detective branch. I paraded for duty at nine
o'clock and was briefed by the duty sergeant and Detective Inspector
Edward Ryan along with the rest of my team. The offices were situated
in a brand-new three-storey building, which we shared with the
Revenue Commissioners, and were adjacent to the Lower Yard of the
historic Dublin Castle.

For the previous two weeks, we had been targeting and carrying out
discreet surveillance on a well-organised south city crime gang. We
believed it was responsible for carrying out a series of armed robberies
on banks and post offices throughout the city. The gang consisted of a
wild bunch of dangerous criminals who were free and easy with the use
of firearms. During the briefing, we received our assignments for the day
and were also informed that two suspects had been arrested in Galway
city the night before in connection with the disappearance of two
women: Elizabeth Plunkett and Mary Duffy. A nationwide hunt had been
under way since 4 September for two Englishmen in connection with the
disappearance of Elizabeth from Brittas Bay in County Wicklow.

Sometime later that afternoon, I was recalled to the unit and told by DI Ryan that Detective Sergeant Pat Cleary and I were to travel immediately to Galway city to assist in the ongoing investigation there. It was after 6 p.m. when Pat and I arrived at Eglington Garda station close to O'Brien's Bridge near the centre of the town.

In the incident room, we were brought up to date with the progress of the investigation and details surrounding the arrest of John Shaw and Geoffrey Evans, the two suspects in custody. They had been arrested the previous night at 11 p.m. by local Gardaí who recognised the registration number of the car provided by a suspicious petrol-station owner. During the briefing, we were told of the dramatic attempted escape made by Shaw earlier that morning.

Shaw had awoken in his cell around half-nine and requested that the station orderly let him use another toilet, as the one in his cell was broken. When permission came back, two Gardaí escorted him to a toilet on the ground floor adjacent to the cells. Within seconds, Shaw had forced his way through the tiny toilet window and had landed in a small yard at the rear of the station.

The two men immediately raised the alarm and gave chase, followed by five or six other officers, out the back door of the station. By this stage, the prisoner had reached Daly's Place, a laneway off Eglington Street. He ran to Brendan's Terrace and into Wood Quay. He got about 200 yards before he was caught and recaptured by his pursuers. There was a brief but violent altercation after which Shaw was subdued and returned to his cell.

I remained in the incident room most of that night making myself familiar with the investigation files on both missing women. There was a stream of detectives coming and going to and from the incident room. I was introduced to Detective Inspectors Hubert Reynolds and John Courtney, who were heading up the inquiry. Following the discovery of shoes and other evidence at Castletimon Wood, near Brittas Bay, it was generally accepted by the team that Elizabeth Plunkett was dead.

All the detectives I spoke to were hoping against hope that the other missing woman, Mary Duffy, might still be alive and had been left at some remote location outside the town. This feeling added an air of urgency to the investigation. Teams of detectives had been interviewing the suspects since early morning in a desperate attempt to discover her whereabouts. At this stage, with every passing hour hopes for her safe return were diminishing. Despite the pressure, Shaw and Evans were giving nothing away.

I got so engrossed in this life-and-death activity that I completely forgot to find myself lodgings for the night. In any case, I found a comfortable old armchair where I could rest during the night. After a meal in a café beside the station, I decided to go for a walk to clear my head. I walked for a couple of miles outside the city past the Ballybrit Racecourse, the venue of the famous Galway Races. As the darkness enveloped me, I imagined a terrified Mary Duffy, tied up, helpless and alone in some abandoned shed or outhouse. And the only men that could lead us to her were asleep in warm, comfortable cells back in the station.

I decided there and then on the course of action I must take. I returned to the station at around three o'clock in the morning. All the detectives had gone home. A couple of uniformed guards were on duty in the public office. I spoke to the station orderly and asked him to take John Shaw from the cell upstairs to the billiard room for interview. I went upstairs to the room and Shaw arrived some minutes later. Before the station orderly left the room, I asked him to leave a Garda on duty outside the door, as I was extremely concerned that the prisoner might attempt another escape. I was also fully aware that my unorthodox action on the night would not be sanctioned or approved by my superiors. Technically, I was in breach of Garda regulations and legal procedures, but these concerns were far outweighed in my mind by my fears for the safety of Mary Duffy.

Shaw and I sat on the floor beside the wall well away from the windows. I introduced myself to him. He was surprised at being taken for interview at that ungodly hour. He looked the worse for wear after his failed bid for freedom the previous day. He was a strong, athletic, six-foot man with piercing dark eyes and a black beard – in any circumstance an intimidating presence. I told him that I was investigating the disappearance of Elizabeth Plunkett and Mary Duffy and that I was satisfied, beyond any doubt, that he and his partner, Geoffrey Evans, were involved. I quietly asked him to tell me the truth. He did not answer. He then placed his head in his hands.

I enquired about the disappearance of Mary Duffy. 'Is she still alive?' I asked.

Silence echoed through the room. There was no reply. I took a breath and slowly outlined to him my well-founded suspicions and the incontrovertible evidence that linked them to the disappearance of Elizabeth Plunkett.

'I had no involvement in anything to do with that,' he replied.

I was clearly getting nowhere, so decided to revert to a general conversation. I asked him about his family circumstances in England. Had he a wife and children? He responded in a friendly manner. 'I have a wife and children,' he replied.

I asked if he was a Roman Catholic and he replied that he was. I suggested to him that we were all innocent little boys one time. I asked him if he remembered his first communion. 'I bet you, John, that your mother was proud of you in your new outfit. Do you remember your confirmation?'

He said that he did and instantly a melancholic look came over his face. He appeared to be staring into the distance and fell silent.

'Do you know what we are going to do, John?' I said. 'We are going to say a little prayer together. Do you remember your prayers, the Hail Mary?'

'I do,' he said.

We began to recite the Hail Mary together. As we got to the second verse, he suddenly grabbed me by the arm and a look of abject terror and fear appeared on his face. His eyes were wild and transfixed. He pointed to the door.

'I see him! I see him!' he screamed.

I felt him clutching me, digging his fingernails into my forearm.

'It's the devil! The devil! He's coming for me,' Shaw roared, his voice echoing through the rafters of the room. His eyes were starting from his sockets as he roared. The door burst open as the Garda on duty rushed into the room.

'Everything is all right,' I said to him, waving him away.

I turned back to Shaw, who began to tremble violently and screamed out again, 'I see her! It's Mary Duffy!'

In that awful instant of hysterical revelation, I realised that Mary Duffy was dead. My heart sank.

'John, what now?' I said.

He continued to tremble. I attempted to comfort him in an effort to get him to calm down. After a brief pause, he uttered a phrase that still reverberates in my mind. 'I'll tell you everything.'

I now knew that I was in the presence of a serial killer.

1

THE HOMESTEAD

I WAS BORN ON 9 MAY 1946 IN THE FAMILY HOME IN CAHIRDOWN, Listowel, County Kerry. I was the fourth youngest of a family of eleven boys and four girls. Both of my parents, James and Mary Ellen (née Moloney), were born and reared in the town of Listowel, as were generations of O'Carrolls and Moloneys before them. As I write this story, 13 of my brothers and sisters are still in the land of the living. My father died in 1978, my mother in 1993, and my beloved sister, Gene, in 1997.

The little settlement in which I lived consisted of a terrace of four homes, one of which my family occupied, and was called the Soldiers' Houses. It had been built for ex-British soldiers who had been severely wounded in action during the First World War. A small limestone plaque embedded in the wall at the centre of the terrace proclaims: 'The Soldiers and Sailors Land Trust'. The houses are situated on the main Tarbert to Listowel road, about a mile from the town, and used to be surrounded on all sides mostly by small dairy farms. Directly in front of the houses and a quarter of a mile away was the main railway line to Limerick, which is sadly no longer in use. Further on, past the Black Wood, the lovely River Feale winds its way slowly down to the Cashen at Ballybunion, where it meets the sea.

Initially, the tenants were obliged to pay a small monthly stipend to the Land Trust. Over the years, as Shakespeare put it, it became 'more honoured in the breach than in the observance' until, eventually, all payments were withheld. Regular written reminders and threats of legal action against the defaulters fell on deaf ears. I remember those official brown envelopes, with 'On Her Majesty's Service' printed on them, being delivered to the house. After a cursory examination, my father would consign them to an old biscuit tin in the sideboard, along with all the other correspondence on that matter. For my father, it was a case of out of sight, out of mind.

From time to time, vague rumours would reach our ears that the Land Trust had been granted court orders to move against us to recover monies that were owed but, after a couple of anxious days and no sign of any such activity, those rumours were soon forgotten. However, on at least one occasion, I remember our neighbour, Pidge Walshe, rushing into our house, having run most of the way from the town, her face flushed and barely able to draw a breath with excitement as she announced that the sheriff and his bailiffs were on their way with warrants to seize our property. On receipt of this momentous report, our neighbours and ourselves were galvanised into a bout of frantic activity. Most of our meagre goods and chattels, which included everything that wasn't nailed down, were removed from the four houses. Tables and chairs, beds, pots and pans, and crockery and ornaments, even the donkey carts, were all thrown over the back railings into our neighbour's field until the place resembled a vast jumble sale. I remember being posted as a lookout along with the other children to raise the alert when we sighted the enemy approaching. It was at once a frightening and exciting time for us.

Eventually, as the hours passed without incident, we gave up our watch. When the crisis had ended, the relieved residents lugged all their belongings back into the houses and peace and calm reigned once more in our little commune.

Despite all the rumours and reports, the bailiffs never came to Cahirdown. I'm not sure even if they ever existed at all. Perhaps they were just phantoms – the figments of the overactive collective imagination of the residents of our settlement – yet the threat of those bailiffs, whether real or not, hung over my childhood like the sword of Damocles.

My father James served as a radio operator with the Royal Engineers in the Great War. He had been in action in France and later in Belgium, where he was severely wounded in Ypres in a mustard-gas attack. After recovering in a hospital in France, he was sent back to the front where he endured two more years of horror and slaughter before that bloody conflict came to an end. He was only a boy of seventeen when he left Listowel and was one of thousands of young Irishmen who answered John Redmond's call to enlist in the British Army. Redmond was a nationalist MP and an ardent supporter of Home Rule. He mistakenly believed that by encouraging local men to fight for King and country the British government would grant Ireland self-government as a reward for its service and sacrifice.

The clergy at the time preached that it was the moral duty of Irishmen to fight in defence of small Catholic nations, like Belgium, which were being trampled underfoot by the German war machine. Many years later, I discovered that this had been the motivation behind my father's decision to enlist. Other young Irishmen who were searching for adventure were influenced by the propaganda campaign spearheaded by Horatio Herbert Kitchener, himself a Listowel man, whose face peering out of that iconic poster with his finger pointed became a symbol of the conflict with the slogan 'Your Country Needs You!'

When the Irish returned from the battlefields of France and Belgium, they came home to a country changed for ever by the Easter Rebellion of 1916. They were regarded by the majority of people not as valiant heroes but as misguided fools who should have been standing shoulder to shoulder with the rebel leader Patrick Pearse and his comrades at the GPO instead of going to fight the Germans for the King's shilling. There were no monuments erected in the Irish Republic to honour the memory of the thousands of young Irishmen who never returned to the land of their fathers.

On the 50th anniversary of the 1916 Rising, the Taoiseach, Sean Lemass, who was one of our most progressive and enlightened politicians ever, stated at a public address regarding the involvement of our countrymen in the Great War: 'In later years, it was common – and I was also guilty in this respect – to question the motives of those Irishmen who joined the new British Army but it must, in their honour and in fairness to their memory, be said that they were motivated by the highest purpose.' One can only hope that the heroism and sacrifice of that lost generation of young Irishmen will one day receive the respect and recognition long denied them.

My father returned to Listowel in 1919 only to get embroiled again in the War of Independence and the subsequent Civil War. This tragedy for our nation came as a result of a treaty that General Michael Collins and other envoys of the fledgling Irish government signed in London with the British, in which they agreed to the partition of the island of Ireland, ceding six counties to remain under British rule. When they returned to Dublin, the government was split down the middle. Hardline Republicans, led by Eamon de Valera, repudiated the treaty and accused Collins and the other envoys of treachery. Former comrades in arms became mortal enemies and civil war broke out.

As in all internecine upheavals, it became a savage and pitiless conflict that tore towns, villages and communities apart, transcended family loyalties and pitted father against son and brother against brother. My grandmother often recounted that she had heard a prominent Republican leader at a public meeting outside the Listowel Arms Hotel state that he would make brother walk in brother's blood for his sacred cause. Terrible atrocities were committed on both sides. In Ballyseedy outside Tralee in our own County Kerry, nine Republican men were executed by landmine explosion as a reprisal for the massacre of Free State forces. The monument erected there in their memory is a stark and disturbing reminder of that shameful period in our nation's history.

It was on the morning of my father's funeral that I learned from an old family friend of an incident that occurred during the Civil War. My father was serving as a radio officer with the Free State forces in Dublin under General Michael Collins at this time. One night while on duty, he discovered the whereabouts of Oscar Traynor, a Republican on the Most Wanted list of the Free State forces. He decided not to pass on this information to his superiors, knowing that to do so would be signing Oscar's death warrant. When his actions were discovered, he narrowly escaped being court-martialled and possibly shot for what was seen as a gross neglect of duty. I don't think my father could have lived with that death on his conscience. After the Civil War ended, Oscar Traynor was elected to Dáil Éireann as a Fianna Fáil candidate in the New Ireland. He went on to become Minister for Justice in the late '50s.

My father's harrowing experiences in the trenches in France and Belgium, and his subsequent involvement in the fratricidal Civil War, left him a changed man. He became a committed pacifist who abhorred violence of any nature. I knew him only as a God-fearing, shy and deeply religious man, and as a gentle and loving father.

He was held in high esteem by all our neighbours, who regarded him as something of a scholar and depended on him to fill in their application forms and write their letters in dealings with various government departments. Although he was a self-educated man, he was a brilliant letter-writer who could cut through red tape and was always successful in organising pensions and grants for our neighbours.

Each house on the terrace had three upstairs bedrooms, while downstairs there was a kitchen and a small scullery. We had an outdoor washhouse and lavatory. There was no heating, electricity or running water, and we would warm ourselves by the cast-iron range in the kitchen that was used for cooking. Paraffin lamps and candles provided all our lighting needs. Barrels under the eaves collected water from the rain for washing and cleaning, and during dry spells we used a donkey and cart to ferry it in from the public fountain in nearby Ballygologue. We got our drinking water from a well about a quarter of a mile from our house.

The outside latrine was a primitive affair comprising a timber seat and a bucket as a receptacle, which was emptied into a hole in the ground and covered with earth. On dark winter's nights I was often called on to do sentry duty for my sisters with an old flash lamp when they had to answer a call of nature. I had to keep talking or singing to reassure them that I hadn't deserted my post. Indeed on these occasions I was a very reluctant soldier, as I shivered with cold and fear in the inky blackness.

Like most children of my generation in those far-off times, I believed that when the sun went down and darkness covered the earth, legions of evil demons were unleashed from the pits of hell to prowl the night.

Belief in this terrible scenario was reinforced at the end of every Sunday Mass when the priest, in a chilling plaintive prayer, called on the Almighty to protect us 'from all the wicked spirits who wander through the world for the ruin of souls'. However, when the electric light finally came to our locality, shining its cold penetrating rays into every nook, cranny and dark corner of our world, ghosts, goblins and demons vanished for ever, like the mists of a May morning never to return.

Some years later, my father installed an Elsan dry toilet system in the little privy, which was a modern wonder for us children. It also made us the envy of our neighbours.

As the North Kerry poet Bob Boland wrote in his 'Ode to a Lavatory':

> Thou art the throne room of soliloquy
> Where each lone patrol with no special art
> Relaxes for expulsion, setting free
> The unfettered waste and the unmuffled fart.

To our right lived Mickey Joe Walshe, his wife, Pidge, and their family. He was a great neighbour and a volatile character but with a heart of gold. Mickey Joe was also a veteran of the Great War, where he had received wounds to his legs that left him partially crippled. When his old war wounds played up, we would hear his wife play the button accordion to lift him out of his melancholic mood.

I was always fascinated by a large framed photograph that hung in his kitchen of him in uniform with hundreds of his comrades on the eve of the first Battle of the Somme, one of the bloodiest battles of the entire First World War. A priest on horseback, also in uniform with a purple stole around his neck and his hands upraised in blessing, is administering a general absolution to the kneeling troops before him in their full battle dress. Often, when I was playing in the house with his grandson, he would point to the picture with tears in his eyes and tell me how only a handful of the young soldiers had survived the ensuing slaughter. As a child, I was fascinated with the picture, though I had no real understanding of the sheer scale and horror of the conflict. Stories of the war had gripped my imagination and I could absorb the awful details as part of a story, a fable set far away from our shores. They had no real substance in a young boy's mind.

To our left were the houses of two other ex-servicemen's families: the Devereuxs and the Fitzmaurices. Next door lived Maggie Devereux, a widow, with her son John Pa and daughter Peggy. In the end house lived Nell Fitzmaurice, also a widow, with her daughter Kathleen and grandson John. They were all wonderful people – their characters cast from the stone of deprivation.

I used to run errands for Nell and buy her daily ration of snuff. Out of curiosity, I used to try a little pinch myself – a habit that remains with me to this day. I will always remember Nell for the many little kindnesses she showed me and my younger brothers, Louis and Philip, whom she loved as if they were her own. As I grew older, I came to realise the burden of pain and sorrow that this ever-cheerful little woman carried with such courage and fortitude. She had endured the agony of seeing almost all her children die before her eyes of the dreaded tuberculosis during an epidemic that killed thousands during the '40s and '50s.

Hardly a single family escaped the scourge of TB, sometimes called the White Death. It killed indiscriminately, taking the old and infirm as well as boys and girls in the prime of their youth. It spread fear, dread and paranoia throughout the land. Families known to have been affected by the disease were shunned and treated like pariahs by friends and neighbours. One of the most disturbing aspects of tuberculosis was that the sufferer looked in radiant good health before being cruelly struck down. Edenburn Sanitorium outside Tralee was often the last earthly destination for many poor victims. To this day, the name Edenburn evokes feelings of dread amongst the older generation in Kerry.

I have described my father as a shy, retiring man. My mother, on the other hand, was outgoing and gregarious. The matriarch of the family, she was a woman of immense presence and personality – a tower of strength who, despite the many vicissitudes life had visited upon her, always remained cheerful and optimistic. She was a great cook and housekeeper who, as one family friend commented, 'could make a dinner from an onion'. She ran the family budget – an almost impossible task on the wages my father earned – and scrimped and saved all her life, denying herself the least little luxury. Apart from a couple of trips to the most popular Kerry seaside resort of Ballybunion each summer, she had no respite from the unrelenting struggle of caring for such a large family. Despite the hardship and poverty of the times, my mother made sure we had clothes on our backs and shoes on our feet and we never went to bed hungry.

There were nine children living in the house when I was growing up. My mother and father slept with my two youngest brothers in the front bedroom and the three girls shared the smallest room at the back of the house. That left me and my three other brothers sharing two single beds in the remaining room. Due to the shoestring budget that my mother had at her disposal, mealtimes were a highly organised operation. Bread, butter, meat and potatoes were strictly rationed according to our needs. Second helpings were never on the menu, though the odd rasher or sausage was bartered among the boys on a Sunday – when we had our only fried breakfast of the week.

As we had no running water or bathroom, our daily ablutions were undertaken using an enamel basin of rainwater and a bar of carbolic soap. During the warm months of the summer, we would follow our mother like ducklings down to the River Feale and she would scrub us clean under the little waterfall. I still have treasured memories of those summer days playing in the water with my brothers and sisters. As a young boy, I fell under the spell of that magical river. The reverence and affection the people of Listowel have for the Feale is no less than the devout Hindu has for the Ganges. During the long summer holidays, I spent many happy and carefree days fishing along its mossy banks. I knew the secret places with names like the Plate, the Table and the Castle Stream where the shy brown trout lay hiding in dark deep pools. I knew the river in all its moods. In summer after a long, dry spell, it became a gentle stream where we swam and played. In winter when it was swollen by heavy rains and burst its banks, it became a raging torrent, dangerous and majestic. The great Listowel playwright and author Bryan McMahon in his beautiful ballad 'My Silver River Feale' sums up better than I could ever hope to the almost mythical appeal that it holds for the people of the town.

> For what are riches when the heart is aching
> And what is wealth when all your senses steal
> To linger for one moment in the gloaming
> Beside your banks, my silver River Feale.

I now realise that it was my mother's resilience and unflinching courage that kept our family going during those hard times. Some of the sacrifices she made during those years did not come without a price, yet throughout her long life she retained her dignity and a sense of humour. She was proud of every one of her fifteen children and I believe that her legacy all these years later is that we still remain a united and loyal family.

Little did I realise at the time how unique our little enclave was. It was only as I grew older that it began to occur to me that being a resident of the Soldiers' Houses carried with it a certain stigma. This was never conveyed openly but nonetheless manifested itself in the condescending attitudes of some of our better-off neighbours.

Every November eyebrows were raised when I set off along with the other children from the houses to sell poppies for the benefit of the Royal British Legion, a charity for ex-servicemen. This practice must have been anathema to many in the staunchly Republican heartland of North Kerry. In my innocence, I was blissfully unaware of such petty prejudices. The Soldiers' Houses formed the happy centre of my little universe. I was then and I am still immensely proud of men like my father and Mickey Joe Walshe, and all the other Irishmen who went off to fight in the Great War.

In that little terrace, I grew up among the kindest, most decent people, from whom I learned the meaning of real community spirit and Christian charity. Over the years, despite the inevitable arguments and minor squabbles, we retained a close and loyal friendship. In the Soldiers' Houses, we shared in one another's joys and sorrows, hopes and despairs, through good times and bad.

Many other colourful characters occupied the kingdom of my childhood, none more so than my good friend John O'Flaherty. He lived alone following the death of his brother in an old, dilapidated two-storey house about a hundred yards from our front door. When I first knew John, he was in his late 50s. He was a man of great intellect and enormous physical strength. He was a talented musician who played the concert flute and was also a brilliant mathematician. John was an intensely shy man who kept to himself and cultivated few friends. Initially, I was a little apprehensive of him, because of his secretive ways.

One day, I was on my way to the well when I met John on a similar mission. We struck up a conversation and by the time we returned home with our buckets of water we had become firm friends. I began calling in to see John on an almost daily basis whenever I was going to the well for our drinking water. As I got to know him better, he started to invite me into his house. Over the next few years, I began to realise what an extraordinary human being he was.

His house, as you might expect of an old bachelor, was a total shambles. Like ours, there was no heating, electricity or any form of sanitation. Yet on many a winter's evening with a blazing fire on the open hearth I listened enthralled as John played tune after tune, many of which he had composed himself. He showed me empty cement bags upon which he had worked out the most complex mathematical equations. He read books on Euclid and Aristotle and was an expert on Irish history. He wrote to professors of mathematics at Oxford and Cambridge universities in his immaculate copperplate hand, challenging them to solve complex problems. I read their replies and from their contents I realised they treated John as an equal and somewhat of an eccentric genius.

He was also a man of gargantuan appetite who could demolish an entire goose or turkey at a single sitting. He cooked for himself and baked his own bread, which he often served up to me in thick slices with my tea. He was a man who, throughout his life, showed little emotion. On one occasion, however, he confided in me his intense loneliness and sense of isolation, and his regrets for not having married and had a family of his own. In the bleak rural Ireland of those days it was often hard for men like John to find a partner in life. Opportunities for young people to meet up with one another in social settings were limited by the constraints imposed by the Catholic Church on such activities and also because of emigration.

Like John, many of the men and women who remained behind to till the land or look after ageing relatives were condemned to lives of quiet desperation. It was not uncommon to find five or more brothers and sisters living in the same tiny cottage into adulthood. One can only imagine in those claustrophobic conditions the sexual tensions and personality clashes, coupled with the mind-numbing boredom and frustration that made their lives a living hell. For many of these forgotten souls, the only contact with the outside world was the weekly excursion to Listowel for Sunday Mass, after which they shopped for meagre requirements. Little wonder then that some, mostly the men, maddened by despair and depression, ended their own lives.

A little further along the road lived another eccentric character. His name was Paddy Lyons. He was known to all and sundry by his nickname Paddy 'the Duke'. He was a fine cut of a man in his early 60s, with a craggy, lived-in face and a mane of unruly hair. He'd had a fearsome reputation as a fighter in his younger days. I again got to know Paddy the Duke on my daily visits to the well. I sometimes called in to his house to give him a bucket of well water and was invited in for a chat.

His cooking arrangements were, to say the least, a little bit unusual. His cooker was a car tyre filled with sawdust and impregnated with diesel oil sitting on the hearth. On many occasions, I saw him standing outside the door gasping for breath while thick clouds of black smoke billowed over his head.

When the Rural Electrification Scheme brought light and power to our locality in the late '50s, the Duke purchased an electric kettle. He put it to good use – or so he thought. He placed bacon and potatoes in the kettle and filled it with water. He plugged it in and went down to Listowel for his daily ration of Guinness. When he returned, the kettle had melted, like the food, into a mush. He went back to the Electricity Supply Board (ESB) shop in Listowel and demanded a replacement. It took him a while to get to grips with this new technology.

He was a kind, hospitable man who took in the odd lodger or passing 'knight of the road' when the notion took him or he wanted company. I still remember the time when 'the Pecker' Dunne and Roger 'True Blue' Walsh took up residence with him. They certainly made for interesting company. To say they were fond of a drink would be the understatement of the year. The Pecker Dunne was a wandering banjo player. With his gold earring, long black tresses and full black beard, he had the fearsome aspect of a swashbuckling pirate. Roger True Blue, a familiar figure in the town, was a lovable old rogue.

One summer morning as I was making my way to the well, I approached Paddy the Duke's house and noticed a car parked outside with English registration plates and a GB sticker. Just then, I saw an elderly couple with a look of abject terror on their faces jump into the car and drive away in a squeal of tyres. I then saw the apparition that had caused the panic. There, framed in the doorway, stood Paddy the Duke, the Pecker Dunne and Roger, all wheezing and spluttering with blackened faces, as palls of thick, acrid smoke swirled around their heads. In the front garden stood a sign announcing 'Bed and Breakfast – Vacancies Within'. I doubt very much that the couple ever came seeking accommodation around Listowel again. I learned afterwards that Paddy had found the sign lying on the road and decided to erect it in his garden. Somehow, I don't think he ever got Board Fáilte approval for his B&B.

During the summer months, my brothers and I worked for our neighbours in the bogs and meadows. We were more than happy to earn a few shillings to help augment the family budget. My mother was also happy at having a few less mouths to feed for the day. One of the people we did seasonal work for was Mons Dillane. He owned a small ramshackle house about three miles outside Listowel down a bog lane, where he lived alone.

He never passed our door on his way home from the creamery in his donkey and cart without dropping in a gallon of buttermilk to my mother, which she used for her daily bread-making. Mons was kind and courteous, and a man of few words. My mother always thought of him as one of nature's gentlemen. When he asked for our help to cut the turf, it was always readily given.

She knew that Mons would feed us well and treat us to such delights as white bread smothered with dollops of strawberry jam. Normally, cutting turf can be back-breaking work, but with Mons Dillane it was a labour of love. We spent most of the day sitting around drinking tea and having the craic.

Mons was fascinated by stories of the Wild West and went to see every cowboy picture in the Plaza and Astor cinemas in Listowel. He was an avid reader of that once-popular genre of literature: the Western. While my brothers and I made an effort to cut a little turf, Mons would sit by the fire reading from one of his treasure trove of novels including those by the great Zane Grey.

Maybe in that romantic landscape of wide, open plains, smiling saloon girls and mean-faced gunfighters, Mons found escape from the boredom and loneliness of his solitary existence. It is many years since Mons rode off into the sunset for ever.

Despite the poverty and deprivation of those days, my parents willingly endured hardships and made many sacrifices to give us a decent education. My father was a committed believer in the value of proper schooling. He saw learning as the only means of escape from the crushing cycle of poverty and servitude. He believed that education set you free.

Thanks to my parents' vision and commitment, our family received the best education available. All my brothers and sisters went to secondary school and many of them to university. I know with certainty that Mum and Dad were immensely proud of all our academic achievements. My brothers and I were educated in the primary school in Listowel and subsequently at St Michael's College, and my sisters at Presentation College in the town.

My father carried me to school on my first day on the bar of his bicycle, as he had done with all my older brothers before me. The first infants' class was upstairs in the Carnegie Library in the town. Mrs Scanlon, who was my first teacher, was a very kind, matronly woman, who did not believe in the belt or the stick and gave us a gentle introduction to the mysteries of reading, writing and arithmetic. The classroom was an Aladdin's cave of bright, shiny toys, and crayons and chalks and slate on which to practise our writing. The toilet was out on the fire escape and consisted of a sawn-off tar barrel that we would pee into. I loved that first year at school and remember Mrs Scanlon with great affection.

I was transferred to the main national school the following year and was in for a rude awakening. There, kind words of encouragement were replaced with the liberal use of the cane for the slightest infringement of numerous rules and regulations. I learned to take my medicine without complaining, but I never forgave or forgot those bullies.

I often remember my fingers being numb for a whole day after an early morning caning and trying to hold back the tears for fear of being made fun of by the other boys. This despicable practice of assaulting defenceless children continued throughout my school days but thankfully has now been consigned to history. Many a child who passed through this vicious system bears the psychological and emotional scars to this day. I received my final beating from one of those sadists when I was eighteen, two weeks before I took the Leaving Certificate. Even now, many years later, I remember that humiliating episode and find it hard to forgive my assailant.

I want to put the record straight that only a minority of teachers resorted to physical punishment. Most of my teachers were kind, considerate and decent people. In my third year at primary school, Bryan McMahon, author, playwright and all-round man of letters, was my teacher. To us children, he was Master McMahon – a truly gifted man who treated us with compassion and left the indelible imprint of his influence on those in his care. McMahon instilled in us an appreciation for Irish literature, poetry and history. He enthralled us with stories of the Red Branch Knights, and the legends of Fionn mac Cumhaill and the Fianna, our Celtic heroes. Sometimes he organised little pageants in the classroom and had us dress up as Irish warriors complete with timber swords and spears to re-enact various themes from our ancient past. He engendered in us a love of all things Irish and taught us to love and respect our culture and traditions.

Before we went to school in the morning, my brothers, sisters and I had a breakfast of bread and tea. Our lunch for the day was two slices of homemade bread wrapped in newspaper. When I was in fourth class, the free lunches started in our school. This consisted of a mug of cocoa and a currant bun. It was a welcome addition to our staple diet of sugared bread. Sometimes during lunch hour, I would visit my grandmother, Kate Moloney, who lived in Charles Street in the town. She would be sitting by the fire, fingering her rosary beads and silently mouthing her numerous prayers, but she was always pleased to see me and slipped me the odd penny when no one was looking. Although she was in her early 80s at the time, she had the robust good health of someone half her age and was still a handsome woman with a full head of snow-white hair tied in a knot at the back of her head. Despite her air of piety, she had her ear to the ground and was only too aware of the frailties and transgressions of all her neighbours on the street. Although she prayed ceaselessly for their salvation, she wasn't quite convinced that they would ever make suitable company for her in paradise.

She lived in a tiny house of just a kitchen with a stone floor and two small bedrooms. There was an outside lavatory, and winter or summer she washed outside in an old enamel basin with cold water from the outside tap. The only access to her room in the loft was via a ladder that she used until she was 90 years of age. I can still see her coming down it in the morning with a hot-water bottle in one hand and her chamber pot in the other, as agile as one of the acrobats in Duffys Circus.

She was a great storyteller and often recounted in vivid detail events of her childhood as if they had happened yesterday. She recalled her mother telling her tales of the Great Famine and how she had witnessed the bodies of the dead being carried on carts to the workhouse in Listowel, their lips stained green from eating grass in a futile effort to stay alive.

She lived with my uncle Bill and took over the rearing of his four children when his wife died. He was a tailor by trade and carried on his business from home. He made all our trousers and jackets for our first communions and confirmations. It was thanks to my uncle Bill that we were always so well turned out on those big occasions. Uncle Bill was a small, slightly built man, who walked with a limp as a result of childhood polio and stuttered when he became excited. He was an irascible, contrary man with a wicked sense of humour and a great fondness for porter. He was the Bobby Fischer of his day where the game of draughts was concerned. Bill was a man with a fierce aversion to craw-thumpers and Bible bashers, and didn't trouble church or chapel for many years himself.

When he was old and lying on his deathbed surrounded by family and friends, he was gently reminded that a visit from the priest might not go astray. My uncle Jim 'the Chum' Moloney, Bill's brother, was being especially persuasive and reminded Bill of the possible perils a man might encounter on the other side of the divide. The Chum was a man who always believed that it was better to be safe than sorry in his dealings with the Almighty. My uncle Bill declined all divine intervention and went to his maker uttering the immortal words, 'I'll take pot luck.' I have no doubt that the good Lord gave Uncle Bill the benefit of the doubt and admitted him through the Pearly Gates.

My uncle Jim lived over the road from us at Bolton's Cross. He was a dental mechanic by trade and the best there was. He worked in the square in Listowel and told me many stories about his work as the chief tooth maker in the town. One of the most bizarre stories was one time when an old country farmer came into his workshop during the big fair day in the town. Uncle Jim said he took out a filthy handkerchief that displayed a full set of false teeth. They were as dirty as the rag that they were wrapped in, he said. The man, who had not a tooth in his mouth, asked my uncle if he could make the false teeth fit his mouth. My uncle asked him where he had come into possession of the dirty, mud-stained teeth. The old farmer replied that he took them from the corpse of his uncle while he was opening a grave to bury a relative. The Chum was horrified that he was looking at teeth taken from a dead man and sent the farmer packing.

Despite his personal troubles – his wife, Mary, had suffered from mental illness all her life – he was a cheerful, good-humoured and extremely witty man. He was a familiar sight in his black Morris Minor around North Kerry and west Limerick, where he was well known as a begging ass. He bought me my first pint of Guinness in a smoke-filled pub in Athea during the holy hour one Sunday when I was only fifteen. My uncle Jim held the unshakeable belief that porter consumed during prohibited hours always tasted better. Many a Sunday in winter he would call and take my brothers and me to Banna Strand to rake for cockles, a delicacy he prized for their aphrodisiac qualities and the stimulation of his taste buds for feed of porter.

Uncle Jim was a splendid athlete in his younger days and was renowned for his physical prowess and feats of strength. His party piece was bending six-inch nails between his teeth, and he regularly took on the Strong Man when Duffys Circus came to town, winning the odd fiver for his efforts. He used to practise weightlifting using axles of the old Lartigue Monorail that used to run between Listowel and Ballybunion.

At his funeral Mass, we were reminded by the celebrant of another instance of Uncle Jim's stamina and perseverance. He recounted how Jim had cycled from Listowel to Cahirciveen to take part in the Munster Athletic Championships. He won several medals in the track and field events, broke a couple of records and cycled home to Listowel later that day. His only sustenance for the day had been a bottle of cold tea and a raisin bun. It is approximately 70 miles from Listowel to Cahirciveen.

My uncle Jim was a larger-than-life character who lived life to the full. He brightened up many a long, dreary winter's night in our house with his lively yarns. He lived long into old age and remained an incurable optimist to the end.

2

HARD TIMES

DURING THE 1940s AND '50s, THERE WAS WIDESPREAD UNEMPLOYMENT,
poverty and emigration in Ireland, yet these many social evils often
brought communities closer together. To quote Dickens in *A Tale of
Two Cities*, 'It was the best of times, it was the worst of times.' Crime,
as we know it today, was almost non-existent. Neighbours helped one
another out in every conceivable way, and nowhere was the spirit of
cooperation more clearly demonstrated than in our little, tight-knit
community in the Soldiers' Houses. What little we had of worldly
goods was shared between us in a generous and open-hearted way.
Over our back railings, tea and sugar and other essential commodities
were borrowed and exchanged in a never-ending cycle. When a farmer
killed a pig, we would all be sure to get a fine parcel of meat and
pudding.

In the mid-'50s, my parents' financial situation was improved with
money my older siblings were sending home from England and
America. We should never forget the debt of gratitude we owe to our
emigrants for the immense financial contribution they made to this
country in those impoverished times. The millions and millions of
pounds they sent home saved many a family from despair and financial

ruin. This vast flow of money into our economy helped to get Ireland back on its feet.

The comings and goings of my own brothers and sisters was a major feature in my childhood. Their arrivals were always joyous occasions, their going a desolation. There was many a heart-breaking scene at Listowel railway station as young men and women said their tearful farewells to friends and families. I remember standing at the upstairs window, with my mother and father waving their handkerchiefs as the train chugged past a few fields away en route to Dublin and my brother or sister leaning out of the train waving their goodbyes in return. For days after my brothers and sisters went away, my parents, especially my mother, would be numb with grief. For the whole day after they left, she would sit staring into the fire, her heart broken, wondering when she would see them again.

Apart from money, my brothers and sisters also sent home parcels from time to time. The arrival of a bulky paper package on the doorstep, especially one from my brother Bob in America, was a source of intense excitement and anticipation in our house. Our neighbours, who could see my uncle Jack, the postman, struggle up the path with one of these packages, would flock into our kitchen to be present at the grand opening. The women would grab excitedly at a dress or a blouse or a piece of costume jewellery, and then parade around in their new finery. The men ended up oversized, with loud check jackets, bell-bottom trousers that flapped wildly around the ankles or flashy neckties a foot wide. We children were happy to get a couple of Hershey bars or other American candy. However, despite these welcome contributions from abroad, the spectre of poverty was permanently perched on my parents' shoulders.

Like most poor families at that time, we had an account at the local grocery shop. It was owned and run by John R. Walsh and his wife, Hannah. They always had a special welcome for my mother, whom they greatly admired and treated more like a friend than a customer.

I drove my mother to Listowel most Saturday mornings for our weekly shopping on our donkey and cart. Billy, our donkey, was a bad-tempered brute with a penchant for biting and kicking. I was on the receiving end of both on many an occasion.

My mother's weekly grocery requirements far outstripped her

meagre family budget, and without the credit facility we had at John R. Walsh's, my mother would have found it impossible to make ends meet. The banks were hostile and forbidding places to the working-class people of that era: requests for even very small loans often fell on the deaf ears of unsympathetic, arrogant and pompous officials, some of whom, at times, took a perverse delight in humiliating the poor who came looking for help. The balance of my mother's grocery bill each week went into a separate account at the back of the ledger. Over the years, this amounted to a very large sum of money. My mother simply referred to this as 'the Bill'.

Its existence was a source of constant anxiety to my mother and gave her many sleepless nights. When the account was finally settled sometime in the mid-'60s as the family fortunes improved, a great burden was lifted from her shoulders. This final repayment heralded more affluent times for the O'Carroll family.

Even as children, we had the savvy to realise that our parents had hardly enough money for the day-to-day running of the household. We responded by doing odd jobs on the local farms, where we earned a few shillings helping with the hay or working in the bogs. During the summer months, the bogs were hives of activity. Almost everybody owned or rented a little bank of turf. My father cut one in Bunahara, a couple of miles from our house. For our neighbours and ourselves, it was the only source of fuel for heating and cooking before the rural electrification scheme arrived; coal and bottled gas were scarce and expensive commodities beyond the reach of most people.

There was a close camaraderie amongst the men and boys who toiled in the bogs. It was energy-sapping, back-breaking work that left even the strongest men exhausted at the end of the day. During the summer holidays, I worked in the bog alongside my father and brothers to harvest our own turf. My mother, who always worried about the dark, cold winter nights, was never happy until she saw the turf home safe and sound in our backyard. In a rare family photograph, our entire clan, all 17 of us and my grandmother Moloney, are seen proudly posing in front of our reek of turf. This was the only moment in time that our entire family was ever gathered together in one location. Thankfully, it was captured for ever due to the quick thinking of my father, who had the foresight to call upon the local photographer, Mr Keane-Stack.

The bogs are deserted now, all cut away, and any evidence of human activity has been covered by heather, bracken and bog cotton. They have once again become the domain of hare, grouse and snipe. Old friends who once wielded the slean (the turf-cutting spade) are gone to their eternal reward and only the wind sighing through the long grasses holds memory of their passing. Those wild and lonely places will always have a special place in my heart.

We also earned a few bob in the meadows, helping out local farmers to save the hay. The horse still played an essential role in the life of the farming community at that time. During the summer months, the distinctive whirring of the horse-drawn mowing machine filled my ears with its soothing, hypnotic sound as it drifted across the meadows. Soon, farm horses would be replaced by tractors; modern machinery and advanced technologies were changing the face of agriculture. The sweet-scented hay was being replaced by silage, destroying the habitat of so much of the native wildlife, and as a result the corncrakes called out no more through the long summer nights. The rural Ireland of my childhood had gone for ever.

In the late '40s and the '50s, only the very rich travelled abroad on their holidays. The vast majority of people, if they could afford it at all, went off for a week to Bundoran or Ballybunion or some other seaside resort. Few people owned cars and most were completely dependent on buses and trains for all their travel needs. Our only holiday destination in those days was Ballybunion, which, during the months of summer, played host to thousands of visitors attracted by its spectacular beaches and caves and the lure of the slot machines.

Five or six times every summer, usually on Sundays, my father hired John Pa Devereux from next door to drive us to the beach. John Pa owned a huge black American car. Those outings were the highlight of our school holidays. The nine-mile journey to and from Ballybunion was an exciting adventure for us children, who rarely saw the inside of a motor car. The resort, with its colourful shop fronts, golden beaches and amusement arcades, was the Shangri-La of my childhood. It will always hold sweet memories of the times spent there all those years ago.

As soon as we returned to school after the holidays, we started looking forward to the next great event of the year: the Listowel Races, held every year in late September or the early days of October.

The racetrack, known locally as 'the Island', is almost completely surrounded by the River Feale, with two bridges across the water to provide pedestrian access. It is a meeting much loved and supported by the racing fraternity, who flock to Listowel in their thousands year after year and have done so since 1858.

Many of the town's native sons and daughters returned there each year, mostly from England, to be united with friends and family for the festivities. For many of the men, this visit home turned into one long drinking session. In their shiny new suits, with the latest hairstyles, they swaggered around spending money as if there was no tomorrow. After the races, they headed off for Holyhead, broken-hearted and penniless, to their grim, lonely bedsits in London, Liverpool, Birmingham and Manchester.

In the weeks preceding the races, the town buzzed with excitement. Talk of the races was on everybody's lips. Shop fronts and houses were freshly painted, and brightly coloured bunting and lights strung around the town. The forthcoming races spurred on even the most lackadaisical and inveterate layabouts to get off their arses and earn a few bob doing odd jobs or selling a few cartloads of turf around the town. My father recounted the story of one small farmer who had a house full of children and a tooth for porter. My father was passing one day, a few weeks before the races, when the farmer called him over to admire a fine pig he had been fattening all year. The farmer looked wistfully at his treasure and, with the approaching celebrations in mind, turned to my father and said, 'God direct me, Jim, will I eat him or drink him?'

On another occasion, the same individual was confronted in Listowel by the local parish priest, who accused him of neglecting the religious education of one of his many sons who was being prepared for confirmation at the time. The old canon fulminated at the boy's ignorance, stating, 'Do you know that when I was examining him on his catechism, he could not even tell me who made the world?'

Unrepentant, the father replied, 'Yerra Canon, for all he will ever own of it, he needn't trouble his arse about it!'

In the days before the races, a steady cavalcade of gaily painted caravans, pulled by piebald ponies with their gleaming brasses and followed by a retinue of goats, dogs and donkeys, rolled past our door as the travelling people from all Munster made their way into town. I remember seeing their red-haired children peering out excitedly from behind their mothers' shawls. In the Tinker's Market, as it was known back then, off William Street, they set up their caravans, amusements, merry-go-rounds and swing boats. Over the coming days, simmering rivalries and old grievances would result in many a black eye and broken nose. Scores were settled in the age-old tradition by fist and boot. Their arrival in the town always guaranteed a busy time for the local Gardaí.

When I was a young boy, my father was employed by the race committee. For the three days of the festival, it was his job to put up on a noticeboard the number of the horses in each race, and the names of the jockeys and trainers. The noticeboard was a huge timber contraption erected out on the course. It was put up for the benefit of those racegoers that couldn't or didn't want to pay the admission fee to the stands. In those far-off days, the stands and reserved enclosures were the sole preserve of the professional classes, gentlemen farmers, clergymen and the merchant princes of Listowel.

For those three days, I helped my father to put up the timber plates on the noticeboard, which was the focal point of the racecourse. All day long, a steady stream of people used to approach my father looking for tips. I doubt if he made them richer with his information; my father was always an enthusiastic but unlucky gambler – at least that's what he used to tell my mother.

From my vantage point on the noticeboard, I could see the horses as they raced around the island bridge and galloped past the stands to the winning post. After the last race was over, we headed for home across the island bridge hungry and weary, with the smell of trampled grass in our nostrils, a pungent scent that still evokes those golden days of my childhood.

On the bridge and in the laneway leading up to the square, three-card tricksters, musicians and assorted beggars plied their trades. When we got home, my mother served us piping-hot bowls of mutton pie in broth to warm us up. Mutton pie was a speciality during the races, but my mother's was the best of all. I always brought her home a few pears or a bunch of grapes with my earnings from the Island. My little offerings were always gratefully received. During the races in

1959, I saw a television for the first time. I remember gazing in amazement through the window of McKenna's hardware shop in Market Street along with hundreds of others.

A lot of water has flowed under the bridge in Listowel since those innocent times. New stands and every modern facility has been built on the course for the racegoer. The old noticeboard has long since been demolished. The traveller clans who once brought so much atmosphere and life to the town come no more. The Tinker's Market, the donkey derby and the old tipster Prince Monalulu, an English chancer who claimed to have African royal blood, long ago passed into history. Listowel is now a thriving, prosperous town and the races – or the Harvest Festival, as it is now known – has gone from strength to strength. Amongst the townspeople and still for me, this event remains the highlight of the social calendar.

After the races were over and the buntings and lights were taken down, normal life resumed in the old town and we children returned to school. Sometimes in November the missions came to town: one week was set aside for the women, one week for the men. The black-robed Redemptorists were the missionaries of choice in our parish. For those few weeks, the local clergy moved aside to give centre stage to these 'Soldiers of Christ'. When they arrived in Listowel, even the hard men of the town, who were known for their drinking and carousing, ran for cover. In those days, the Catholic Church was still a great monolith, supreme and unchallenged. The princes of the Church still retained the respect and total obedience of their flocks; the parish priests still prowled the laneways and boreens of rural Ireland after parish-hall dances looking to catch unsuspecting courting couples in the act. If caught in a field or behind bushes, they would be beaten out with the help of a gnarled Blackthorn stick.

When I was a young boy, my father took my brothers and me along to the men's mission in our local parish church. In that dim half-light of flickering candles, the missionaries would ascend the pulpit as a hush settled over the expectant congregation. After the perfunctory 'My dear brothers in Jesus Christ', they were soon in full flow. In voices quivering alternately with emotion and rage, they cajoled, scolded and reprimanded the menfolk of Listowel for their sinful ways.

With their righteous anger echoing in the eaves and every corner of the church, they prophesied hell and damnation and the wrath of God on those wretches cowering before them, beating their breasts in collective supplication. It was clear to me from listening to them that Sodom and Gomorrah were only trotting after the goings-on in Listowel. That night in my bed, I prayed to God to forgive me for the sins that I didn't know I had committed and to save me from the eternal fires of hell.

On the last night of the mission, with lighted candles in our hands and the suffocating odour of incense in our nostrils, we renounced the Devil, renewed our baptismal vows and went home, the spectre of hellfire ringing in our ears, hearts and souls. We had been convinced that there was only one outcome in our lives after death: eternal damnation.

During one such ceremony, now an essential part of local folklore, the missioner was calling for a more spirited denunciation of the Devil. 'Do you renounce the Devil and all his pomps and wiles?' he asked of the congregation.

'We do,' came the response.

Still not happy with the volume, he asked the question twice more, interjecting, 'Men of Listowel, put your hearts into it.'

This inspired the congregation to shout, 'We do', but one voice was even more fervent, adding the appendage, 'We do, and fuck him!'

After the missionaries left, the religious fervour in the town subsided and the townspeople returned to their 'auld sins'. The threat of damnation faded and was replaced by the normal exigencies of living and the acceptable failures of human desire. One well-known character who was himself the subject of a witch-hunt by the local clergy because of his alleged insatiable sexual appetite contemptuously dismissed the black-souled missionaries' moral crusade. He said it would have no more effect on the menfolk of Listowel than a blackbird's piss would have on the water levels of the great Grand Coulee Dam.

The heat of temptation was far more potent than the fire of hell and, after all, Christmas was just around the corner.

I will always remember that time of year as a child as amongst the happiest days of my life. My parents always ensured that Christmas was a very special time for us children. Ever since I can remember, it was the same ritual every year. My father would make a big ceremony of bringing down the decorations from the attic the week before. Each decoration had its own place and even now, 50 years on, I remember that the cardboard Santa Claus with the gammy leg always went under the Sacred Heart picture and the crib sat on top of the old wireless set.

My mother would have been busy making cakes and plum puddings for weeks before and filling the house with delicious aromas. These goodies, along with a tin of biscuits, a bottle of whiskey and a dozen of minerals, were put under lock and key by my mother until the big day. Like the keeper of the crown jewels, she wore the key to the press around her neck on a string.

Late on Christmas Eve, my brothers and I collected our presents in John Joe Dillon's shop in Listowel. We had being paying a couple of pence a week off them in the Christmas Club since September when we went back to school. We were the happiest children in the world as we headed for home clutching our precious toys. Every year, I bought myself the same things: a gun and holster, and a sword.

Later that night, with faces scrubbed and wearing our best clothes, we were marched down to Midnight Mass. When we returned to the house, we were treated to cake, biscuits and glasses of Nash's lemonade, which my mother had released from quarantine. It was one of the few nights of the year that we were allowed to stay up late to play with our toys. All my life, when a match is struck and that first whiff of sulphur reaches my nostrils, I am transported back to those Christmas Eves long ago when we played with our new cap guns.

On St Stephen's Day, we were always up bright and early to get ourselves ready to 'go out on the wren'. This was an age-old tradition in Kerry and was more important to us children than Christmas Day. The custom is commemorated in the famous ballad 'The Boys of Barr na Sraide' by the Kerry poet Sigerson Clifford:

> With cudgels stout, we roamed about
> To hunt the gay droelin,
> We searched for birds in every furze
> From Litter to Dooneen,
> We jumped for joy beneath the sky
> Life held no print or plans,

> And we boys of Barr na Sraide
> Who hunted for the wran.

Before leaving the house, we blackened our faces with burnt cork and disguised ourselves in old tattered clothes. With our preparations complete, my brothers and I would head off in pairs into the countryside. For the next eight or nine hours, we trudged from house to house, singing our songs and receiving anything from a penny to a half-crown as a reward for our efforts. In the houses where we performed an encore, we would be rewarded with cake and lemonade, as well as the occasional glass of Maltevina tonic wine.

We were made welcome in most houses, as we had a reputation for being good singers with a wide selection of songs and ballads in our repertoire.

In fact, my second-youngest brother, Philip, won the final of a prestigious all-Ireland singing competition called the Crock of Gold. It was sponsored by Gael Linn, the Irish language organisation. He won £50, a small fortune in those days. Encouraged by Philip's success, I subsequently entered a singing competition in McFadden's Travelling Roadshow during its annual visit to the town. I was beaten in the final by a local crooner, who charmed the judges with a fine rendition of that popular song at the time, 'How Much is that Doggie in the Window?' I had to be content with the consolation prize of a ten-bob note. Any hopes and ambitions that I might have harboured about a singing career were cruelly dashed that night: I had been beaten by a boy with a pronounced stutter who sang through his nose and sounded like a bull-frog in the mating season.

When other children were buying comics and sweets with their pennies, my brothers and I bought books of songs and ballads from old Bob Cuthbertson, who had a printing shop in William Street in town. Every Saturday when I was a small boy, we listened to the radio programme sponsored by Walton's music store in Dublin after the midday news. Only Irish songs and ballads were featured on the programme and I learned many of them by heart just by listening to them. When I was growing up in Cahirdown every family celebration ended up with a sing-song.

At the end of that long day, we would head for home tired but happy, our pockets bulging with coins. We then counted our money into neat piles on the kitchen table. When the other wanderers returned, we compared our earnings and boasted of our narrow escapes from savage dogs and wild bulls. Between us all, we often brought home around £40 for our day's work, a small fortune back then. Needless to say, it was a godsend to my mother, who eagerly awaited the annual windfall, which she used to help pay the Christmas bills. Remembering the childhood Christmases of long ago still awakens in me feelings of intense happiness that time will neither diminish nor dispel.

* * *

The carefree days of my childhood had come to an end, and in the autumn of 1960 I enrolled in St Michael's College, Listowel. During the summer holidays, I got my first real job working as a waiter in the Cahernane Hotel in Killarney and went back to work there every summer for the next four years. In 1961, the council supplied us with running water and my father bought his first motor car, a Ford Anglia. The O'Carroll family was going up in the world at last.

The following year, an event that was happening halfway across the globe intruded upon our peaceful life. This event was the Cuban Missile Crisis at the height of the Cold War and brought with it the threat of imminent nuclear annihilation. It is almost impossible now to convey the sense of dread and terror that swept through the country. It was the topic of conversation on everyone's lips. Work and all social activity almost came to a halt as people huddled around their radios in frightened groups listening for the latest news bulletins. As the crisis deepened, people flocked to churches and chapels to pray for deliverance; in our house, the family rosary was never said with such conviction. Added to our woes was the apocalyptic prophecy that three days of darkness was on its way, heralding the end of the world. This was believed by many Catholics around the world to be the Third Secret of Fatima, which the Pope had not revealed for fear of causing widespread panic and fear across the globe.

Thankfully, our prayers were answered. The world didn't come to an end and there was a universal sigh of relief as the missiles sailed back to Russia.

The only other memorable event of those years occurred in November 1963 with the assassination of John F. Kennedy. Like most people on the planet, I too remember where I was when I heard the news: I was on my way home from college after study when I met my neighbour, Mickey Shea, on the way into town and he blurted out the grim tidings. I ran home to find the whole family in tears. News of his death affected us all as if he had been a family member. In almost every rural house at the time, there was a picture of Kennedy alongside Pope John 23rd and The Sacred Heart. During Kennedy's visit to Ireland, there had been a huge outpouring of national pride that one of our own, the great-great-grandson of a poor immigrant, had become leader of one of the most powerful countries on earth.

In June 1964, I sat my Leaving Certificate and was pleased when I got honours in six subjects – I went down in maths, which I had always detested. I was utterly disappointed when some weeks later I failed to get the call for teaching. I had my heart set on getting into teacher-training college in Dublin to become a national schoolteacher. Sometime in early September, the president of St Michael's College, Father Daniel Long, called to see me at home and offered to pay my fees for an arts degree in University College Dublin. I was greatly moved by his offer, but I felt I could not accept his charity.

In early October that year, embittered by my failure to become a teacher, I headed across to England with my first cousin, Paddy Moloney. We travelled by train to Dublin and took the cattle boat from North Wall to Holyhead in Wales. It was my first time on a boat and I suffered terrible seasickness. During the entire crossing, the cattle bawled and stamped and drunken navvies staggered over sleeping bodies on their way to and from the bar. From Holyhead, my cousin and I took the train to Paddington Station in London, where we went our separate ways. Paddy had family in London and I went to stay with my brother, Vincent, and his wife, Molly, in Woking, Surrey.

On Monday morning, I started as a tea boy with a civil engineering company on the outskirts of Woking where Vincent was a ganger. I earned £20 a week making tea and running errands for the workers, who were mostly from the west of Ireland. They were tough-as-nails, hard-drinking men who could work the pick and shovel all day without tiring. Although I was as green as grass, they tolerated my inexperience and shortcomings with a benign indifference; however, they were not men to be trifled with, as I soon found out.

The old veteran navvy who worked the cement mixer was known as 'the Sheep'. He hailed from County Galway and lived in a tiny mobile home close to the building site. One morning as I was driving by in a dumper truck, I accidentally hit his home, knocking it off its stand. The Sheep, who was cooking breakfast at the time, lost his balance and his fine pan full of eggs and rashers ended up on the floor. I was just about to go back and apologise when a shovel flew past my ears, almost decapitating me. Discretion being the better part of valour, I ran for my life. Some hours later when he had cooled down, he accepted my grovelling apology and saw the funny side of it. We became good friends, in fact. Some weeks later, he gave me the full guided tour of the Irish pubs in Cricklewood and Camden Town.

Towards the end of that year, my career as a tea boy came to a sudden and fiery end. While trying to light the stove one freezing cold winter's morning, I accidentally poured petrol instead of diesel on the smouldering coals. I was lucky to escape with minor burns, but the canteen, a large timber structure, went up in flames. All the workers' personal belongings stored in the canteen were also destroyed in the blaze. I decided to terminate my employment there and then, and took off like a scalded cat.

My brother was highly embarrassed by this debacle but relieved at my narrow escape. He did advise me, however, in the interests of safety – chiefly my own – to find alternative employment. Within days, I was working for another civil engineering firm, laying cables for the Post Office. We had to dig trenches one foot wide and two feet deep with a pickaxe and shovel, a back-breaking job.

At the end of the first day, my hands were red raw and blistered. At the end of the second, I was in agony. One of the workers, seeing I was close to tears from the pain, advised me to urinate on my hands, as it would help to toughen up the skin. At that stage, I came very close to ending my career as a navvy. But I soldiered on, and little by little my hands healed. Over the next few weeks, my muscles hardened, my stamina increased and I started to feel like a real navvy. I was 18 years old, earning good money and on top of the world.

Inevitably, I began going to the pub every night with my mates after we finished work, much to the disapproval of my older brother, who was a teetotaller at the time. When I ran low on funds, I went to the 'subbie', like all the others. I began to drink heavily and frequent the less salubrious taverns. In one such establishment on St Patrick's night in 1965 all hell broke loose and I was caught up in the middle of a vicious row between rival factions of fellow Irishmen. Bottles, glasses, fists and boots went flying in all directions. At the height of the disturbance, the police arrived and waded in with batons swinging. Sadly, my head got in the way and I woke up sometime later in a police cell with a lump on my head the size of an egg. Later on, I was interviewed by a sergeant and managed to convince him that I was an innocent customer caught up in the fracas. I was released without charge, nursing a monster headache and thanking my lucky stars that I hadn't been brought before the magistrates.

Unfortunately, it would not be my last involvement with Woking Police. A week later, I was cycling home late at night through the centre of the town when I was stopped by two uniformed bobbies on the beat. I was pulled off my bike into nearby bushes and battered around the head and shoulders with their torches. This attack was sudden and unexpected, and I didn't even get a chance to defend myself. As they walked away, one of them turned around and said, 'That'll teach you, Paddy. Remember the Railway Bar?' I suffered cuts and bruises but never mentioned what happened to another soul. The Railway Bar was where the riot had broken out on St Patrick's night and I later heard that a number of their colleagues had been injured in the row. My two assailants had obviously tried to even the score and mete out their own form of summary justice. After those incidents, I cut down on the booze and began to get a bit of sense.

In June that year, I went home to Listowel to see my parents. During that visit, an event occurred that would change the course of my life. One night, under the pretext of having to get some forms signed, my father inveigled me into going with him to the local Garda station. It was my first time inside the door of that, or any other, Garda barracks. Before I knew what was happening, I was being measured and weighed by the local sergeant. For the next hour and a half, my father and the sergeant sat singing the praises of a career with the guards. I was told that I would have a wage every week come rain, hail or shine, clothes on my back and a good pair of boots on my feet for the rest of my life. After much cajoling, I finally gave in and filled in the application form to join An Garda Síochána.

Up until that night, I had never for one moment considered a career as a policeman. My father seemed mighty pleased with himself as we supped a pint together in John R's after leaving the station. The more I thought about the events of that night, the more I was convinced that my father, having heard of some of my escapades across the water, had decided to put a stop to my gallop the only way he knew how.

Two days later, I went back to England. I was employed as a labourer on a building site in Guildford, Surrey, within days. The three bricklayers, all brothers, who gave me the job came from London's East End. They were a tough bunch, but they treated me OK and paid me well. After a couple of weeks, they took a shine to me and invited me up to London at weekends to meet their families and friends.

In the bars and clubs, I noticed that the brothers were treated with more than a little respect by the bouncers. Wherever we went drinks appeared out of the blue from all sides, but I never saw them put their hands in their pockets. Although I was pretty naive at the time, it began to occur to me that the brothers did more than lay bricks.

One Monday morning, I turned up at the site as usual. I started up the mixer and laid out the mortar and bricks along the boards. The brothers never appeared and at around eleven o'clock in the morning, a police car drove in on the site. A policeman approached me as I was working and said, 'Paddy, you won't be needing that today,' pointing to the mortar. He was smiling from ear to ear as he told me that my employers were locked up, having been caught red-handed carrying out a warehouse robbery in London that weekend. I switched off the mixer, gathered my traps and left. I never saw the brothers again nor ever heard what became of them. Following the sudden termination of my employment in Guildford, I went back to laying cable again for the Post Office.

In September that year, I got news from my father that I had been called to undergo a medical examination in Dublin by the Garda authorities. I returned to Dublin, where I underwent the medical, and afterwards returned home to Listowel. I had left home a wide-eyed, inexperienced youth untutored in the ways of the world. I returned home two years older and ten years wiser. I had met many Irishmen who were old before their time from years of alcohol abuse and the wear and tear of brutal manual labour, and I didn't want to end up like those unfortunates in ten or fifteen years. With the introduction of modern machinery in the building and civil engineering industries, the days of the pickaxe and shovel were numbered and a way of life for generations of Irishmen was coming to an end. I feel privileged that even for a short time I shared the hardships, enjoyed the company and was a paid-up member of that hardy breed.

I suffered random instances of racial abuse and intolerance because of my Irish background, but overall found the English people to be kind and polite. All in all, I enjoyed my self-imposed exile and my experiences in these years would later stand me in good stead in my chosen career.

After I returned to Listowel, I worked for a couple of months as a labourer in the construction of the ESB power station on Tarbert Island in the Shannon estuary. Deep excavations and massive earthmoving machinery had turned Tarbert Island into a sea of mud. On 8 December that year, at around six o'clock in the evening, Sonny Wynne was killed on the site when the tractor he was driving overturned, pinning him underneath. I helped to carry his lifeless body on a makeshift stretcher across to the canteen, where we laid him out. He looked as if he had fallen asleep. One hour earlier, we had spoken together and made plans to go dancing that night. Sonny was around my own age. I was deeply shocked by his death, which forced me for the first time to confront my own mortality. Sudden, violent death would be no stranger to me in the coming years.

During this time, when I was living back in the family home, I was involved in an incident that resulted in one of the most serious altercations between my father and me. It all began when I was involved in a car accident on my way home from work. A close friend and work colleague was driving and I was sitting in the front passenger seat.

Earlier that dark winter's evening after finishing work, we had gone straight to the local boozer, where we consumed a skinful of pints. The visibility was very poor as we drove back to Listowel that night along the narrow bumpy road and my friend, who was very short-sighted, even without a cargo of porter on board, collided with an oncoming cement lorry. Our car ended up on its roof in the ditch. We crawled out of the wreck virtually unscathed except for some bruising and cuts to our faces from smashing into the windscreen.

Even in our drunken state we realised that we had very narrowly escaped serious injury or worse. After getting back on the road, we flagged down a passing motorcyclist, who brought us into Listowel. After that I went straight home. On seeing me, my parents were shocked and upset. I must have looked like something the cat dragged in, with my bruised and bloody face, and covered in mud from head to toe.

Though still a little dazed and confused from my ordeal, I explained to them in a shivered and slightly incoherent manner that I had been involved in a traffic accident and was lucky to be alive. Their shock and relief soon turned to anger, however, when they realised that I was very drunk. My usually very mild-mannered father read me the riot act about my drunken ways and accused me of being a disgrace to my family. I had never seen my father in such a temper. Such was the ferocity of this tongue-lashing that, for once, I was stunned into silence and never once retaliated. After having being duly chastised, I slunk way to my room to lick my wounds.

When I got home from work the following night, I was sore and sorry and still smarting from the events of the previous night. The atmosphere in the house was tense and edgy. After dinner, my father took me to one side and during a heart-to-heart talk he confessed that he was very concerned about my drinking and advised me to take the pledge for the foreseeable future. He was so genuinely upset and worried about me that I agreed to go on the wagon.

My father was overjoyed at my response and, in a rare display of outward affection, he hugged me. From that night on, I never again had a cross word with my father. That weekend I went to the local priest, took the pledge and became a probationary member of the Pioneer Total Abstinence Association.

My good resolutions didn't last too long and I was soon back enjoying my few pints. My father eventually accepted that, like most of the menfolk in the O'Carroll clan, I too was cursed with a tooth for the drink.

3

BOOT CAMP

I FINISHED ON TARBERT ISLAND BEFORE CHRISTMAS AND ON
29 December 1965 my father dropped me off in his old Volkswagen
Beetle at the gates of the Garda Training Centre in Templemore. We shook
hands and said our goodbyes. Much of the confidence I had felt earlier
drained away when my father's car disappeared from view and I walked
through those forbidding wrought-iron gates. In my old, battered suitcase
I had all the kit that I had been instructed to bring along, namely:

One suit of plain clothes
Two complete changes of underwear
Two shirts
Three towels
Two suits of pyjamas
One shaving kit – complete
A comb, hairbrush, nailbrush, boot brush and clothes brush
A toothbrush and toothpaste
Three pairs of black or navy-blue socks
Two pairs of black boots or shoes (new or in good repair)
One pen (ballpoint or fountain)

Inside I reported to the Guard Room, where my name was ticked off in a ledger by a Garda on duty. Over the next few hours, other new recruits kept arriving in dribs and drabs. Eventually, about 50 of us were milling around the room like lost sheep. At around 4 p.m., we were ordered into a loose formation of four abreast and marched to an assembly hall. There we were addressed by a Garda officer who, after a few brief words of welcome, ordered us to raise our right hands and swear to do our duty without fear, favour, malice or ill will. From that moment, I became a member of An Garda Síochána. After the short ceremony, the officer's closing words left us in no doubt that we were in for a rough ride over the coming months.

Later that evening, before we had supper, we were allocated our sleeping quarters, which were laid out in cubicles off a long, narrow corridor. Each cubicle was separated from the next by a low timber partition and contained three iron beds, a wash-hand basin and built-in presses. Communal showers were located at the end of each corridor.

That night as we settled in, we received an unexpected visit from the assistant training officer and his senior inspector, who roared at us to stand to attention. As we stood beside our beds clad only in our pyjamas, we were questioned in depth about our family backgrounds, our drinking habits and our motives for joining the force. From their aggressive and hostile attitude, I got the distinct impression that life in Templemore would not turn out to be a bed of roses. First impressions are rarely wrong.

The following morning, reveille sounded at 7 a.m. from the Tannoy system with a noise that would wake the dead. We showered, dressed and had a breakfast of stodgy, cold porridge, hard-boiled eggs and stale bread. The pervasive, obnoxious smell of the eggs filled the dining hall – a smell that I have detested ever since. We were then marched to the stores, where we were issued with our kit. I received one tunic, two trousers and shirts, a baton, a pair of handcuffs and a button stick.

Afterwards, we all attended a barber and came away looking like convicts. I would be subjected to this pointless exercise three or four times each week for the duration of my stay there. What institution in the world would subject its inmates to so many haircuts in one week? I never fully understood whether the purpose of this bizarre ritual was an exercise in humiliation or to create a pension scheme for the barber. Maybe the training officer was just worried that we would all get nits.

The following morning at 9 a.m., resplendent in our new uniforms, we marched under the clock tower out in the front square for our first inspection. My class had been designated December A and B. In the square, we were made to stand to attention in lines two abreast to await the dreaded inspection. You could hear a pin drop as the assistant training officer and his inspectors walked along each line. Despite the most careful preparations, every morning some unfortunate individuals were reported for having dirty uniforms or shoes, having a hair out of place or other such trivial infringements. One also had to be on alert in case some joker tipped cigarette ash on you as you hurried out, a fate I suffered on a number of occasions.

After morning parade, we were marched in from the square and went straight to our classrooms. There I began my apprenticeship in legal studies under the tutelage of Sergeant Ned Sheppard, a fatherly and understanding man. After I came to grips with the archaic and abstruse language of the law, I began to make steady progress and found, to my surprise, that I possessed an aptitude for it. We were also instructed in all aspects of police duties, most notably those contained in the *An Garda Síochána Guide* and the *An Garda Disciplinary Code*. The *Garda Guide* contained the A to Z of policing and was our bible. It was venerated almost as much by the hierarchy in Templemore.

It was an indispensable book that I would consult on an almost daily basis for the next 30 years. The code was a weighty tome of 1,000 pages, outlining the dos and don'ts for every member of the force in their public and private lives. Earlier on in my career, while on holiday, I left my youngest brother, Louis, in charge of the house and of our slightly retarded Airedale terrier, Homer. Louis deserted his post and Homer wreaked havoc and destruction on our property. The rampaging dog took particular delight in devouring the Garda Code, which hardly had a page left intact; however, not even Homer found the code palatable and its regurgitated remains were scattered the length and breadth of the house.

Twice a day, we were marched out onto the square for drill practice. This aspect of our training appeared to be given a very high priority in the overall curriculum. The drill instructors, mostly ex-army men, were tough, experienced masters of the parade ground, who were blessed with a vast lexicon of insults and explosive tempers. During those first feeble attempts at marching, we stumbled and stamped about like drunken men with two left feet. Our pathetic efforts were greeted by a torrent of invective from the drill instructor and howls of laughter from the other trainees. Gradually, we would learn under the ever-watchful eyes and relentless tongue-lashing of our redoubtable instructors, and would some day amaze family and friends with our parade-ground expertise.

Apart from drill instruction and police-duty classes, much emphasis was placed on physical training. We spent at least an hour and a half each day in the well-equipped gym, where we were put through our paces by the PT instructor, Sgt Reggie Barrett. Reggie also taught us unarmed combat, swimming and boxing. Another important element of the training was first aid, civil defence and firearms, particularly on the .38 Webley and Scott handgun. Sergeant Barrett trained every day and was in superb physical condition for a man of his age.

During unarmed combat training, he showcased his skills, flinging us to the floor like rag dolls time and time again. He didn't spare our pride or our bones. He put the fear of God in us about the dangers we would face on the mean streets of Ireland. He was also a trained boxer himself and insisted that every recruit learned the rudiments of that manly sport. To that end, he arranged regular boxing matches between the various classes.

I had never boxed before but after a few successful scraps, fancied myself as a bit of a pugilist. However, during one of these bouts, my budding career came to a sudden and painful end. My opponent, a trainee Garda motorcyclist, who was built like a brick shit house, dealt me a haymaker, sending me crashing to the canvas with a broken jaw. The next day, with my face looking like a high fiddle, I was taken by ambulance to Dublin to Dr Steeven's Hospital, where I underwent an operation. My jaw was wired together for the next three weeks and I was transferred to the Garda hospital at headquarters in the Phoenix Park to recuperate.

It was an ancient building that was more of a nursing home than a hospital, but it was spotlessly clean and the food was great. It was staffed entirely by Garda orderlies and presided over by a matron. My fellow patients were mostly recovering alcoholics, which I later found out to my cost. As they were confined to their beds, I ran little errands for them to the stores and wet canteen. One night, I was returning with cigarettes and a couple of naggins of whiskey when I was confronted by one of the Garda orderlies. He went purple with anger and castigated me for bringing in liquor to his patients. He seized the contraband and stormed off. When I arrived back to the ward red-faced with embarrassment and empty-handed, they only laughed at my innocence. They had led me to believe that they were suffering from life-threatening diseases.

I enjoyed the relaxed, friendly atmosphere in that place, but all good things come to an end and before I knew it, I was once again back in Templemore. It took me a couple of days to get into the routine of the place. From Monday morning till one o'clock on Saturday, we did not have a minute to ourselves. The Tannoy blared out its musical commands throughout the day, telling us when to get up, when to go to bed and when to turn off the lights at night. To my surprise, I readily adapted to this strict way of life and actually began to enjoy it. But even Sunday didn't bring respite from the gruelling schedule. We were roused from our slumbers as usual at 7 a.m. by reveille. After breakfast, every recruit in the depot, and most of the staff, assembled in the front square. Led by the assistant training officer, we were marched in formation down the tree-lined avenue to the Church of the Sacred Heart, a distance of about half a mile. In that era, there was no room in Templemore for atheists, agnostics or freethinkers! We filed in to the seats like schoolboys on First Communion Day. After Mass, which was usually celebrated by the doddering old Canon Fogarty, we were marched back up to the depot, where we disbanded.

We had the rest of the day to ourselves. On certain Sunday nights, we attended the dance at the Las Vegas Ballroom; however, after one or two dances we had to beat a hasty retreat back to the depot for the eleven o'clock curfew. There were always some recruits who would dash into the Guard Room red-cheeked and out of breath with only seconds to spare. Our only other recreational activities were the odd film or concert in the assembly hall.

As I stated earlier, I had little difficulty in adapting to the strict code of conduct demanded of every recruit during training. After all, I had signed up to be a member of a disciplined force and fully accepted the implications of that decision. However, as the weeks went by, the regime became so oppressive that I, and most of my classmates, found the situation unbearable. The daily inspection became little more than an exercise in public humiliation and an opportunity to bully and intimidate the recruits. The most minor infringement of the rules and regulations ended up with a visit to the training officer for a severe dressing down. Even as we lay in our beds at night we remained under the close supervision of the training inspector, who prowled the corridors outside our cubicles into the small hours.

To add insult to injury, we were confined to the depot during the weekends as punishment for trivial breaches of the rules. On one occasion, we suffered this fate because it was alleged some recruits had put holy medals into the collection boxes at Sunday Mass. This atmosphere became more intimidating following the dismissal of several of my colleagues as a result of their failure to pass the in-house exams. It was hard to see these men, who had become as close as brothers, with their ambitions so cruelly and arbitrarily dashed, and this caused further tension and distress.

Some weeks before my final exams, an incident occurred that almost ended my career before it began. One evening, I was looking for a quiet place to study, where I would be free from interruptions. I found the ideal room for this purpose on the ground floor below my dormitory. The following morning, as I prepared for inspection, I suddenly realised that I had left my cap and tunic behind in the room. I rushed down to retrieve them and discovered to my horror that the room was locked. I returned to the dormitory in a panic and disclosed my awful predicament to my classmates. Things went from bad to worse when they told me that there had been a public announcement on the Tannoy to say this particular room was out of bounds to all recruits as exam papers were being stored there.

My heart fell into my boots as I took in the probable consequence of my actions: as innocent as they were, it was likely that they would be interpreted in an entirely different light and would lead to instant dismissal. As only sickness or infirmity would excuse me from the morning inspection, I decided there and then to resort to drastic action. I took a razor blade and made an incision an inch and a half across my right knee. By drawing a small brush that I used to clean my uniform across the wound, I disguised the origin of the cut. I quickly reported to the duty sergeant and told him that I had fallen down the stairs, injured my knee and was unfit for duty. Later in the morning, I went to see the medical officer who was, to say the least of it, sceptical of the real reason for my injury but let it pass. As I limped back to my room, I realised that my desperate remedy would succeed in gaining no more than a temporary reprieve.

In the dormitory that night, worried classmates rallied around the condemned man with words of advice and encouragement. Some suggested that I admit to my heinous crime and fall on my knees for mercy; others disagreed, saying that the felony would be fatally compounded if it was discovered that my injury was self-inflicted in an effort to cover up my actions. An innocent molehill had now become a mountain of guilt up which, like Sisyphus, I was rolling a stone to the summit only for it to roll back down to the bottom. It looked like I had nowhere to go, so I packed my bags for that ultimate eventuality.

At around eleven that night, at the height of our increasingly desperate discussion, the entire depot was plunged into darkness as a result of a fortuitous power cut. In an instant, I leapt at this God-given opportunity that had opened up to me. I raced down the stairs and stole out under the clock tower and into the front square, and located the room where my tunic and cap were still under lock and key. I managed to force open the window and enter the room.

Groping around like a blind man in the darkness of a dungeon, my breath coming in gasps, I searched for the items that, if found by superiors, would surely ring the death knell of my career. I would have never made a cat burglar, that's for sure, but by combing every inch of that black space for what seemed like an eternity I managed to put my hands finally on the tunic and cap.

Grasping my prize, I made my way back to the window, praying and hoping that the power cut would last and returning light would not expose me. I hopped out through the window and, with perspiration glistening on my brow, made my way back through the front square, under the clock tower and up the stairs. With indescribable relief, I opened the door of the dormitory and slipped into my room.

Within a minute, the depot was a blaze of light as the power kicked in. My colleagues were jubilant and amazed at the extraordinary stroke of luck that had saved my bacon. In darkness we always pray for light, but not on this occasion – the darkness was my saviour that night. With my heart thundering in my chest from a mixture of fear, adrenalin and excitement, I unpacked my suitcase and fell exhausted into bed.

The last couple of weeks of training passed without incident and, to avoid the fate that had befallen several of my friends, I immersed myself in my studies. Despite the pressure of the looming finals, I detected a growing mood of optimism among the class as the hour of our deliverance edged closer and closer. On the square, we were drilled close to exhaustion by the anxious instructors fearful that we would tarnish their reputations on the big day as we passed by the assembled brass.

We finished our final exams and that night we celebrated with a massive booze-up in our favourite local watering hole. The party was somewhat tinged with sadness at the absence of our classmates who hadn't made it this far. The following day, we were allocated to our new Garda stations. Kevin Colleran, a native of Dublin, and I were allocated to Rathfarnham Garda station in south County Dublin. In May, classes A and B marched proudly under the clock tower into the square for the passing out parade. To the rousing music of John Philip Sousa, we gave a faultless display of our marching skills much to the relief of Sergeant Liam Wall, our instructor.

The following day, I boarded a train at Templemore with Kevin. During the journey, I reflected on the events of the previous 22 weeks with mixed emotions. I was definitely glad to see the back of the training centre, but on the other hand, I knew I would miss the friendship and camaraderie there, which had been forged during our tough times together.

I had accepted the regime of discipline as a necessary element in our training, but I could not accept the injustices, oppression and lack of humanity I had witnessed there. The experience left me with a legacy of deep-rooted distrust and a permanent residue of anger and resentment towards certain authority figures. This attitude would surface from time to time and land me in hot water right through my career.

The train pulled in at Kingsbridge station in Dublin, where we were collected by a Garda van and driven directly to Rathfarnham station. On our arrival, Kevin and I were welcomed by the sergeant in charge. Once we had handed over our transfer documents to him, he duly directed the barracks orderly to record this momentous occasion with an entry in the station diary. We were now officially members of the Rathfarnham station party and of the 'M' district. After the formalities had been completed, Kevin left for his home in Churchtown, which was little more than a mile away. The barrack orderly then took me on a quick tour of the station, including the living quarters, which were to be my home for the next three years.

The station, a two-storey detached brick building, is located on the southern side of the village on Butterfield Avenue. I shared a large bedroom at the end of a long corridor on the first floor with three colleagues. It contained four iron-framed single beds, four grey, steel bedside lockers and two enormous antique wooden wardrobes. The walls, like almost every surface in the station, were painted battleship grey and matched perfectly the linoleum on the floor. I was later supplied with two stiff linen sheets, two regulation grey blankets, two linen pillowcases and a feather pillow. The one redeeming feature in the room was its large fireplace. I still have fond memories of lying in my bed on cold winter nights enjoying the warmth of a blazing fire fuelled by coal 'borrowed' from the official supplies.

The three other single bedrooms along the corridor were occupied by the more senior members of the station party. The station's sergeants and detectives also had offices on this floor. The drying room, public office, cells, and our private living room and kitchen were situated on the ground floor. At the rear of the station, a garage was provided for the safe storage of our bicycles, which each Garda was required by regulation to possess.

Directly in front of the garage, and neatly stacked at the back wall of the station, was a big pile of solid concrete blocks. Wandering around the yard one day, I noticed them and, being curious by nature, asked old Ted, who did odd jobs around the station, as to their purpose. He told me that they had been delivered a few years ago by the Board of Works and were to be placed against the windows and doors in the event of a nuclear attack.

My new home, although drab and austere, would nevertheless, because of the elaborate defence measures taken by the authorities, be a safe haven in the event of atomic Armageddon.

4

ON THE BEAT

THREE DAYS AFTER ARRIVING IN RATHFARNHAM, I REPORTED FOR DUTY in the public office. I was inspected by the station sergeant, a grizzled, old veteran. He looked me up and down to check that I was in possession of all my accoutrements, namely notebook and pen, baton and handcuffs. It was entered in the station diary that I had reported 'clean and regular' for duty. After a cursory briefing, the station sergeant finally wished me well in my new career and sent me forth amongst an unsuspecting public. As I headed up to the village on my first assignment, any nervousness or fear that I might have had were soon dispelled as I contemplated the great adventure that hopefully lay ahead of me as a member of that much-revered and unique institution An Garda Síochána.

Sometime around noon as I was patrolling the main street, I got my first taste of action. I was informed by a passer-by that a traffic accident had occurred on Rathfarnham Road beside the garage. When I arrived at the scene, I was approached by an irate bus driver who complained loudly and bitterly about women drivers. It turned out to be an open and shut case. I spoke to a nice middle-aged lady, who had reversed her car out of her driveway onto the main road and into the path of an oncoming city-bound bus. The poor woman was hysterical and in a state of shock. I wrote down the particulars of both parties in my brand-new notebook and took rough measurements of the scene. I then administered the official warning under the Road Traffic Act to the unfortunate woman and told her that I would be prosecuting her for dangerous driving. Although I felt sorry for her, I was nevertheless pleased with myself that I had handled the matter like an old pro. I was also looking forward to my first prosecution case in the District Court.

As events turned out, I would have to wait a little longer for that experience. A couple of days later, I was called aside by one of the detectives at the station and told to take no further action against the woman involved in the accident as the matter had been settled. I discovered that the driver of the car was the wife of a prominent local businessman and politician. In a police jargon that I was soon to become familiar with, the case had been 'squared'. It was the first time, but it wouldn't be the last, that I would square a case at the request of a colleague.

As I never sought to gain any advantage, either monetary or otherwise, by acquiescing to such overtures, I did not believe that my actions in any way compromised my integrity or my commitment to uphold the law. Most of the cases squared would have been minor traffic offences or breaches of the Public Order Act. In the close-knit community that was Rathfarnham at the time, many of the residents were on first name terms with the local Gardaí and would approach them for help if they got into trouble. Most of these minor cases were squared, not least of all because the ordinary working man could not afford to hire solicitors to represent them or to pay the fines that would be imposed by the courts.

I have no doubt that there are many people today who would regard our tolerance towards minor law breakers at that time as unacceptable and unprofessional. I would argue that it was not so. I believe that the law should always be dispensed with clemency, compassion and common sense, and this was our style of community relations almost 40 years ago. Those people to whom we gave a break were often the first into the station with information about any serious crimes that had been committed in the area.

Those early days went by in a blur, each filled with new and exciting experiences. I took to my role as village law man like a duck to water. From my first faltering steps on the beat, I realised with a deep conviction that I had found my true calling in life. This sense of belonging was reinforced by my posting to the leafy environs of Rathfarnham. At that time, the village was a peaceful and friendly suburb nestling in the foothills of the Dublin mountains. Rathfarnham translates into English as 'Rath of the Alders'. The village was well serviced by a number of grocery shops, four pubs, two churches, a bank, a courthouse and a rosary-bead factory.

Close by and lording over all, the massive ramparts of Rathfarnham Castle kept their centuries-old vigil over the town's inhabitants. The castle was built around 1583 to defend the village and the surrounding countryside from the marauding Wicklow clans, the O'Tooles and the O'Byrnes. It was given a peaceful purpose in more recent times when in 1913 its south-western section was opened by the Jesuit Order as a retreat house.

Indeed, Rathfarnham and its hinterland are steeped in history and folklore. The great Irish patriot Robert Emmet resided for a number of months in the Old Orchard House, a stone's throw from the Garda station, when he was planning his ill-fated rebellion of 1803. The insurrection failed and he was subsequently captured and executed. Two roads in the neighbourhood were named after important women in his life: his faithful domestic servant Anne Devlin and his fiancée, Sarah Curran. William Butler Yeats, the poet, playwright and Nobel Prize-winner for literature, had his last home in Riversdale House on Willbrook Road, just outside the village.

Patrick Pearse and his brother Willie, two of our greatest nationalist heroes, lived a short distance from the village at the Hermitage on Grange Road, part of which they converted into St Enda's School. Both were shot by a firing squad, along with the other leaders of the rebellion, for their participation in the unsuccessful uprising of 1916. Although seen as a failure by many at the time, it was the catalyst for the War of Independence a few short years later, which ended British Rule in 26 of the 32 counties of our country. The last surviving member of the Pearse family, Senator Margaret Pearse, was still in residence in the Hermitage in 1967. After her death in 1968, the

Hermitage and grounds passed into the ownership of the state and now house the Pearse Museum.

The surrounding hills and mountains of Rathfarnham are also rich in antiquities, including megalithic tombs, passage graves, standing stones and dolmens. The same hills offer breathtaking panoramas of Dublin city and bay. I spent many happy, carefree days both on and off duty trekking through the lush, fertile glens and the majestic heather-covered mountains of that spectacular landscape.

As was to be expected, being one of the more junior members of the station party, I was landed with more than my fair share of 'sticks'. These were the tasks that the more experienced old hands avoided like the plague. They included traffic-point duties on freezing cold winter mornings and fatigues duty in the station. When engaged in the latter, I was a regular Mrs Mopp, cleaning and sweeping the floors and tending the fires in the public and sergeants' offices.

During the first months of my posting, a local woman was employed to cook lunch for us on weekdays. It was a case of 'first come, first served' and the devil take the hindmost. This arrangement didn't last for long and after her departure we fended for ourselves. Due to the all-male environment, there was the inevitable clash of personalities resulting in occasional heated argument and at times brief pugilistic exchanges, but overall we were like one big, happy family. I forged bonds of friendship that have stood the test of time for over 40 years.

The wages were very poor back then and after I had paid for the food and accommodation, I had very little left. To survive from week to week, along with the rest of the lads I opened an account in a shop in the village. It was called Butterfield Stores and was owned by three lovely old ladies, all sisters. It was a tiny little grocery shop with only the bare essentials for sale. My daily purchase of tea, sugar, bread, milk and the occasional packet of rashers was recorded meticulously in a battered, old ledger. Although my account was seldom in the black, they never let me leave the shop empty-handed.

On my paltry wages, there was little scope for social activity and I had to content myself with the occasional pint of stout when I was in funds; however, the fact we were all in the same boat seemed to make it a little more tolerable. Indeed only three of the men in our station out of thirty-two owned a car at the time; the rest of us relied on shanks's pony or a bicycle.

Yet, as usual, the authorities expected us to keep up appearances even though, as the old phrase goes, 'We didn't have a pot to piss in.' The deterioration of our financial position and the consequent loss of morale eventually led the staff association to confront senior Garda management in the Department of Justice. After a series of meetings attended by thousands of angry Gardaí, the government became alarmed and agreed to set up a commission of inquiry to examine our grievances. Judge John Conroy was appointed to head up the commission.

The subsequent report led to a vast improvement in Garda pay. More importantly, it forced senior management to adopt a more humane, fair and enlightened attitude in their dealings with the force. While all this agitation and unrest was going on, I was learning my trade on the laneways, boreens and quiet village streets of Rathfarnham.

It seems laughable today that we should have been employed in collecting statistics from the local farmers for the Department of Agriculture but back then it was considered an important duty, as was enforcing the provisions of the Noxious Weed Act, which obliged land owners to remove the ragwort plant from their property or face prosecution and fines. There was also the occasional house-breaking spree or drunken row at the weekend, but Rathfarnham was, in general, a peaceful place.

My ambition to be the next Sherlock Holmes looked very far down the road at that point. My first big day out in the Court of Petty Sessions was to prosecute one of the local parishioners for not having tax on his car. I was never happy about issuing summonses to decent people and only did enough to get the sergeant off my back.

Apart from the duties I have already described, I was required to be barrack orderly on a regular basis. This meant that I was employed in the public office answering telephones, manning the radio and dealing with the public. The shift covered a 24-hour period. At midnight, I locked the front door, changed into my pyjamas and assembled the old iron bed in the office. Most nights, I was able to get to sleep for a few hours, but other nights, when a prisoner was in the cells, I never closed my eyes, as I had to inspect him every half-hour and and record each visit in the station diary. On one occasion, a violent prisoner broke free as officers were taking him to the cells and he attacked me in the bed while I was asleep. After that, I slept with the baton under my pillow. A prisoner might consider a guard in pyjamas as a pushover, but if a baton was produced it would be a different matter.

I spent my first Christmas in the station that year and it turned out to be a unique and highly enjoyable experience. The week before, we really got into the Christmas spirit, and put up a tree and decorations in the public office and also in our own private quarters, transforming their drab interior to a warm and homely little oasis.

Throughout the week, a steady stream of local publicans dropped in with cases of spirits and barrels of porter and beer. We set up a bar in the kitchen with the kegs of beer and Guinness on draught. We entertained friends and local people, as well as visiting colleagues who normally dropped in at that time of year. On Christmas Day, we tucked into steaming plates of turkey and ham that had been kindly delivered from the kitchens of the lads who were married, who took pity on us, knowing that we were missing out on our own family dinners. That night, we held a party in the kitchen and the sing-song went on well into the early hours of the following morning. This tradition carried on in Rathfarnham for many a long year. Even after my transfer from there, I always returned on Christmas Day to see old colleagues and friends.

In June 1968, I went back to Templemore for four weeks to complete my training. Although there had been some relaxation of the draconian regime, I still found it a grim and unwelcoming place. I then returned to Rathfarnham and resumed the quiet and uneventful life of a country Garda. As I was, by this time, an almost fully fledged member of the force, I was getting the occasional assignment as observer in the district patrol car. From the older and experienced drivers, I was beginning to learn what real police work was all about. I was soon becoming a dab hand at settling domestic disputes, traffic accidents and the almost daily task of driving wandering horses, escaped from the traveller encampments in the district, to the pound in Churchtown, where they would later be redeemed by their owners on payment of a small fee.

However, on one occasion, which I now put down to inexperience,

I got involved in an escapade that could have lost me my career, as I was still a probationer when it happened. On the night in question, I was assigned as observer in the patrol car. The driver and I had earlier received an invitation from Mick McCarthy, the owner of the famous Embankment pub in Tallaght, County Dublin, to a dinner dance, which was held every year around November for the management, staff and invited guests. Mick was a close friend of mine and a fellow Listowel man. The venue that year was the Hibernian Hotel on Dawson Street in Dublin. We decided to join them in their festivities and, against all regulations, headed for the city, parked the patrol car down a side street and turned up at the hotel in full uniform. There we were greeted by the affable and gregarious Mick, who was delighted to see us and escorted us to the top table to the amusement and curious stares of the other guests.

Two hours and a good number of pints later, I got involved in a fracas with the legendary Luke Kelly, of the famous ballad group The Dubliners, and another individual. The row broke out in the downstairs toilets and to this day I can't remember what caused the hostilities, but I think I gave a good account of myself under the circumstances. After this unseemly mêlée, my colleague and I decided to beat a hasty retreat from the hotel. On the way back to Rathfarnham, I pondered on the possible consequences should our ill-fated foray to the Hibernian Hotel come to the attention of our authorities.

Two days later, I was called into the office of the sergeant in charge. I had a knot in my stomach, as I guessed the game was up. I was presented with the damning evidence: a photograph of me looking drunk and dishevelled in uniform, which had been taken outside the Hibernian Hotel by a snapper from the *Irish Press*. The photographs had been on display outside the newspaper's headquarters on Burgh Quay.

The sergeant informed me in ominous tones that a full investigation was under way into the affair and hinted that I might be packing my bags if the worst came to the worst. I left the office with a heavy heart and for the next few days was on tenterhooks, wondering if before long I would be buying a one-way ticket back to old Blighty. Thankfully, my fears proved to be unfounded. Although I was found guilty of numerous breaches of discipline, to my great relief I was let off with a severe written reprimand. I learned later that but for the plea for clemency from the sergeant, a fellow Listowel man, I would have been given my marching orders. As a result of gross stupidity, inexperience and booze, I had come to grief. I vowed there and then that in future I would keep my nose clean, work hard and try to redeem my tarnished reputation. That whole experience brought home forcibly to me the truth behind that wise old saying, 'The ale house has overwhelmed more men than the ocean.'

In January 1969, I returned to Templemore for a month on a motorcycle training course. When I returned to Rathfarnham, I was appointed official motorcyclist on my unit. I was issued with a smart new uniform that included riding jodhpurs, black-leather leggings and a special motorcycle greatcoat. Although I had no previous experience, or indeed interest, in bikes I became an avid enthusiast and I really relished the freedom and scope that the motorbike offered. In my new role, I was able to pursue and check out suspect vehicles and respond speedily to calls for assistance from colleagues and members of the public. It provided a perfect method for patrolling mountain roads and forest tracks, and I soon became familiar with every nook and cranny of the extensive territory of the Dublin mountains.

Shortly after this appointment, I had the first major success of my career. I was instrumental in the capture of a notorious burglar. He had been operating in the area for over ten years and was believed to be responsible for a large number of break-ins. He had become the prime target for the local detective unit, but, despite the best efforts, he continued his nocturnal activities with impunity. He proved himself to be a very careful operator, as he never left fingerprints or any other forensic evidence at the scenes of the crimes.

On night patrols, I was alert for any activity that might indicate the whereabouts of this daring and resourceful criminal. I tried many cunning stratagems and ruses to trap the elusive quarry.

One particular night, I was about to stop and check out the driver of a red Mini whom I saw acting suspiciously in a housing estate. As I approached on foot, the driver switched off the headlights and drove away at speed. I pursued him through a maze of side streets and got a good look at his face and the registration number of the car. I can still remember the number. He eventually gave me the slip, so I returned to the station and reported the matter to the detective on duty. The next morning, as a result of this information, the detectives raided a house in the Rosemount area of Rathfarnham.

During the search, the detectives uncovered an Aladdin's cave of stolen property; they had to get a lorry to remove it all. The burglar turned out to be an outwardly respectable married man. He admitted carrying out scores of other burglaries in the area. He never fenced away any of his ill-gotten gains, but squirrelled them away in garden sheds and his attic. During his subsequent trial, medical evidence showed that he was suffering from a severe psychiatric condition. I was commended by the police commissioner for good police duty and received a reward of £5 for the recovery of the stolen goods.

Around that time, however, I was involved in two other incidents from which I did not emerge quite so fortunate. These incidents illustrate in dramatic fashion the dangers that lay in wait for the unsuspecting police officer in the most unlikely circumstances whilst carrying out so-called routine duties. I had always accepted that in the role of police officer risk to life and limb is part and parcel of the job and, in any case, it was never a career for the faint-hearted.

The circumstances surrounding the first of these incidents began to unfold around midnight one night with a phone call to Rathfarnham station, where I was on 24-hour barrack orderly duty. On the other end was a frightened, hysterical woman telling me that her husband had gone mad on poitín. He had attacked his best friend and was rampaging through the house, breaking furniture and windows. She went on to say that she was terrified that her husband would attack her and her baby son. I tried my best to calm her down and to reassure her. I told her that I would send a patrol car without delay and immediately tried to make contact with the district patrol car on our antiquated radio system, but to no avail. Within minutes, the same distraught woman was back on the line, sounding even more distressed and panic-stricken. She said her husband had made another brutal assault on his friend, who was now lying unconscious in the front garden. She then said she was hiding behind the sofa in her sitting room, holding on to her baby. I again made frantic efforts to contact the patrol car, but to no avail. Fearing for the lives of the mother and baby, I decided to go immediately to their rescue. I hurriedly donned my motorcycle gear and baton, and headed off at breakneck speed leaving the station unattended, a cardinal sin at the time. En route to the scene, I tried over and over again to make contact with the patrol car but with no success. However, in the forlorn hope that it might be picking up my signal, I gave out the particulars of the incident and requested urgent assistance.

In little over ten minutes, I pulled up at the house in a respectable middle-class neighbourhood. There were lights blazing in every window upstairs and down, and the front door was wide open as I approached it. In the front garden, I saw a man lying on his back. His face was covered in blood and he was moaning softly. There was no sound of any description coming from the house. I entered through the hall door and went in to the sitting room. I saw broken glass, upturned chairs and smashed ornaments scattered all around. In the midst of all this chaos, there was a young man sitting placidly on an armchair in front of the fire. He had a glazed, vacant look in his eyes and he did not seem to notice or acknowledge my presence. Just then, I heard a frightened whisper and saw a young woman clutching a baby peering out from behind the sofa. I helped her up and escorted her and the baby out of the house and onto the roadway. The poor woman was in a pitiful state, wild-eyed with terror from her ordeal. Between sobs, she told me that her husband, whom I had seen in the house, and his friend, who was now lying prostrate on the ground, had gone on a drinking binge in the house. They had between them consumed two litre-bottles of poitín and cans of beer. She said her husband went completely berserk and attacked his friend, and that she feared for her own life and that of her baby as he rampaged around the house smashing everything he could lay his hands on. I told her to get help from her neighbours and called an ambulance for the injured man.

I went back into the house with the intention of arresting her husband for the savage assault. As I entered the sitting room, without any warning or provocation whatsoever he jumped out of his chair and lunged at me with a knife. I blocked the blow with my baton, which I had drawn as a precaution. He chased me around the sitting room and hall and into the kitchen, slashing and stabbing at me for all he was worth with a long-bladed carving knife. I managed to get a few blows in myself, but he had the strength of a madman and they appeared to have little effect on him. It was a desperate situation and I began to think I was done for.

I cannot recall now how long this life-and-death struggle lasted for, as time seems to get distorted in these situations; however, I do remember three of my colleagues bursting into the house and overpowering my attacker. It was a timely rescue, as I don't think I could have held out much longer. I finally collapsed onto a chair in utter exhaustion. It was then I noticed that chunks had been taken out of my baton by the knife and realised what a close shave it had been for me.

My assailant was never charged with any offence. The friend he had seriously assaulted refused to press charges against him. It turned out that this deranged individual was a pillar of the community and held a senior position in local government. Overtures were made to me from both internal and external sources not to proceed with a prosecution against him. I was assured that his violent behaviour that night was completely out of character and due entirely to the consumption of the poitin. I was told of his suicidal state, and his sorrow and remorse after his night of madness.

After a final tearful plea from his wife and a lot of soul-searching on my behalf, I agreed to drop all charges against him. I subsequently read in an FBI report that more police officers lose their lives dealing with domestic disputes than in any other situation.

During the other incident I recall, although less dramatic, I received serious injuries to my arm. It began on a peaceful Sunday afternoon while I was on routine motorcycle duty in my district. I picked up a message on the radio from the control room at Dublin Castle to the effect that youths were breaking into cars in the car park of the Mount Argus church and monastery off the Kimmage Road in Harold's Cross. When I arrived at the scene, I saw that a number of car windows had been smashed and radios ripped out of the dashboards. I immediately began a search of the grounds for the thieves. Minutes later, I saw two young thugs acting suspiciously close to the bank of a little river that runs through the grounds. As soon as they saw me, they split up and ran off in opposite directions. I ran after one of them, who I recognised as belonging to a notorious criminal family from a nearby housing estate.

Despite being hampered by my bulky motorcycle gear, I managed to catch up with him as he tried to cross the river. I attempted to put him in an arm lock in order to handcuff him, but he put up such violent resistance that I was unable to do so. During the ensuing struggle, we splashed and thrashed about in the middle of the river and eventually I lost my balance and fell, dragging my prisoner down with me. In trying to regain my balance, I struck my left hand on a piece of rusty corrugated-iron sheeting that was submerged in the water. I felt a searing pain in my arm and realised that I had done myself a serious injury. When I looked, I saw a gaping, ragged wound on my hand and wrist that was pumping blood. In the confusion, my prisoner saw his opportunity and legged it. I struggled onto the bank of the river, where I was helped by a small crowd of people that had been attracted by the commotion. Somebody with knowledge of first aid used a necktie as a tourniquet to stem the bleeding. The Rathfarnham patrol car arrived on the scene soon after.

One of my colleagues helped me into the rear of the car and sat beside me holding the tourniquet as we headed for the Adelaide hospital in the city. By the time we arrived at Accident and Emergency, I had lost a lot of blood and was starting to feel dizzy. I was immediately seen to and put on a drip. It needed 31 stitches to close the deep wound on my wrist. The Australian doctor who attended me told me I was lucky to have received such prompt attention, as I had severed an artery, potentially a very dangerous injury. I spent a number of hours in hospital before finally being discharged. Unfortunately, in the following days the wound became infected and I became very unwell with a high temperature.

It was a month before I recovered sufficiently to return to work. I subsequently arrested and charged the youth who had caused me such pain and trouble. He pleaded guilty in court to a number of charges, including larceny, obstruction and resisting arrest. He received 12 months in jail for his little crime spree.

Around August that year, after I had recovered from my injuries, I availed myself of some leave and went down to Listowel to visit my mam and dad. One day during my stay, I decided to go trout fishing on the beautiful Feale with my brother, Vincent. It was an ideal day for our purpose, warm and overcast with a slight breeze. We went to our favourite haunt, the Castle Stream, and began to fish for the wily and elusive sea trout. We had barely cast our lines into the river when we were confronted by the water bailiffs, who demanded to see our fishing licences. As we did not have any, we had to surrender all our tackle and rods, much to the anger and indignation of my brother. I had to physically restrain him from subjecting the two officials to a second baptism in Feale water.

To avoid a prosecution under the Fisheries Act, which would have landed me in hot water with the police authorities, I gave my uncle James's name and address instead of my own. Some months later, he was summoned before the local District Court and fined £12. I ended up paying the fine and the legal expenses, a not inconsiderable sum of money at the time. My poor uncle, who took the rap for me and had to endure the taunts of his old cronies, was quite indignant that his previously unblemished character had been sullied by this conviction. I reminded him that it was a form of poetic justice: in his youth, he had been one of the most prolific poachers on the river. In the summer of 1969 when my holiday ended, I returned to the station and the idyll that was Rathfarnham. However, storm clouds were gathering in those parts of our island still under the rule of Her Britannic Majesty.

Since the previous IRA border campaign had ended in 1962, the North had remained relatively peaceful. There had, of course, been the inevitable sporadic outbreaks of sectarian violence, especially during the Loyalist marching seasons. However, since 1966, the 50th anniversary of the 1916 Rising, which was also celebrated by the nationalist population in the North, tensions between both communities were at breaking point. The vast majority of the Loyalist Protestant population was implacably opposed to any nationalist aspirations of closer ties with the Irish Republic, or indeed to granting them the most basic of human rights and freedoms.

The Province was a tinderbox waiting for a spark to ignite it. Inevitably, the centuries-old animosity, hatred, fear and suspicion that simmered between those two warring tribes like a dormant volcano erupted in all its fury in the summer and autumn of 1969.

A civil-rights association called the People's Democracy had been formed in October of 1967. The aims of the association, which were loosely based on the civil-rights movement for black citizens in the

United States, were to seek social justice and equality for the Catholic nationalist community, who, for centuries, had been treated as second-class citizens in their own country.

A number of very successful demonstrations and marches were held across the North in 1968. There was, of course, violent opposition by Loyalist diehards to these displays of nationalist resurgence. On 5 October, 23 November and 4 December, demonstrators were attacked by Loyalist mobs in Derry city, Dungannon and Armagh city.

Undeterred, the civil-rights movement planned another march, this time from Belfast to Derry city. They set out on 1 January 1969. All along the route, they were attacked by Loyalist mobs and re-routed time and time again by the Royal Ulster Constabulary. On 2 January, the march reached Burntollet Bridge outside Derry city. Here the marchers were confronted by RUC officers and units of the feared and hated Ulster Special Constabulary, known as the 'B' Specials, a Protestant sectarian force that did not have in its ranks one single Catholic. The peaceful marchers, without the slightest provocation, were then violently attacked by the so-called forces of law and order under the full glare of the TV cameras. It was a horrifying, frightening and ugly spectacle. Men and women were brutally attacked to the ground and hit with batons. So many of them were seriously injured, it took a fleet of ambulances to remove them to hospital.

Later on, the remnants of the march were attacked again, this time by Loyalist thugs, at Irish Street in Derry city, where 15 more marchers were seriously injured. The television images of the demonstrators being bludgeoned and terrorised by the security forces caused shock, revulsion and condemnation around the world. A Pandora's box had been opened. More than 3,000 people would pay with their lives over the next 25 years in what would euphemistically become known as the 'Troubles'.

When I returned for duty after my little sojourn in Listowel, I had to face up to the fact that irrevocable changes were taking place little more than 100 miles away. In July and August alone that year, ten people were killed, sixteen factories were burned down, 170 houses were destroyed in arson attacks and nearly 500 more damaged by petrol bombs. In Belfast, 60 Catholic-owned public houses were attacked and 24 burned to the ground. As a result of Loyalist intimidation, almost 2,000 families had to flee their homes, 1,500 of them Catholic.

By August, the RUC and 'B' Specials had lost all control of the situation. The British Government dispatched the Queen's Regiment to the North to restore law and order and to protect the beleaguered Catholic community, especially in the cities. Originally welcomed as saviours, these same British troops would turn their guns on the very community that they were supposed to be protecting. On 10 October, the British government announced that on the recommendations of Lord Hunt's committee the Ulster Special Constabulary, the 'B' Specials, would be disbanded. This news filled the Loyalist community with dismay. In the Protestant estates of Belfast, serious rioting erupted. An RUC officer was shot dead on the Lower Shankill Road by a Loyalist terrorist, the first such officer to be killed in the Troubles. The Irish government began establishing army camps along the border. These five posts were situated at Dundalk, Castleblaney, Cavan, Finner and Dunree.

Events were unfolding that would soon herald the end of our peaceful and tranquil life in the South and even threaten the very existence of the state. As W.B. Yeats wrote of the 1916 Rebellion: 'A terrible beauty was born.'

We in An Garda Síochána became the thin blue line that stood between anarchy and the rule of law. Many of my colleagues would pay the supreme sacrifice over the next 30 years. As events worsened in Northern Ireland, rumours started to circulate that Loyalist terror groups, like the Ulster Volunteer Force, were preparing to attack targets in the Republic. Units of the Irish Army were deployed to protect power stations and public and government buildings against attack. In my own district, soldiers were stationed to keep watch on the television mast and building on Mount Kippure, high up in the Dublin mountains. Further information gleaned by intelligence sources revealed a plot by a terrorist group to poison the water supply in Dublin city and the suburbs.

Incredible as it now seems, the government of the day took the threat seriously and ordered Garda protection of the reservoirs. There were two reservoirs in my district, one at Bohernabreena and the other at Woodtown.

I did my fair share of duty protecting the latter armed only with a baton and an ancient walkie-talkie. It was a lonely posting in an isolated place – eight hours listening to the sound of the wind in the pine trees and the eerie sloshing of the water through the viaduct and the pipes. When I heard that a young seminarian had drowned himself in the reservoir some years before, it did nothing to relax my state of mind. I also knew that I was on a fool's errand. I had no chance of protecting the water supply against a terrorist unit armed, as I was, with only a baton. It was a typical arse-covering exercise by the authorities, who could claim in the event of an incident that they had taken appropriate measures. Luckily, nothing did happen and the only interruption of my watch was the occasional badger foraging for supper in the undergrowth.

One night during that period, at around three in the morning while I was on motorcycle duty, I received a call on my radio directing me to go to the ESB sub-station in Carrickmines, County Dublin, where an explosion had been reported. I immediately returned to the station and asked the duty sergeant for permission to arm myself with an official revolver before responding to the call, reminding him of the UVF's threats to attack installations. He refused point-blank. I argued that I needed such protection in the event that I came face to face with an armed terrorist and was infuriated by his refusal, which was not simply illogical but was effectively putting my life in danger.

However, as soon as his back was turned, I forced the lock on the gun cupboard and helped myself to two guns and ammunition. I loaded the weapons and placed them in the pockets of my greatcoat. I left the station, mounted my motorcycle and headed off to Carrickmines. When I arrived, other Garda units were at the scene. It later transpired that it was nothing more sinister than the transformer exploding because of some technical problem. Before leaving the scene, I displayed my hardware to startled colleagues in an act of bravado which I would subsequently regret. I drove back to the station and returned the revolvers and ammunition to the gun closet in the sergeant's office.

A couple of days later, I was confronted by the duty sergeant, who had heard through the grapevine about my latest exploit. I had to apologise for my reckless behaviour and for disobeying orders. I received a stern warning and was told that any repeat of my insolent insubordination would see me back working on the pick and shovel.

5

FAMILY MATTERS

AS EVENTS TURNED OUT, IT WOULD BE ANOTHER THREE YEARS BEFORE Loyalist paramilitaries would venture south and unleash death and destruction on the streets of Dublin. However, in the early months of 1970, a more immediate threat to the security of the state was the activities of a renegade gang of former IRA men styling themselves Saor Eire. Meaning 'free Ireland', Saor Eire was a legitimate political organisation founded in the 1930s, which had long since ceased to exist. This shadowy Republican splinter group did not come into existence officially until March or April 1969, although they had been importing illegal firearms from Britain for a number of years and hiding them in dumps in the Dublin and Wicklow mountains. Their aim, like all the other unlawful Republican terrorist organisations, was to overthrow the legitimate government of the Irish Republic and replace it with a 32-county all-Ireland republic using force of arms.

In 1970, reports were circulating that this group were planning to kidnap certain government ministers, including the Secretary of the Department of Justice Peter Berry. This information caused deep concern and resulted in the beefing up of security measures on those individuals.

Most of the members of this gang were well known to the police and their photographs had been circulated in our official police gazette, *Fogra Tora*, in October 1969. That year the gang had carried out a number of daring armed robberies on banks on both sides of the border, netting thousands of pounds for their cause.

As late as February 1970, the gang had raided the Hibernian Bank in Rathdrum, County Wicklow, taking over the entire village, cutting telephone lines and hijacking cars. As we carried out our duties protecting banks and post offices, we were mindful of the warning contained in our gazette that this gang were armed and dangerous and would not hesitate to use lethal force if confronted in pursuance of their activities.

On 3 April that year, I was having breakfast in Rathfarnham station when I heard the terrible news that Garda Dick Fallon had been shot dead by an armed gang during a bank robbery at Arran Quay. I remember vividly to this day my feeling of shock, revulsion and anger. My colleagues in the station were stunned by the news and many of them were close to tears. I was due to travel home to see my parents in Listowel but like hundreds of other Gardaí, I cancelled my leave. The subsequent funeral was a very emotional affair. There was a huge outpouring of public grief as his cortège passed. I stood solemnly to attention along with thousands of my colleagues to form a guard of honour along the city streets. Many bystanders and comrades wept openly as the coffin, draped in the tricolour, passed by.

Garda Richard Fallon was the first member of the force to be killed on duty since 1942. His murder by violent subversives sent shock waves through the government. Tragically, Dick Fallon would not be the last. Over the next 30 years, another 13 members of the force would be slain in the course of their duties, almost all at the bloody hands of the Provisional IRA and other subversive organisations. I was involved in the investigation of eight of those murders. The shooting of Garda Fallon and the threat to kidnap government ministers highlighted the dangers posed to the security of the state by the activities of these paramilitaries.

Shortly afterwards, hundreds of men were drafted in to the Special Branch unit in response to the deteriorating situation. Fallon's death also dispelled the notion that we in the Republic would remain unscathed as the North was descending into anarchy and civil war.

During this time, I was doing a steady line with Kathleen Murphy, a native of Edinburgh, whom I met in Dublin in 1968. I remember that warm, sultry June night at the Television Club in Harcourt Street. My search for romance wasn't going too well and because of the stifling heat and choking cigarette smoke I decided to postpone my quest for another night. I left the club and went walking up Rathmines Road towards the station. About a mile away, I heard a little inner voice telling me to return to the club. Against my better judgement, I turned around and headed straight to the same place. I was only minutes back when I met Kathleen. I was instantly attracted to her and asked her for a dance. She was my type: dark-haired and voluptuous, with beautiful brown eyes.

After the dance, we sat down together in a corner and had a chat and a drink. I introduced myself and told her that I was from Listowel, County Kerry, and was a policeman. Kathleen told me she was from Edinburgh and worked for an insurance company in the city centre. When she heard my name and where I came from, she seemed a bit taken aback. She then went on to tell me that two weeks previously she had been hitching a lift on the Belfast Road near the airport on her way to take the ferry home to Scotland. She said a man pulled up in a car and offered her a lift, and it turned out that he was also heading to Larne to catch the ferry to Scotland. Kathleen told me that she had had a pleasant journey with this extremely polite man who bought her lunch on the boat and then drove her up to Edinburgh, and even dropped her off at her own front door. She said she remembered his name as Liam O'Carroll from Listowel in County Kerry.

I told Kathleen that Liam was my brother and I produced a photo of him, which I had happened to take a few weeks earlier, from my wallet. She instantly recognised him. I think at that moment we both realised that fate may have brought us together. We left the Television Club hand in hand and are still together, despite all our ups and downs, thirty-eight years and five children later.

At this point, I was still living in the station and sleeping in my old room; however, as each of the older residents moved out to get married their rooms were refurbished for official use. This new policy would soon mean the end of the old tradition of members of the force living and sleeping in Garda stations. As 1970 was drawing to a close, I was the last remaining tenant there.

In early October that year, my father James suffered a severe stroke on a visit to Dublin with my mother. He was rushed to the Mater Hospital, where he hovered between life and death for more than a week. He survived and lived for another ten years entirely paralysed on one side and unable to speak. It was the first time that serious illness had struck my immediate family, and I was naturally extremely upset. I returned to the station about 12.30 a.m. one night after visiting him in hospital. I headed up to my room, undressed and got into bed.

I lay awake for a while in silent prayer for my stricken father. Suddenly, I became aware that my bedclothes were being slowly pulled downwards and I sensed I wasn't alone in the room. I switched on the light and jumped out of the bed. I got a vague uneasy feeling, but I put it down to my imagination. I got back into bed and fell into a deep, untroubled sleep, and I thought no more about it. The next night I visited my father in the hospital with the rest of my family and again got back to the station at about one o'clock in the morning.

Garda Mick Clancy was in his bed in the public office. After having a little chat with him, I went upstairs to my room. I remembered the strange events of the night before, so took the precaution of placing my baton and rosary beads beside me on my locker to be ready for all-comers. I switched off the light and almost immediately I sensed a presence in the room. Again, I felt my bedclothes being pulled slowly downwards towards my feet. Suddenly, I saw the tall figure of a man dressed in old-fashioned clothes standing beside the bed. I could see his face clearly as the street lamps outside illuminated the room.

I froze for a moment in terror before letting out a blood-curdling scream and jumping out of bed. In my panic to escape from this terrifying spectre, I pushed a heavy timber wardrobe aside as if it were a matchbox. I took off like a scalded cat down the corridor, where I met Mick, who had been awakened by all the commotion. I told him of my ghostly visitor and he made me a cup of tea to calm my nerves. He swears to this day that my hair was standing on end as though I'd had an electric shock.

I slept in an armchair for the rest of that night and moved into digs the following day. I was the last resident to leave the official accommodation. Within months, my old bedroom was converted into the District Detective Unit office.

Subsequently, other former residents of this haunted room have come forward and told me that they too had strange experiences over the years. One man in particular said with the utmost sincerity that he too had seen the ghostly apparition of a man dressed in turn-of-the-century clothes in that room. He assured me that he was also sober that night. I heard that when workmen were building the station back in the late '30s or early '40s, they claimed to have seen an apparition of a man in that same room. I was to learn later from an old Rathfarnham man that part of the station was built over an ancient burial ground.

Around May that year, the political scandal that became known as the Arms Crisis convulsed the nation and rocked the Fianna Fáil government headed by Jack Lynch. It had emerged that monies allocated by the government to alleviate hardship and distress amongst the nationalist peoples in the north of Ireland had been spent instead on guns and ammunition to be used in the event of a doomsday situation to defend the Catholic population.

A number of Fianna Fáil ministers were sacked from the government and others, including the ex-minister Charles J. Haughey and a serving Irish Army officer, were arrested and charged but later found not guilty by the courts. As a result of this debacle, the Fianna Fáil government was split down the middle in its policies on the north of Ireland, and the people were bewildered and a little frightened at these extraordinary events. The well-meaning but totally undemocratic actions of those involved at the highest ranks of government gave many of us in An Garda Síochána real concerns for the continued safety and security of the state.

I am still of the opinion that our fears at that time were well founded. One incident in particular that I myself was involved in reinforced that belief. One night during that period, I was on security duty at the home of Liam Cosgrave on Scholarstown Road in Rathfarnham. He was at that time the leader of the opposition in Dáil Éireann, our seat of government. At around two o'clock, he drove up unaccompanied in his own car to the front gate where I was on duty. I opened the gate and saluted, and he drove in. A few yards up the driveway, he stopped the car and walked back towards me. He told me in a calm, steady voice that a man who had appeared to be armed with a handgun tried to stop his car near Templeogue Bridge. He'd been on his way home from a late sitting of the Dáil. Seeing the walkie-talkie around my neck, he told me to get on to Rathfarnham Garda station immediately for assistance.

Within minutes of putting in the call, several carloads of armed Special Branch detectives arrived at the house. Although a detailed search was made of the area around Templeogue village and the bridge, no trace of the armed man was ever found. Several senior officers also called and spoke to Liam about this incident. Armed detectives remained at his home for the rest of the morning but nothing untoward happened at the house that night or, thankfully, any time afterwards.

When the senior Garda officers had left, Liam Cosgrave invited me into his house. He made tea and sandwiches, which we ate in the kitchen of his modest bungalow. During our conversation, he told me we were living in strange, troubled times. I told him that my father had been a Fine Gael activist in North Kerry all his life, and had held him in very high esteem as a man and a politician. I found Liam Cosgrave to be a kind and courteous gentleman with a warm sense of humour. I marvelled at his calm, unruffled composure after enduring such a frightening ordeal.

Back in those far-off days, the District Court sat on the first Tuesday of each month in the little courthouse in Rathfarnham village. It was an old, unheated and rather dilapidated building dating back to 1912. On the day of the sitting, which was always a very important day in the station, a Garda was employed at the courthouse. His duties included opening up the building, lighting a fire in the judge's little antechamber and reserving a parking space on the road outside for the judge's car. This was normally done using a few chairs from the courthouse, as back then we didn't even have traffic cones.

When the District Justice arrived, the Garda would greet him with a salute and assist him in parking his car, He would then carry his bags and escort him into the courthouse, and remain at his service for the duration of the court. The Garda was also expected to make a cup of tea and provide light refreshments, if requested by the District Justice.

I was assigned from time to time on this very important duty. In those days, most of the business of the court was taken up with licensing applications, the prosecution of road-traffic offences, breaches of the peace and minor assaults. Occasionally, the local detectives would arrive with handcuffed prisoners, who were charged with more serious crimes such as burglary or larceny. I always found it a pleasant and interesting tour of duty. I enjoyed the courtroom atmosphere and was fascinated by the cut and thrust of legal arguments between the various parties. From attending this court of petty sessions, I learned and absorbed the finer points of the law of evidence that would later stand me in good stead in the more austere surroundings of Green Street and the Four Courts.

I remember one cold winter's day when I was on court duty. I had done all the usual tasks and had a big fire blazing in the judge's room. I had reserved a parking space and was waiting out on the street for the arrival of his lordship. At around 11.30 a.m., the District Justice pulled up in a car driven by the court clerk. I went over and opened the passenger door, stood back and saluted. As he got out of the car, he stumbled and almost fell. To my amazement, I realised he was drunk and practically had to carry him into the courthouse.

Inside his chamber, he slumped down into a chair. At this stage, I was joined in the room by an irate court clerk who quietly whispered in my ear that the judge was drunk – as if I had to be told! I offered the Justice a cup of tea or coffee, which he declined. He then caught me by my jacket and ordered me to get him a large gin and tonic. I looked to the court clerk for guidance, but my furtive glance was intercepted by the old Justice, who snarled at me to get him his drink without delay.

I left and went up the village to the Castle Inn and returned a couple of minutes later with a large gin and tonic concealed in a brown paper bag. I handed it to the judge, who swallowed it down in one gulp. He handed me back the empty glass and demanded a replacement. No money had changed hands as of yet. I trotted off back to the pub, where I again ordered a large gin and tonic from the bemused proprietor.

I returned to the courthouse and handed the drink over to the judge, who downed it again in one go. By this stage, the courthouse was filling up with witnesses, defendants, prosecuting Gardaí and solicitors. The court clerk had already announced a delay in proceedings. I returned to the judge's chamber to find him fast asleep. The court clerk and I tried to wake him but to no avail. Seeing the hopelessness of the situation, he announced to all that the court was adjourned to a new date, details of which would be posted up on the door in due course.

I cleared the court and locked it up. I went back to the judge's room with the court clerk and found the judge sitting bolt upright in his chair. On seeing me, he immediately ordered another gin and tonic. At this stage, the court clerk, who was at the end of his tether, told the judge he was getting no more drink and he was taking him home. Together we helped him into the car, and they drove away. I posted a new date on the courthouse door for the adjourned proceedings.

I never got payment for those gin and tonics, but I never begrudged them to that poor man. Drink is an awful curse, but I'm the last man to cast aspersions on any poor devil who succumbs to her deadly charms. The judge had a chronic alcohol problem and I never saw him again as he died shortly afterwards.

As 1970 drew to a close, my father, who had made a slight recovery from the stroke, was moved from his nursing home in Dublin to the hospital in Listowel by ambulance. I accompanied him on that long, sad journey. Against all the odds, he had survived and we were grateful to God that he had been spared. I spent that Christmas at home in Cahirdown with my family. The following year would turn out to be a very special year in my personal life and career.

In June 1971, my brother Joe was ordained to the priesthood in an ecclesiastical extravaganza at St Mary's Parish Church in Listowel. His Grace, the Archbishop of Alaska, Joseph T. Ryan, his sister Margaret and a retinue of Monsignors and priests arrived in Listowel in a cavalcade of black Mercedes for the ceremonies. They were there at the invitation of my brother Tony, a Holy Ghost Father, who at the time was based in Alaska.

On a sunny June morning, our family and half the population of Listowel packed to capacity our beautiful church. Archbishop Ryan, a giant of a man standing almost 6 ft 5 in. tall and with a mane of steel grey hair, was the principal celebrant at the Mass. He was arrayed in the most magnificent vestments and cut a splendid figure on the altar surrounded by dozens of other priests in equally sumptuous robes. After he ordained my brother, he pronounced in a booming voice that Joe was now a priest for ever according to the Order of Melchizedek. That was a joyous and moving moment for all the family.

Afterwards, the beaming Archbishop emerged into the bright sunshine to bless the hundreds of people waiting in the square outside the church. For almost an hour they filed past, each in turn kneeling in homage to acknowledge his blessing or kiss his Episcopal ring. He later confided in Tony that he should have worn his Alaskan gold nugget ring that morning. As you can gather, he wasn't the most modest of men I ever met! It was a great occasion for the town – after all, it wasn't every day that a prince of the church honoured Listowel with his presence.

We celebrated the joyous event with day-long festivities in the Central Hotel in Ballybunion attended by hundreds of guests. The hotel was closed for the day to all except those attending the ordination party. No expense was spared and a marvellous time was had by all. The free drink throughout the day was especially appreciated and enjoyed by an army of veteran drinkers from the town thanks to the largesse of the Archbishop. Some days later, His Grace bade farewell to Listowel and returned to Alaska.

When all the excitement subsided, my newly ordained brother headed off to his new post in Lancashire. He has remained a labourer in those vineyards until this day and in 1996 celebrated his silver jubilee as a priest. Some months later, my brother Tony left the priesthood and took up a teaching post in a school in San Francisco. He is now happily married with three children.

Tony had given the best years of his life to the Church. He spent many years teaching in Ireland and subsequently four years in the mission fields of Alaska, but became disheartened and disillusioned at the number of his fellow priests, including some of his closest friends, who were leaving the ministry. He could no longer tolerate the lonely isolation and the unnatural and unrealistic demands of a celibate life, and decided to call it a day. He was not alone: over a hundred thousand priests worldwide have left the ministry since then.

One year previously, my brother Michael, who had been ordained a number of years earlier in Clonliffe College for the Dublin Diocese, had also chosen to call it quits. He later received a doctorate in public health and has spent the last 30 years working in the poorest countries in the developing world. His wife is Nicaraguan and they have two daughters.

When Michael and Tony left the priesthood, my parents were devastated; it was as if there had been a bereavement in the family, such was their sense of grief and loss. Over time, they got over their bitter disappointment and fully accepted the decisions their sons had made, taking some consolation in seeing them happily married with children in the following years.

Both brothers went through an extremely difficult and painful period following their departure from the ministry. Turning their backs on the priesthood was denounced by many of their colleagues as nothing short of scandalous. Without the benefits of any support group or counselling services, they had to endure rejection by old friends, social banishment and a degree of public opprobrium. I still admired their courage and integrity for facing up to the reality that they had lost their vocation: rather than live a lie, they were prepared to face a very uncertain future.

At one time or another, eight of my siblings were in religious orders. I am at a complete loss to explain the factors and influences that attracted them to that life like moths to a flame. However, one possible explanation might have been the constant activities of the recruiting sergeants of God's army, who travelled the length and breadth of Ireland calling to every college, school and convent in the ceaseless quest for suitable candidates. In those innocent times, we were all filled with religious fervour from a steady diet of religious magazines, like the *Sacred Heart Messenger*, with stories from the Far East, extolling the glamour and adventure of life with the Foreign Missions and the guarantee of a bed in heaven in the next life. In those far-off days, it should be remembered that a son or daughter in holy orders conferred a high degree of honour and respectability on many a humble household. Mercifully, I was never enamoured by vows of poverty, chastity and obedience.

My father was a deeply religious man, who lived and breathed his

Catholic faith on a daily basis. My mother, on the other hand, had a certain laissez-faire approach to religion and believed in the dictum *Laborare est orare* – to work is to pray – which seemed particularly apt for someone who was coping with 15 children. Either way, I never once heard them encourage any of my brothers and sisters to enter the religious life, although my father did insist that each of us pay the strictest adherence to our spiritual obligations. Come hell or high water, we all had to kneel down at night and recite the family rosary to which he had a great devotion. Any unfortunate neighbours who happened along at the time were dragooned into taking part in our family worship as well. My father, who was one of the old school, believed that 'the family who prays together, stays together' and, by and large, his faith in that creed in relation to our own family has not been misplaced even after all these years.

In August that year, applications were sought from suitable candidates to go forward for interview for appointment to the Crime Task Force, a new and novel policing initiative to be staffed entirely by uniformed personnel. I applied for a position on the unit and my application was recommended and I went for interview in Dublin Castle. Shortly afterwards, I was thrilled to get notification that I had been successful.

In September, I was appointed to the very first uniformed Crime Task Force. I left behind the rolling hills of Rathfarnham for the hustle and bustle of the city. I was excited at the prospect of real action and I was not to be disappointed on that score.

Our unit was based in the lower yard of Dublin Castle. The twenty-two-man unit was headed by two fine officers, Superintendent Tim Farrell and Inspector Michael Hanrahan. At our first briefing, our role was clearly defined by Superintendent Farrell as follows: 'This unit will concentrate and confine its entire activities on the prevention and detection of crime in the city centre with special emphasis on the entire north docklands area.'

We were provided with unmarked police cars, motorcycles and the most up-to-date walkie-talkies. However, Superintendent Farrell went on to explain that the ethos and spirit of the unit was based on old-style policing, which we would implement through intensive patrolling. The units were to saturate areas of high-crime activity, targeting known criminals and putting them out of business. Over the coming months and years, the task force would earn the well-deserved reputation as the most efficient and successful unit in the fight against the rising tide of crime and lawlessness.

I spent two years on the unit and gained valuable experience that would assist me in the years ahead. From our very inception, we made our presence felt by intense and sustained activity. In those early days, we were so enthusiastic that we hardly stopped to take a meal break. We became the scourge of petty and professional criminals alike and chalked up hundreds of arrests in that first year.

We adopted a 'zero-tolerance' policy for all kinds of criminal activity long before that term became a sound bite for certain politicians. The criminal fraternity soon learned to have a healthy respect for the men of the task force, or the X-ray unit, as they sometimes referred to us (X-ray being the call sign of our walkie-talkies and car radios). The unit was particularly effective in combating the very high level of thefts on the docks at that time. There were pubs in the docklands area where stolen goods, ranging from a needle to an anchor, were bought and sold with impunity.

On 24 September, I married Kathleen, my girlfriend of three years, in a civil ceremony in Kildare Street registry office in Dublin. I was still half in uniform, having come straight from court. During a brief and impersonal service, Kathleen and I exchanged vows before our two witnesses, and the registrar duly pronounced us man and wife. We went through the civil marriage in Dublin because under Scottish law I would have to have been resident there for three weeks before we could be legally married – time that I did not have.

After the wedding, Kathleen and our witnesses, Harry and Alice, went to Davy Byrnes pub in Duke Street for a few celebratory drinks. Kathleen stayed for a while before heading back to her job at the insurance company. I stayed behind with Harry and Alice and had a few more. I paraded for duty in Dublin Castle that evening a little late and slightly tipsy. I apologised to my boss and explained that I had got married earlier that day. There were gasps of disbelief all round. My boss shook his head and told me I should be on my honeymoon with my wife. I informed him that it was out of the question, as I had given a cast-iron guarantee to the parish priest in Rathmines that I would not engage in any such activity until we were married by the Holy Mother Church. He continued to question me with a look of complete bewilderment on his face.

I could see with every passing moment he was becoming more and more sceptical about my story. I explained that I had indeed got married that day in a civil ceremony in the registry office with the permission of Catholic authorities in Dublin. I further explained that Kathleen and I intended to have a full Catholic wedding in Scotland later that year. It came as no surprise to me that everyone should have been so shocked, as it was almost unheard of at the time for two Catholics, and especially a member of An Garda Síochána, to get married in a registry office. Until then, I told him, I had to give a solemn undertaking to those same Church authorities that Kathleen and I would not live together as man and wife. For weeks afterwards, I was subjected to unmerciful slagging from the lads on the unit.

Ten days later, on 4 October, Kathleen and I tied the knot for the second time in the beautiful St John's Church in Corstorphine in Edinburgh. This time my brother Joe performed the nuptials and solemnised our marriage under the rules of the Church. Now we could consummate our marriage without fear of eternal damnation!

Afterwards, we had a truly memorable celebration in the nearby Harp Hotel, where Kathleen's mother, Brigid, worked as a cook. By this stage, I had been back and forth to Edinburgh with Kathleen three or four times a year and had been welcomed with open arms into her family. Kathleen's mother came from outside Dungloe in County Donegal and her father, John, was born in the little rural mining village of Fauldhouse in West Lothian. He had been a career soldier and had travelled the world with his regiment, the Royal Scots. When he had a few drams on board, he would boast of how he had marched 'from Kabul to Kandahar'. He was also a former welterweight boxing champion of the regiment and not a man to be trifled with. He was a big, gregarious, honest man, whom I much admired and, over the years, I developed a great friendship with him. I think because of her father's military background, Kathleen understood the life she was letting herself in for, as the wife of a policeman. In the three years we were going out, she rarely ever complained when I was late for a date or had to cancel it altogether because of work commitments.

From the beginning, Kathleen was a pillar of support to me. When we drove out of Edinburgh for our honeymoon in the south of England, I knew that I had a loving, loyal partner and friend who would stand by me through thick and thin in the years ahead.

On returning home, we moved into a flat on Howth Road to begin our married life. Towards the end of November, I was back again with my unit. I was enjoying this new and exciting phase in my career, where every day brought new challenges and experiences. In the fictional world of the police, as depicted on our television screens in programmes like *The Bill*, *Inspector Morse* and the many other similar series, every day is an action-packed adventure for our heroes in blue; in reality, much of the everyday police work is routine, repetitive and not at all glamorous. But at the same time it's never boring. I believe that a sense of humour and a large dollop of common sense are indispensable when facing the trials and tribulations of police work, and one needs to have both in abundance when the need arises.

I recall one such occasion while on routine motorcycle patrol in the city centre. I answered a call to a disturbance on board a ship in Alexandra Basin on North Wall. When I arrived at the scene, I was confronted by a gentleman in naval uniform looking like a drowned rat. In an extremely agitated state he told me in broken English that he was the captain of a ship called the *Nea Thea*, which was moored alongside the quay wall. He said there had been a mutiny on board and the crew had thrown him overboard and that he was lucky to escape with his life.

When other members of the unit arrived at the scene, we boarded the ship and spoke to the crew. It was little more than a floating rust bucket. The living quarters were filthy and the crew looked half-starved and neglected. One of them, who spoke a little English, admitted that they had indeed thrown the captain overboard. He said that they had not been paid in six months and had subsisted on tinned food and little else for the past month. I explained to him that it was a serious matter to throw their captain into the sea. Neither he nor the rest of the crew seemed to care less. The ship, a grain carrier, was owned by a Greek businessman but registered in Liberia. We later took the captain away to the Bridewell Garda station for his own safety.

Over the next few days, we were stationed on board, keeping a watch on the ship and its crew.

The Seamen's Mission on Abbey Street was informed of the crew's dire conditions and officers from that worthy organisation brought food and money to them. After a number of days of stalemate, the Greek owners, at the request of the captain, transferred money to a Dublin bank to pay its staff's wages. The captain, who had by now recovered his dignity after his unceremonious exit from the ship, was strutting around the Bridewell Garda station in his full regalia, demanding that we arrest and clap in irons his mutinous crew.

No such action was taken and a couple of days later, when passports and papers were sorted out, the captain and crew were repatriated to their native homelands. As to the fate of the *Nea Thea* I cannot remember now, but I doubt she ever sailed the high seas again.

6

BLOODY MASSACRES

IN JANUARY 1972, I WAS INVOLVED IN THE DRAMATIC ARREST OF A bank robber at a house in Ranelagh village in the south city. I was on motorcycle patrol when I heard a call for assistance over my police radio. I met other members of my unit, including Sergeant Maguire, who had also answered the call for assistance to the scene.

While we were there, a member of the public informed us that one of the gunmen who had robbed the local bank had gone into a house on Ranelagh Road. We sealed off the house and when a search warrant was obtained, we raided the building with the help of armed members of Special Branch and local detectives. We succeeded in arresting the bank robber and also recovered a large sum of money.

Later, at Donnybrook Garda station, the bank robber admitted that when we had entered the house he was in possession of a .45 revolver. When we searched the house, we found the gun. It was fully loaded. It later transpired that the bank raiders were members of the subversive organisation Saor Eire and the bank raid was a fundraiser for their cause. In a photograph published in the *Irish Independent* on 7 January 1972, Sergeant Maguire and I can be seen taking the prisoner into custody outside the house.

Later that month, on Sunday, 30 January, an event took place that convulsed the island of Ireland, north and south. The Parachute Regiment of the British Army shot dead 13 protesters during disturbances in the Bogside area of Derry. Initially, it was called Ireland's Sharpsville, but soon became known simply as 'Bloody Sunday'. The cold-blooded murder – for that's what it was – of innocent, unarmed civilians sent shock waves around the world. In Dublin, there was a flurry of intense diplomatic activity. The Irish Ambassador was recalled from London and our Minister for External Affairs, Dr Patrick Hillery, was dispatched to the headquarters of the United Nations in Washington and to other world capitals to seek support for our government in the crisis. The government also declared the following Tuesday a day of mourning and ordered the national flag to be flown at half-mast on all public buildings. The entire country was numbed with shock at the callous killing of so many young men. The iconic image of that day seared for ever in all our memories is that of Father Daly waving his white handkerchief as he ministered to the dead and dying amidst a hail of bullets.

This event also brought back bitter memories amongst many people of another Bloody Sunday on 23 November 1920. On that date, auxiliary soldiers of the British Army drove into Croke Park, our national stadium, where a football match was in progress, and shot dead 12 spectators.

Television images of the massacre in Derry and eyewitness accounts of the slaughter changed the mood of the people in the Republic from grief to anger, perhaps mixed with guilt for having turned a blind eye to the wretched conditions of our fellow countrymen north of the border since the partition of Ireland. Huge rallies and marches were planned to protest at the British Embassy on Merrion Square in Dublin. Across the water, the firebrand nationalist Mrs Bernadette Devlin assaulted then Home Secretary Reginald Maudling in the House of Commons. The British Prime Minister, Ted Heath, promised an independent government inquiry but rejected calls for a full international investigation. In the North, the nationalist population engaged in a massive display of protest and defiance at the shootings.

John Hume, along with leaders of the Social Democratic Labour Party and others, had called on all civil servants to withdraw their services forthwith. Insult was added to injury when the British Home Secretary refused to express sympathy for the families of the dead. On Tuesday, 1 February, a crowd of up to 10,000 protested outside the embassy on Merrion Square. The protests were mainly organised by Sinn Fein and Kevin Street and Gardiner Street, the political wings of the two major IRA factions.

At six o'clock that evening, I was detailed for duty at the embassy along with other members of my unit. We were in regulation uniform without protective clothing or riot equipment. As darkness fell, we were pelted with missiles, and petrol bombs exploded around us. The crowd seemed resentful towards us. We were booed and jeered at incessantly. It was an ugly, tense and dangerous scene. During one episode, a hail of petrol bombs set the passport office on fire, less than 25 yards from the main embassy building. When units of the fire brigade tried to intervene, they were showered with petrol bombs and missiles. During the next few hours, a number of running battles were fought between protesters. About 15 Gardaí were injured and some protesters arrested. The disturbances continued well into the night.

On the following day, 2 February, the day of the Bloody Sunday victims' funerals, I was detailed again that evening for duty at the embassy. The entire square was packed with protesters. Estimates on the size of the crowd would later range from 25,000 to 30,000 people. There were at least 700 or 800 Gardaí on duty there. Again, as on the previous day, as soon as darkness fell a barrage of missiles and petrol bombs was directed at the embassy and its defenders. A number of Gardaí around me were struck with missiles and had to receive medical treatment, mostly for head injuries.

At one stage, a leading Sinn Fein supporter and known hard man tried to drive a lorry through our cordon. I was among the group of Gardaí who smashed the windows and windscreen on the truck, and pulled out and arrested the driver. The truck was shunted down a side street. All the time, a steady hail of petrol bombs exploded at the main doors and ground-floor windows of the embassy but made little impression as massive steel shutters had been installed at these points. At one stage, we parted our line to allow protesters through with a mock black coffin, which they placed outside the main entrance.

Shortly afterwards, a kind of hush fell on the crowd, and two men wearing black balaclavas sprinted up the steps of the embassy and left an object at the main doors. Seconds later, there was a deafening explosion and the steel doors of the embassy were ripped apart. It was a frightening incident. For a brief moment, panic and confusion spread through our ranks; however, we quickly regrouped. I later learned that the bomb had contained more than 5 lb of gelignite. The explosion was followed by a shower of petrol bombs that set the building ablaze.

I decided to leave my position and approached the senior Garda officer present, a very experienced and capable man. I put my concerns to him about the worsening situation and how I feared for the safety of my colleagues, who were hopelessly outnumbered. I pleaded with him to call out the army, who were on standby behind the embassy. He snarled at me to get back to my position and said that he alone would make that decision. He looked completely unperturbed and calm in the midst of all the noise and turmoil. In any event, it was now too late. The embassy was blazing out of control, fanned by high winds.

A number of Dublin Fire Brigade tenders tried to get to the building, but they were driven back by the protesters with shouts of 'Let it burn, let it burn!' and 'No arrests, no arrests!' Sinn Fein stewards wearing armbands were passing up and down our lines, telling us to stay back and we wouldn't get hurt. The entire scene was becoming more surreal with every passing moment. Some of the protesters had by now gained the first-floor balconies of the embassy and were waving tricolour flags to the wild cheering of the crowds.

Many of us who stood there that night were no less appalled than other citizens of the state at the Derry killings and harboured a certain ambivalence about our role there. Many of us weren't too distraught at seeing this symbol of British rule going up in smoke. The building, of course, had been evacuated long before. As the embassy burned out of control, the anger and resentment of the huge crowd began to dissipate and people began to leave the square. Only a hardcore of troublemakers and Sinn Fein activists and supporters continued the protest.

When they refused to disperse and continued throwing missiles and petrol bombs, the order was given to draw batons and charge. I took off in full battle cry with the rest of my comrades. Within five minutes, we succeeded in clearing all the protesters from the square. It was a fast, furious and bloody action, but thankfully there were no serious injuries reported in the aftermath. Order was restored. The Irish government apologised to the British government and promised full compensation for the destruction of the embassy.

In a subsequent interview, Neil Blaney TD probably summed up the feelings of the majority of people in Ireland when he was quoted as saying he 'shed no tears for the embassy'. To this day, I suspect the government, or elements within it, witnessing the extraordinary scenes of anger and outrage at Merrion Square, became indifferent to the fate of the embassy. It was only when the building was a smouldering ruin that we had been ordered to end the protest. Most of the time, we were little more than observers, and only token measures were taken to prevent its destruction. I also think that it was a wise, courageous and correct decision made by the senior officer to whom I spoke not to use the army to protect the embassy. I did not agree with his decision at the time but then I was young, inexperienced and hot-headed. If there had been loss of life, it could have had catastrophic consequences for the peace and stability of the country during that volatile period.

The events of Bloody Sunday and the subsequent inquiry by Lord Widgery fill the pages of the newspapers more than 30 years on. The latest public inquiry chaired by Lord Saville has just come to an end at the Guildhall in Derry and we are still awaiting the final report.

In the aftermath of Bloody Sunday, a large swathe of the nationalist population in the North, who had heretofore shunned the men of violence, turned to the Provisional IRA as their protectors. Many hundreds of idealistic but, I think, misguided young men and women swelled the ranks of the IRA in the months and weeks following Bloody Sunday. The incidence of bombings and shootings in 1972 increased to unprecedented levels, resulting in the highest death toll in the 30 years of the Troubles.

The repercussions of Bloody Sunday were also felt closer to home. Some time after the event, I was observer on a patrol car with a colleague who was much older and more experienced than I. During our tours of duty, he would often make references to the actions of the British Army on the Bogside on that infamous day in an angry and emotional way and would get visibly upset as he spoke about it. This Garda later became involved with the Provisional IRA and helped them to acquire a large quantity of commercial explosives to be used in bombings on mainland Britain. He was later arrested and convicted in the Special Criminal Court, and imprisoned in Portlaoise Jail for two years. I have no doubt that the shootings in Derry had a major influence on his decision to throw his lot in with the Provisional IRA.

How many other members of the force crossed over to the other side we shall never know. I knew at least three others, one a high-ranking officer who was on the payroll of the Provisional IRA for many years. He retired from the force on a full pension, his activities known only to me and one other officer. This man's involvement with the IRA was not out of misguided patriotism but for the monetary rewards. It was inevitable that we would have some defections; however, I am immensely proud to say that the overwhelming majority of the force throughout the long years of the conflict remained faithful to their country and loyal to their oath of allegiance to the state.

The remainder of 1972 saw a dramatic escalation in IRA activity in the north of Ireland. In the Republic, the Provisional IRA was busy restructuring its organisation, and training and equipping its volunteers. Guns, ammunition and explosives were being channelled to them through means of illegal arms shipments. They were also engaged in other activities, such as robbing banks and extortion and protection rackets to fund their activities.

There was also the threat of Loyalist retaliation and hardly a day went by without a series of bomb scares in the centre of Dublin. Every bomb scare had to be checked thoroughly and because we were on patrol in the city my unit was spending most of its time responding to these calls. We were constantly evacuating buildings and streets, and searching for suspect devices and vehicles. It created a climate of terror and fear for ordinary people going about their daily business. These bomb scares also caused a major disruption to the commercial life of the city centre, as people were afraid to shop or socialise there. At the time, the public was only too well aware of the death and destruction caused by these terrible devices, especially the car bombs.

On 1 December, I was driving a personnel-carrier van. That fateful night, I had eight other uniformed Gardaí on board. Our role at the time was to carry out security patrols in the city and respond to all reports of bomb scares. Sometime around eight o'clock, as I parked close to the Dáil, we heard a massive explosion, which seemed to be coming from the O'Connell Street area. Almost immediately, there was a call over the radio from Garda control that a bomb had exploded in Sackville Place, close to Liberty Hall. We were at the scene in less than five minutes.

It was like a battlefield. Smoke and fumes filled the air; injured people were walking around in a daze, blood streaming down their faces, their clothes in rags. The bodies of two CIE bus company workers lay beside the mangled remains of the car used in the bombing. The blasts injured 127 people. It was my first experience at the scene of a car bomb, and I found it a deeply harrowing ordeal. We helped the wounded into a fleet of ambulances and later worked to preserve the area for forensic examination.

At the time the bombs went off, the government was sitting late into the evening debating a controversial piece of new legislation called the Offences against the State (Amendment) Act 1972. One of the major clauses of the Act was a provision to allow the word of a Garda chief superintendent to be accepted as hard evidence in court that a person was a member of the IRA. When news of the bombs reached Government Buildings, the opposition party, Fine Gael, which had been wavering in support of the proposed legislation, immediately abstained from the vote and the Act was carried by 69 votes to 22. The Fianna Fáil government led by Jack Lynch was the sponsor of that Act.

It was later claimed in a report in the *Evening Herald* by journalist Jim Cantwell, dated 21 August 1973, that the Irish government had been given evidence by the Garda Special Branch that two members of the Special Air Services of the British Army were wanted in connection with the bombings. The two men were named in that report. It was believed in the highest echelons of our government at that time that British intelligence was involved in undercover operations in the Republic and had infiltrated our own intelligence agencies. The two SAS suspects are, to my knowledge, still wanted for questioning in this jurisdiction in connection with the murders of George Bradshaw and Thomas Duffy, the two CIE employees killed in the blast.

It is my opinion, and many others in the country would agree, that the bombs were detonated to influence the vote of the Irish government on that Act, whose passage through the Dáil had been problematic but which made it immediately following the bombings.

This Act would be a major factor in the fight against the IRA and its enactment would suit the policy and aims of the British government in its own fight against terrorism.

* * *

My two years in the Crime Task Force came to an end in September 1973. I would have dearly loved to stay on but two years was the maximum assignment to this unit. Kathleen and I had by then moved from our flat on the Howth Road to a house in Tallaght with our first child, Conor. I returned to Rathfarnham and was appointed relief driver on the patrol car – although my first love was still the motorcycle.

I soon settled in, carrying out the mundane but essential duties in the community that I served. Between routine patrols, there were reports of traffic accidents to respond to, along with alarms from banks and private residences, almost always set off accidentally, and domestic disputes. In quieter moments, especially in the early morning, we would patrol the mountain roads high up in the Featherbeds, Glenasmole and Bohernabreena and the Sally Gap.

As well as being places of great natural beauty, there was always a possibility of intercepting stolen cars or coming across IRA activities in the Dublin mountains. Down through the years they have been the traditional training grounds of the IRA. During one of those early-morning reconnaissance patrols, we came upon an old woman bent under the weight of enormous message bags. I felt sorry for her and a little concerned that she was all alone in such a remote place. I stopped the car and asked her if she wanted a lift, and where she was headed. She said she was going to Rathfarnham village. She appeared to be a little bit reluctant to accept my offer, but eventually sat into the rear seat. I attempted to engage her in conversation on a number of occasions, but she was having none of it. A while later, we dropped her off in the village and returned to the station to have some breakfast.

As I pulled up the car, I heard a sloshing sound. I opened the rear door and saw my uniform cap floating in a pool on the floor by the place the woman had been sitting. Whether out of fear or excitement, she had lost control of her bladder in the car. Because I was the one who had acted as Good Samaritan, my partner Kevin said that I should clean up the mess. We had a good laugh about it later, but I was very dubious about giving lifts to old bag ladies again.

On another beautiful morning in the summer of 1974, I paraded for the early shift in Rathfarnham station. My partner for the day was a young recruit newly arrived from Templemore. After leaving the station, I decided to pick up my .22 rifle and ammunition from the house and bag a couple of plump rabbits for the pot. I knew where lots of them would be nibbling the grass in the morning sunshine. After I picked up the gun, I headed for Marlay Park in Rathfarnham. I was aware that Dublin County Council had recently purchased the estate from Raymond Love, the millionaire racing magnate, although it turned out the house still belonged to the family.

When I got to Marlay Park, I told the recruit to remain in the car and listen to the radio. I went off with my rifle and returned ten minutes later with two fat rabbits after a successful hunt. I was in the process of putting the rabbits in the boot of the patrol car when I heard a woman screaming nearby. I had been under the impression that nobody was living on the estate. I looked up and there in the upstairs window of the lodge house I saw the florid, angry face of the lady of the house, who was leaning out the window. Miss Love was the sister of the previous owner. I stood there shamefaced with embarrassment, still clutching my trophies under her fearsome gaze. My pathetic and insincere apologies for the intrusion seemed only to make her more angry. By now, she was leaning so far out of the window that her ample bosom was almost resting on the windowsill.

She was shouting that I was a disgrace to the uniform and that my days as a Garda were numbered; she would report me to the Minister for Justice as soon as he arrived at his office. I drove off with threats of further dire consequences ringing in my ears. My young observer was in a state of shock. He was close to tears as he saw his fledgling career in ruins. I assured him that I would accept full and complete responsibility for the entire affair.

I returned to the station and informed the sergeant on duty of my predicament. The sergeant said it was indeed a grave situation and that I should report the matter personally to the superintendent when he arrived in his office. When he turned up at the station, I reported to his office. I knocked on the door and he invited me in. He was changing from his civilian clothes into his uniform. As I blurted out my news and Miss Love's threats about the Minister for Justice he went into a paroxysm of rage. He started hopping around his office in white long johns with one leg still in his trousers, struggling to keep his balance and shouting all sorts of names at me, both uncomplimentary and unprintable. I think what really annoyed him was that he had granted me the licence for the rifle.

I was severely reprimanded for my behaviour but, thankfully, was saved from a more severe punishment. I had to hand in my rifle and ammunition to the station for safe keeping in case I was tempted to go on another early-morning safari. I didn't get it back again until the superintendent retired.

Some years later, I was called as a witness by Miss Love to give evidence in a personal-injury case in the Civil Court. Afterwards, we had a cup of tea together and she thanked me for my attendance. At one stage, I saw a flicker of recognition in her eyes as we spoke, but she was too much of a lady to mention the past. We parted the best of friends.

In the early months of 1974 because of the almost daily threat of car bombs in the city centre, I was often detailed with others from the station to parade for duty at Pearse Street and Store Street Garda stations to assist our hard-pressed colleagues there. A huge amount of manpower and overtime payments were expended on these operations.

There were no bomb warnings on 17 May, yet at approximately 5.30 p.m. three car bombs exploded within minutes of one another. The bombs exploded in Parnell Street, Talbot Street and South Leinster Street. About 90 minutes later, another no-warning car bomb exploded outside a bar in Monaghan. Thirty-three innocent men, women and children were killed in the blasts. The scenes of carnage and destruction at all four sites were described by eyewitnesses as like scenes from hell. On the day of the bombings, I was on duty in Rathfarnham. I was directed to parade for duty the next day in Store Street Garda station.

In Store Street, I was detailed to go to Talbot Street to assist other members in sealing off the affected streets while forensic teams combed through the rubble and debris for evidence. Talbot Street and parts of Gardiner Street were like a war zone. Shops and other business premises were completely destroyed. Every window within a 100-yard radius was smashed and a carpet of glass and other blackened debris littered the streets. Motor cars that were parked as far away as 50 yards were completely destroyed. Even a day later, the smell of fumes and smoke seemed to hang in the air.

Later, when I was leaving the station with a colleague from Rathfarnham, we were approached by the duty sergeant and asked if we would help out at the city morgue, next door to the station. He said that the regular mortuary attendants were severely traumatised and exhausted, and needed help. We agreed, and reported there immediately.

Nothing could have prepared us for the ghastly, nightmarish scenes we walked into. I had never seen so many dead bodies nor human forms ripped apart. For the next couple of hours, we assisted as best we could mainly helping to coffin the dead. Many of the victims had suffered appalling mutilations; some had lost legs, others had lost arms. One poor man that I helped coffin had lost both his legs. There was a pile of amputated limbs in the corner of the room; many still wrapped in bloody bandages. Some of the victims had suffered horrific facial injuries from flying glass and car parts and were unrecognisable, deprived in the parting moment of life of their identity. We witnessed images that day that would haunt us for the rest of our lives. It seems strange, but I remember just one of the victims that I helped to coffin and lay out. She was a beautiful young girl. Her name was Josephine Bradley. She was from Kilcormac, Birr, County Offaly. She was only 21 years of age. To this day, I think about her and remember her lovely, peaceful face.

When I left the morgue, I had very mixed emotions, anger being the uppermost at the heartless, cruel and inhuman cowards who had caused so much death and sorrow. My colleague John was ashen-faced and hadn't a word to say.

I felt so bad myself that I needed a drink. We went into Lloyd's pub on North Earl Street, where I had two large whiskies. I think my colleague, who didn't take a drink, was a little uncomfortable, as we were still in uniform, but the way I was feeling that day I didn't give a damn. I later took him home to my house for a meal. Halfway through dinner, he rushed from the table and was violently sick. It had been a terrible day for us. One leading government minister at the time described the bombings as 'without exception the worst single outrage in these islands caused by man against man since the end of the Second World War'.

Nobody was ever charged in connection with those bombings. It is my understanding, incredible as it may seem, that to date no suspects have ever been questioned by An Garda Síochána in connection with this mass murder. Author Don Mullan revealed in *The Dublin and Monaghan Bombings* a letter sent from the Royal Ulster Constabulary to the solicitors representing the Dublin and Monaghan bereaved, dated 28 August 1996, which states:

4(a) A number of persons were arrested and interviewed in relation to the theft of vehicles.

4(b) A number of persons were arrested and interviewed in relation to these murders.

5 Details arising from the interviews as well as other material were passed to An Garda Síochána at various stages of its inquiry.

Despite those reports and other evidence gleaned during the Garda investigations in Dublin and Monaghan that identified some of those Loyalists who planned and carried out the bombings, no attempt was ever made by our own government or the Garda to extradite those believed responsible for the bombings. Incredibly, the investigation of 33 murders started in May and was wound down in August, just over two months later, although officially the file was left 'open'. One senior officer who was involved in the original investigation told me that he knew the identity of at least three of the bombers.

In the report on the bombings published by John Wilson of the Victims' Commission on 5 August 1999, it is stated: 'My information comes in the main from reportage which suggests, among other things, that the Garda investigation had identified the probable culprits very quickly, but then ran into difficulties.' Further in the report he states that 'agents of a friendly government may have had a hand in planning and executing the crime'.

Perhaps the real reason that the authorities in the Republic never demanded the extradition of those who were believed to be responsible for the bombings was because of concerns for the security of the state. If the British authorities had agreed to our request for extradition at the time, there was a very real likelihood that they in turn would have demanded and expected a reciprocal agreement. Our government would then have had to hand over IRA men who were wanted by the British government for multiple shootings and bombings in their jurisdiction.

I have no doubt that if the Irish government of the day had gone down that road, the guns of the IRA would have been turned on members of the government, the judiciary and ourselves and that it would have precipitated a slide into civil war. Perhaps our government did choose, rightly or wrongly, the lesser of two evils. One way or another, it was a spurious, painful and unjust outcome for the relatives of the victims. I wish to add my small voice to the undeniable demands of the 'Justice for the Forgotten' campaign in seeking a full public sworn inquiry into this whole sad affair. As Shakespeare's Hamlet states, 'Foul deeds will rise, though all the world o'erwhelm them, to men's eyes.'

One of the advantages of being stationed in an outlying post like Rathfarnham was that we were always the first to be called on to supply reinforcements in the city centre stations when required for special duties. When on duty away from our station, we were paid travel allowance, subsistence and overtime payments, always a welcome addition to the budget.

From 1972 onwards, a large contingent of officers were required to be on standby in Portlaoise Garda station in case they were needed to deal with riots or violent protests inside or outside the town's prison. At that time, Portlaoise Prison, a grim fortress with maximum-security status, was used solely to house those who were convicted of subversive crimes in the state. Within its walls were incarcerated many dangerous individuals, men who had been convicted of murders, bombings, bank robberies or kidnappings. Most of them were members of the Provisional IRA.

Despite the massive security measures taken, which included the presence of heavily armed soldiers, acres of razor wire and tank stops, there had been a spectacular escape by 19 prisoners in 1974 after a bomb was exploded near the governor's office and blew a gaping hole in the perimeter wall. In 1975, in another escape attempt, a prisoner was shot dead by the soldiers on duty there. Later that year, during yet another attempted breakout, a huge earth-moving machine reinforced with heavy steel plates was used to batter down the perimeter wall. On this occasion, the army foiled the attack and nobody escaped. The IRA unit behind the planned breakout had christened the monster earth-moving machine the 'Bridget Rose' after Dr Bridget Rose Dugdale, the IRA activist. Dugdale was a middle-class Englishwoman who had joined the ranks of the IRA in Dublin. In 1974, she was the leader of an IRA unit that raided Russborough House. She was later convicted for the theft of paintings worth £8 million. She was something of a heroine amongst Republican hardliners.

During 1974 and 1975, I was one of hundreds of Gardaí from all over the city who were bussed down on a daily basis to carry out security duties in Portlaoise town. In the early days, we were all based at Portlaoise Garda station. It was a fairly loose arrangement and with the permission of our sergeants, we were allowed into the town to have our meals. After a very short while, the authorities discovered that some of my colleagues were frequenting public houses in the course of their perambulations around the town and coming back to the station half-cut. As a result, we were all confined to barracks. But even that decision was changed a short time later and we were all bussed directly to the prison. There we were deployed in groups of twos and threes at intervals on each landing.

The prison was run along the lines of a prisoner-of-war camp, as the inmates did not regard themselves as common criminals. They only took orders from their superiors and were not allowed to speak to the prison officers without their permission. The prisoners neither acknowledged our presence nor spoke to us; overall discipline was maintained by a senior IRA man who had been appointed the officer commanding (OC) by his fellow inmates.

Every night at lock-up time, each prisoner stood at ease outside his cell door. For a few moments, there would be complete silence.

Immediately, the OC would bark out the command and all the prisoners would snap to attention, salute smartly, fall out and enter their cells. It was a very impressive display and also a little intimidating.

As you would expect, the atmosphere in the jail was always a little bit tense and uneasy, with the constant threat of trouble and disorder simmering away beneath the surface. We maintained as unobtrusive a presence as possible and in all the months I did duty there, I never saw any trouble.

However, I myself had a slight altercation with one of the prisoners over a rather trivial incident. I was on duty at Portlaoise on Easter Monday, the anniversary of the 1916 Rising, which is a national holiday in the Republic of Ireland, marked by ceremonies and wreath-laying to commemorate the birth of our nation. The Republican prisoners were in good spirits and celebrated the day as best they could in the confines of the jail.

I was stationed on the top landing that night when a couple of prisoners brought out guitars and flutes and started a sing-song. Soon, all the prisoners in the jail had joined in, until the whole building was filled with the lusty strains of 'A Nation Once Again', 'Kevin Barry' and many other rousing rebel ballads.

Forgetting where I was for a moment, I joined in with a few choruses. A very senior Republican prisoner approached me and told me to keep my mouth shut, that he did not want to listen to any Free State bastard singing their songs. I protested that they were my songs as well, but it cut no ice with him. A few minutes later, a prison officer came to tell me that some of the IRA high command had objected to my presence. For the sake of a peaceful coexistence, I was sent to another landing for the night.

In the September of the same year, I was sent on another quite different mission. This time it was to Buncrana in County Donegal. In the early hours of Sunday morning towards the latter end of the month, I paraded with about 100 other Gardaí in the courtyard of Dublin Castle. There we boarded two buses and headed off into the dark. Only when we were on the road were we informed of the purpose of our journey. The senior sergeant on board told us that we were going to Buncrana to assist the local Garda force. He said that reliable evidence had been received that a group of IRA volunteers and their followers from the Bogside in Derry were intent on causing a riot in Buncrana that night. He went on to say that we would not be advertising our presence in the town for tactical reasons.

It was still dark when our two buses glided unnoticed through the gates of the town's Convent of Mercy. The nuns gave us a very warm reception and dished up a fine breakfast. All that day, they fussed over us like doting maiden aunts, bringing us innumerable plates of sandwiches, pots of tea and mounds of cakes. Despite the hospitality of the sisters, that long, sleepy Sunday dragged by very slowly. As night fell, we waited for news of any impending trouble but all was quiet and peaceful. Later that night when we were about to call it a day and head for home, we got an urgent request for assistance from a local Garda who was on duty in the town.

He said that a drunken mob had gathered and was creating a serious disturbance. We were immediately ordered into line by our sergeants, who marched out of the gates and down the main street. We marched in formation through the town close to where the rioters had assembled beside a number of Ulster buses. As we approached them, we met with a hail of stones and bottles. A number of my colleagues were struck and injured in that first salvo. Without further ado, we were ordered to draw batons and charge.

As we closed in on them, I had my eye on a bottle-throwing skinhead, who appeared to be one of the ringleaders. I made sure that he was the first to go down and stay down. It was a swift but brutal engagement and, in minutes, we had them on the run and scattering to the four corners. We took no prisoners that night; we herded them on to buses to lick their wounds and told the drivers to take them back across the border to Derry. After they had left, we returned to the town to be greeted by the townspeople, who thanked us for our help. The rioters never returned to terrorise and intimidate the people of Buncrana again.

* * *

On the home front, my second child, Margaret, was born in June 1974. Kathleen had her hands full coping with two small babies. I must confess I was no renaissance man and my parenting skills left a lot to be desired, but thankfully Kathleen was an extremely competent and devoted mother, which more than made up for my ineptitude. I was also living and working in the same district, which allowed me during my hours of duty to call and check on Kathleen and the babies, as we had no telephone at the time.

Although I had spent six happy years in Rathfarnham and my current position as patrol car driver suited my domestic situation, nevertheless when 1975 dawned I decided to seek new opportunities and challenges at the first chance I got. It had been my ambition from the very beginning that one day I would become a detective officer. After eight years in uniform learning my trade, I felt it was time to pursue that career path. Fortuitously for me, applications were invited in March of that year from suitably qualified uniformed personnel to be considered for appointment as trainee detectives. I jumped at the chance and immediately applied for the job.

I went for interview before a panel of senior detective officers, and a couple of days later I was called in by my superintendent and told that I had passed the test with flying colours. I was over the moon at the news. Just after my 29th birthday, I left Rathfarnham station for the last time resplendent in my brand-new suit to begin the next phase of my career in the Central Detective Unit in Dublin Castle.

For my first year, our unit was based in a dilapidated, old building in the grounds of the castle. We later moved to brand-new offices around the corner in Ship Street, which we shared with the Garda Fraud Squad, the Garda Drug Unit, the State Solicitors' Office and a branch of the Revenue Commissioners. The whole building was called Osmond House.

The Central Detective Unit was also known as the Flying Squad. Our main role was the targeting and surveillance of the most active major criminals operating in the city. Highly organised gangs with access to firearms were beginning to emerge and would soon be a regular feature of the Dublin criminal underworld. The drug scene was confined mostly to the use of cannabis, the preferred recreational substance of the time, but soon that would change as a heroin epidemic hit the streets of Dublin with all its attendant horrors. The gathering and collating of criminal intelligence was also a major and integral part of the functions of the unit. I spent a good deal of my time working undercover and on surveillance duty on motorcycle.

It was exciting and interesting, and not without its dangers. On one occasion at least I had a narrow escape. This night, I was on surveillance duty in the city, watching the activities of a particular criminal gang who had carried out a number of daring bank robberies in Dublin and its surrounding counties. The leader of the gang was an ex-British paratrooper with a fearsome reputation for violence. Around midnight, I saw the gang leaving a well-known city-centre watering hole, get into a car and drive off in the direction of Dorset Street. There were four of them in the car, including the gang boss, who was driving. They drove out past the airport and on to the main Dublin to Belfast road. Just beyond the Coachman's Inn pub, they turned right for Kinsealy.

This whole area is a maze of narrow lanes and back roads. On one of those quiet and unlit roads the driver of the car must have seen the lights of my motorbike and realised, or at least suspected, that he was being followed. I saw the brake lights come on in the distance and suddenly the car was speeding back down the road in my direction. In a dramatic reversal of roles, I was now the one being hunted.

I immediately switched off my lights, turned my bike around and headed back in the direction I had come. I had only travelled a short distance when I saw an opening into a field on my left. I drove my motorbike well into the field before cutting out the engine. I let the bike topple over on its side while I was still seated on it and remained completely still. Seconds later, I heard the sound of a car as it screeched to a halt on the roadway, close to where I was.

I heard angry, agitated voices and suddenly the headlights of a car were shining across the field. I looked around and saw that I was surrounded on all sides by cabbages. I remained completely motionless. After a few minutes, the field was once again plunged into darkness and I heard the car drive away at speed. When I felt that the coast was clear, I mounted my motorcycle, left the field and headed back towards the city. I was unarmed at the time and was fairly shaken by my experience. I have no doubt that if that gang had caught me that night, I would have been lucky to escape with my life.

During those early years, the day-to-day running of the unit was in the very capable hands of Detective Inspector Edward 'Ned' Ryan. Ned was a larger-than-life Cork man with a wry sense of humour. A non-drinking workaholic, his great pleasure in life outside his work and family was his weekly game of cards. To the major gangland figures on the Dublin crime scene, Inspector Ryan was a relentless and implacable adversary. They feared but respected him, as he had a reputation for being fair but tough. For me, as an aspiring detective, Ryan became for me a role model whom I admired and emulated, and later he also became a trusted friend.

During the five years I spent in this unit, I was involved in the investigation of some of the most serious and shocking crimes that occurred in the country. None turned out to be more controversial than the investigation into the robbery of the mail train at Sallins, County Kildare, on 31 March 1976. At 3.02 a.m. that day, the Cork–Dublin mail train was halted by armed men. The raiders boarded the train and removed 12 bags of registered mail, which contained among other items £215,906 in cash, the property of Allied Irish Banks. At 3.16 a.m., the alarm was raised and immediately a full-scale investigation got under way.

Prior to the train robbery, some of the gang took over a house in nearby Celbridge posing as members of the Garda. No one in the family was injured, but the gang stole their car and used it for the hold-up. Later, a family member would identify one of the gang involved in the incident.

Almost immediately after the hold-up, intelligence reports and confidential information filtering through the Garda headquarters pointed in only one direction: that the Irish National Liberation Army had carried out this daring raid. The INLA was the military wing of the Irish Republican Socialist Party led by Seamus Costello, its founder. Costello had split with the Official IRA and set up this party at the start of December 1974.

In the subsequent follow-up operations, more than 150 detectives were involved in the arrests and interrogation of members of the INLA. All were arrested under the provision of Section 30 of the Offences against the State Act, 1939, and were detained in various Garda stations in the city, the majority of them in Bridewell Garda station. I was involved in the arrests and interviews of three of those detained, including John Fitzpatrick and Osgur Breathnach.

In early April, Brian McNally, Edward Noel 'Nicky' Kelly, John Fitzpatrick, Osgur Breathnach, Michael Barrett and Michael Plunkett were charged with robbing the train. They were each released with a surety of £10,000. None of the six men charged had any previous convictions. Nine other persons were arrested and questioned in connection with the crime and were released without charge.

Almost from the very beginning, the case was mired in controversy. Certain elements in the Intelligence Section of the Garda Special Branch believed that the Provisional Irish Republican Army (PIRA) had carried out the raid and not the INLA. The case would resume later, but in the interim, Ireland's first serial killings occurred, shocking the nation and taking up all my attention.

7
·······
A TALE OF HORROR

ON SATURDAY, 28 AUGUST 1976, A 23-YEAR-OLD WOMAN, ELIZABETH Plunkett, was enjoying a weekend in Brittas Bay with a group of friends. That evening, they retired to McDaniels pub. Among the group was her boyfriend, Damien Bushe, and his sister, Mella, who had just returned from a holiday with Elizabeth in the south of France. The women stood out in the crowd because of their deep tans.

When Damien got into a heated argument with one of the group about the sale of a car, Elizabeth intervened and asked them to stop. She told them they were there to enjoy themselves and to hell with the car until Monday. When the argument continued, she jumped up from the table and stormed out of the pub. It was a case of the heart ruling the head, but the spontaneous emotional reaction was to have dire consequences. Just a short time earlier, two English drifters on the run from rape charges in Britain were driving towards Brittas Bay, where they intended to rob caravans. Geoffrey Evans and John Shaw were a very dangerous duo.

As they neared their destination, Geoffrey, who was driving that night, began to talk about women. So they drove around looking for some. When they saw a girl standing at a corner, Shaw got out and

Evans stopped beside her. It was part of a ghastly plan. Only one would remain in the car, so that the potential victim would not be intimidated by two men. Evans asked the woman if she wanted a lift, but she declined the offer because she said that her friend would be there in a minute. Little did she realise how close she had come to death on that sultry August night. Elizabeth Plunkett by a cruel twist of fate was not so lucky.

Evans and Shaw drove away and the hunt continued. They saw Elizabeth walking towards nearby Arklow. She was the perfect victim for these men; she was a stunning-looking girl in the wrong place at the wrong time.

'She will do,' was predator Evans's chilling remark. Their evil plan was put in place. Shaw got out of the car.

Evans drove by, then turned the car, an old Austin A40, back in the direction of Elizabeth. He stopped the car and asked her where she was going. She replied that she was heading for Dublin. Evans told her that he was going in that direction himself and that he would be happy to give her a lift. Once she was in the car, he drove on a short distance and picked up Shaw, who jumped into the back seat. The trap was sprung.

Just over a week later, the men burgled a house in Cashel, County Tipperary, and stole over £500, a princely sum at the time. Some days later, they arrived at a caravan site in Barna, just outside Galway, and bought a mobile home from the proceeds of the robbery. They carried out a series of robberies in Connemara and brought all the stolen property back to their lair. In Clifden, they stole a green Ford Cortina outside a garage. They did an amateurish paint job and replaced the registration plates with those stolen from another car.

They travelled across the country to continue their crime spree, targeting caravan parks in County Wexford. In order to disguise their identities, they applied for and were issued two provisional driving licences in the names of Roy Hall and David Ball. They gave the address of an English friend, Chris Outram in Fethard, as their own.

On the evening of 22 September, they were back in County Galway. They pulled in at a shop and petrol station in the tiny, picturesque village of Maam in the heart of Connemara. The shopkeeper noticed the poorly executed paint job and the Dublin registration plates and was surprised when one of the men asked for £3 worth of petrol with an English accent. His attempt at polite conversation was ignored and the unfriendly manner of the duo aroused his suspicions.

Shaw and Evans drove off in the direction of Leenane. It was 7 p.m. The shopkeeper wrote down the registration number of the car in a ledger. He remembered a newspaper article about two Englishmen wanted for questioning about the disappearance of a woman in County Wicklow, so the next morning he contacted local Gardaí and supplied particulars of the car and descriptions of the men.

After leaving Maam, the pair had travelled to Westport in County Mayo and later to Castlebar. As they drove, they saw a young woman outside a telephone kiosk. It was after 11 p.m. and she was alone on the deserted street. Mary Duffy, a local girl aged 23 with a petite build, had finished work in a coffee shop. She had just rung the garage where her brother, Michael, worked and left a message to pick her up on the Breaffy Road.

Shaw asked Evans to stop the car. He got out and grabbed hold of her. As he dragged her to the car, she started to scream. He punched her hard and forced her into the back seat. Evans drove into the darkness. Another victim had fallen prey to these evil hunters.

* * *

This is how I came to be face to face with John Shaw in the middle of the night on 28 September. He had cracked a few minutes earlier and was about to spill the gory details of his disgusting killing spree. I asked him if he wished to make a statement about the murders of the two girls and he agreed. He was still in a highly emotional state, his voice trembling and his eyes wide, as if he had just woken up from a terrible nightmare.

I called for the guard on duty outside the door to wake Detective Tom Connolly, who had travelled from Dublin with me and was sleeping in the upstairs bedroom, and tell him to join me immediately in the billiards room. Tom had been working on the team investigating the disappearance of Elizabeth Plunkett.

I told Tom that Shaw had decided to make a full statement about how he and his partner, Geoffrey Evans, had murdered the two women.

After his legal rights were explained to him, we began to take a written statement from him. He told us that he was separated from his wife and three children, who all lived in England. He had been born in Lancashire and had come to Ireland two years earlier with Evans. On 5 August 1976, he went to live with another English chap, Chris Outram, at Fethard, and Geoffrey had come to stay on 27 August.

Shaw seemed somewhat relieved as he started to recount his heinous story. This is what he said:

'On Saturday, August 28th 1976, I got the loan of a car from Frank Walsh of Fethard. Walsh is a friend of Outram's. The car was an Austin. Geoffrey and I left Fethard in the car on the Saturday and we drove to Dublin. We went there to collect suitcases of Geoffrey's at the railway station along the quays. We collected them about four or five in the evening. We had a meal in the city. We decided to go to Brittas Bay, County Wicklow, and break into some caravans. Somewhere outside Arklow, we went into a pub on the main road and had a few drinks. I don't know the name of the place. We left it after a few hours. We then drove on towards Brittas Bay. We were talking about girls and Geoffrey said he was going to pick up a bird and have it off with her. He said he wanted a small bird. Geoffrey was driving and we drove around the roads for a while looking for a bird.

'We saw one standing at a corner. Geoff stopped and asked her if she wanted a lift. I had got out of the car and walked up the road at the time. This girl told Geoff she was waiting for someone and he picked me up again. Shortly afterwards, we saw another bird on the road and Geoff said, 'She will do.' She was walking down towards Arklow. We passed her. Geoff stopped and I got out.

'He turned the car and went back and picked up the girl. He then picked me up. I sat in the back and the girl was in the front seat. She was wearing pants and a jumper with writing on it. We drove to the woods with her. She told us she had a row with her boyfriend. She started to scream in the car and we stuffed tissues into her mouth. When we got to the wood, we dragged her out of the car. We climbed over a wire fence that was across the road there. We went into the woods with her. We had a hold of her. We told her to lie down and she did so.

'We took the suitcases out of the car and put them on the ground beside her. Geoff told me to take the car. I went away in the car and left Geoff with the girl. I parked the car in a car park on the main Dublin road at a pub. I walked back to where Geoff and the girl were. I was gone about five hours and it was coming light when I got back. I saw people coming along the road, trying to stop cars, and I got in over a gate. When I got back to Geoff and the girl, I saw that the girl's hands were tied.

'Her clothes were on. I took off her pants and had intercourse with her. She was struggling all the time. Geoff went a short distance away while I was having intercourse with her. He then returned and he had intercourse with her. Geoff said he would go back for the car and he told me to kill her while he was away. He said to me "Remember what happened in England?" Geoff went off for the car and I had intercourse with the girl again. When Geoff came back, he said "Why haven't you killed her?" He said again "Remember what happened in England?"

'I took a nylon shirt out of one of the cases. I put the sleeve around her neck and choked her. She was then dead. It was then about six in the morning of Sunday. We left her in the forest and went to the caravan site and broke into a few caravans. Sometime after midnight, we returned to the forest with the car.

'We carried the dead girl to the car and put her into the back seat. I think Geoff had her shoes and watch. We drove down to the caravan site again. We got a lawnmower out of a shed at one of the caravans and a rope. We put her into a boat. We tied her on to the lawnmower with the rope. Geoff and I rode out into the sea. Geoff threw her out and she sank.

'We came back in again and went to a pit in a field behind the caravans. There was a fire there and we burned the girl's pants and jumper. We stayed in Brittas that day and the police came along and spoke to us. We stayed on around the caravan park until sometime late that night or Tuesday morning. We then returned to Fethard. We stayed with Outram again until September 10th '76. While we were there, we done a few strokes around that area.

'We left Fethard on September 10th 1976 and Chris drove us to Limerick. We came on to Salthill then and we bought a caravan. We stayed in this caravan, we pinched a car in Clifden – Geoff pinched it, not me. A few days after that, we were in Castlebar one night. It was about twelve o'clock. Geoff was driving. We saw a girl on the road, walking along. Geoff stopped the car. I got out and went over to the girl. I grabbed a hold of her and dragged her to the car. She started to scream. I put her into the back of the car and sat in beside her.

'She told me her name was Mary. We headed for some place near Clifden. While Geoff drove the car along the road, I had intercourse with the girl. I took off her pants and jacket. I took off only her pants. Somewhere along the road, I started to drive and Geoff got into the back of the car with her. She didn't scream but said, "Don't do me any harm."

'We got to a forest and stopped. We pulled her out of the car. Geoff pulled off her clothes. We both had intercourse with her. Geoff gave her some pills to take – he gave her five or six pills. She took them and got a bit dazy. Geoff told her that they were sleeping pills and he would take her home. I wanted to let her go and Geoff said we couldn't. I got a cushion out of the car and put my hands around her neck and killed her. We threw her into the back of the car with her clothes. Geoff said that he had picked a spot to dump her.

'When she [was] alive, Geoff [had driven] off in the car and [had come] back again to me in the forest. He [had been] to our caravan and got some food and the pills. We [gave] her some sandwiches and barley water. When Geoff returned, he had a cavity concrete block in the car. There was also a rope. Geoff was away about four hours [*sic*]. He went away in the morning after we took the girl and he returned that evening. While Geoff was away, I had intercourse twice with the girl. I saw fishermen fishing in a river close by. Geoff had intercourse again with her when he came back.

'The girl was with us for more than 24 hours before I killed her. We brought her up the road a short distance from where I killed her. We took her out of the car. I tied a concrete block onto her with the rope. Geoff tied an anchor and a brick onto her. We broke into a shed beside the lake. We took two oars out of it. There were a number of boats on the lake. We put the girl into the boat and went out on to the lake. It was dark.

'We dumped her into the lake and I think she sank. I will show the spot to you today. We burned all her clothes on the way back to the caravan. We left the boat back in the same place and put the oars in the shed. The girl had big leather boots and wore two rings. We took off the rings and threw them in the forest. We returned to Salthill and went to our caravan. The night we picked up the girl, Mary, in Castlebar we had a roof rack on our car. We took it off the car somewhere.

'I am sorry for what I have done and I want to help in every way to find the two girls that I have killed. There must be something wrong with me.'

John Shaw's stark and terrible confession ended there. At 6 a.m., after listening to this tale of horror, we returned Shaw to his cell. We were in a state of shock from the full scale of the nightmare and the callous, cruel deaths inflicted on these women, recounted during the confession in such a matter-of-fact way. Later that morning on hearing that the game was up, Evans made a full statement outlining his part in the murders.

In the afternoon, Shaw and Evans were brought to the scene of the crime at Lough Inagh. On the journey back, they pointed out to the investigating team where they had dumped her clothing and their tents and sleeping bags. Later that evening, the prisoners were driven back to Wicklow Garda station.

I was in the back of one patrol car handcuffed to John Shaw and as we drove eastwards through the dark he made a chilling admission that he was glad they had been caught because he said they were going to kill one woman every week. A subsequent investigation revealed his threat against women was no idle fantasy. Some days prior to the abduction and murder of Mary Duffy another young woman had an amazing escape from the deadly clutches of the two killers. This incident came to light following the newspaper and media reports of their dramatic arrest and subsequent court appearances in connection with the murders.

Their intended victim on that occasion was a young nurse who was hitching a lift near Oranmore on the outskirts of Galway. She described to detectives that seconds after getting into the car, she got a bad feeling about the two polite, smiling Englishmen. As they drove through the village, she persuaded them to stop the car, having somehow convinced them of her need to use the toilet. For whatever reason, they stopped the car and let her out. She went into a local pub and escaped out through the toilet window. A finely honed sixth sense or her mother's prayers saved her from certain death.

We arrived at Wicklow station about midnight. As I was placing Shaw in the cells, he turned to me, shook my hand and said that he had just remembered that it was his son's birthday and would I send him a birthday card on his behalf. By a sad coincidence, Elizabeth Plunkett's body was washed ashore that same evening at Duncormick on the south Wexford coast.

In February 1978, John Shaw was sentenced to penal servitude for life for the murder of Mary Duffy, fourteen years for rape and two years for false imprisonment by Mr Justice Costello at Dublin's Central Criminal Court. In the December, Geoffrey Evans was sentenced to penal servitude for life for the murder of Mary Duffy. Almost a fortnight later, Evans was sentenced to 20 years' penal servitude for the rapes of Mary Duffy and Elizabeth Plunkett. He was found not guilty by direction of the judge of the murder of Elizabeth Plunkett.

Both killers subsequently appealed against their convictions on the grounds that their constitutional rights had been violated, as we had held them for longer than the 48 hours allowed by the Offences against the State Act. The court held that it was our belief that Mary Duffy might still have been alive and that we had an obligation to do our utmost to find her, even if that meant a violation of their constitutional rights. In a landmark and far-reaching judgment, the Supreme Court rejected their appeal. Judge Griffin stated, 'If a balance is to be struck between one person's right to liberty, for some hours or even days, and another person's right to protection against danger to his life, then in any civilised society in my view, the latter's right must prevail.'

John Shaw and Geoffrey Evans are now the longest-serving prisoners in the Irish penal system. I believe any parole board or government agency, before contemplating the release of these psychopathic killers back into society, should consider the sickening depravity of their crimes still undiminished by the passage of time. They would do well to remember Shaw's chilling vow in his words to me: 'I am glad we were caught, we were going to kill one a week.'

8

JUSTICE ON THE RAILS

IN THE MEANTIME, THE MAIL-TRAIN ROBBERY CASE WAS TRUNDLING
through the courts with no end of problems cropping up along the line.
On 9 December, the District Court dismissed the case because of the
failure of the Director of Public Prosecutions (DPP) to furnish the
defendants with the book of evidence. The charges were dropped
against the six and they walked out of the court free men.

Their freedom was short-lived, however. A week later, four of the
original six were re-arrested – Kelly, Breathnach, Plunkett and McNally
– and charged before the Special Criminal Court with stopping the mail
train with intent to rob the mail, and larceny of mailbags. All four were
remanded on £5,000 independent bail. At the time, the DPP had also
ordered the arrest of John Fitzpatrick and the direction to charge him
with the same offences as the other four, but he could not be located
and was never charged with these offences. Michael Barrett, the
remaining accused, was never re-arrested nor did he stand trial due to
lack of evidence.

The first trial began in the Special Criminal Court on Green Street
on 19 January 1978. There were 109 witnesses listed in the book of
evidence, mostly Gardaí. I was involved in the interrogation of Osgur

Breathnach and had taken verbal admissions from him regarding his part in the robbery. It was only the second time I had given evidence in the Special Criminal Court, which is situated in the heart of the bustling fruit-and-vegetable markets in the north inner city.

It is an impressive old granite building and many famous trials of bygone years were conducted behind its grim walls. In the hallway inside the main doors beneath an iron rail on the wall from the original dock, there is a plaque on the wall that states, 'Hurrish the Sweep, the last person to be publicly whipped through the streets of Dublin.' I always found the atmosphere in that oak-panelled courtroom oppressive, intimidating and unnerving, and the witness stand there one of the loneliest places in the world.

A couple of weeks into the trial, it became obvious that one of the judges was unwell and was finding it difficult to stay awake and alert, especially as the courtroom could get quite warm and stuffy. On a number of occasions, barristers from both sides were dropping books and having coughing fits to wake him up. As the trial progressed, the situation with the judge became even more acute. He was finding it difficult to stay upright in his chair, his eyes were closing and his head seemed, at times, to be resting on the bench. One did not have to be a medical expert to realise that Judge O'Connor was a very sick man and unfit for the rigours of a lengthy, complicated and politically sensitive trial. Certainly the interests of justice were not served by allowing him to remain on the bench, as he was almost comatose during most of the trial. It was at once almost farcical yet extremely poignant to see the poor man trying to carry on, as he was literally dying in front of our eyes. It was inexplicable and deeply disturbing, despite the weight of the evidence presented by Patrick McEntee SC and his defence team in the High and Supreme courts, that all their submissions on the unfitness of the judge to continue the trial were rejected.

On the 15th day of the trial, McEntee SC, acting on behalf of Osgur Breathnach and Michael Plunkett, asked that the court discharge itself because Judge O'Connor appeared to be sleeping during much of the proceedings. When the court refused his application, McEntee took his application to the High Court in order to stop the trial. The High Court refused his application. The defence barristers then appealed against this decision in the Supreme Court. They lost there as well and the trial continued. A month later, as the trial was entering its 65th day, Judge O'Connor died, and it was abandoned.

The second trial of the four accused opened again in the Special Criminal Court on Thursday, 10 October 1978. The following day, Michael Plunkett was discharged and released without any stain on his character. The only evidence against him had been personal identification, which was found to be unsatisfactory. The trial of the other three continued.

As with the first trial, it attracted huge media publicity. During the trial most of the Garda witnesses, myself included, were accused by the barristers of committing assault and battery of their clients and extracting false incriminating statements from them while in custody.

On Monday, 11 December, when the court resumed after the weekend recess, only Osgur Breathnach and Brian McNally appeared in the dock; Nicky Kelly had done a runner to the States, where he lived as a fugitive. On 14 December, after a trial lasting 43 days, the Special Criminal Court found Nicky Kelly, Osgur Breathnach and Brian McNally guilty on both counts of the indictment. The court sentenced McNally to nine years' penal servitude and Breathnach to twelve, while Kelly was sentenced to twelve years' penal servitude *in absentia*. Breathnach and McNally appealed against their convictions in the Court of Criminal Appeal. In May 1980, the court upheld their appeals and they were released from Portlaoise Jail after serving 17 months in custody.

On page 23 of its judgment, the Court of Criminal Appeal states:

> Notwithstanding the fact therefore that the applicant also made detailed and serious allegations of physical cruelty and threatening behaviour by An Garda Síochána prior to the making of these statements, this court is satisfied that it cannot and should not interfere with the decision of the court of trial, which of course had the opportunity of seeing and hearing all the witnesses concerned, that these allegations were untrue.

On page 29, the decision of the court is given:

> . . . working on the basis that all the primary findings of fact made by the court of trial are correct and beyond the reach of

> correction in this court, we are not satisfied beyond reasonable doubt, nor do we think that the court of trial was entitled to be satisfied beyond reasonable doubt under either head of the test laid down by the Supreme Court in Shaw's case that the statements made by this applicant were voluntarily made or the manner in which they were made satisfied the basic requirements of fairness.

The court had decided that the statements of Osgur Breathnach should not have been admitted in evidence, and that without them there was not enough evidence to connect him with the crimes charged. His appeal against conviction and sentence was upheld by the court.

In another judgment delivered by Mr Justice Ronan Keane on 20 December 1991 in relation to discovery proceedings taken by Osgur Breathnach against Ireland, the Attorney General, myself and seven other Gardaí, it states:

> It has already been held by the Court of Criminal Appeal that the primary facts found by the Special Criminal Court could only have led to the inference that the interrogation of the plaintiff which culminated in the making of incriminating statements by him did not comply with fair procedures and to the further inference that the statements could not be regarded as voluntary.

The factors referred to by this court in reaching this conclusion were principally the place and time at which the inquiry was conducted and the unexplained failure to comply with the plaintiff's request that a solicitor be present during the interrogation.

In the case of Brian McNally, the Court of Criminal Appeal quashed his conviction on the grounds that the verbal statements he made should not have been admitted in evidence at his trial as they were taken in breach of the 'Judge's Rules'. The Judge's Rules are not rules of law but are there for guidance when taking statements and must be obeyed. The court also held that McNally had been held for 44 hours before making any admissions and had been interrogated for long periods of time in the small hours of the morning in circumstances, they said, that amounted to oppressive questioning.

I, like all my colleagues involved in the investigation of the mail-train robbery and subsequent trials, as you would expect, was not very happy at the outcome of the Court of Criminal Appeal, but as a servant of the state I accepted the decisions of the court, it being the only and final arbiter of law in the land. We had carried out duties under difficult circumstances to the best of our abilities and believed the matter to be at an end. In fact, my troubles in this controversial affair were only just beginning.

All of us who were involved in this investigation and the subsequent trials were relieved that at least the Court of Criminal Appeal had dismissed the allegations of abuse, mistreatment and assault by the appellants while in custody. However, certain sections of the media continued to label many of the detectives involved in the investigation, including myself, as the 'heavy gang'.

On 4 June 1980, Nicky Kelly was arrested at Shannon Airport, having returned voluntarily to face the music. He was taken to the prison at Portlaoise to begin his 12-year prison sentence, imposed on him in 1978. He also appealed against his conviction in the Court of Criminal Appeal. The judgment of that court was delivered in April 1982 by Mr Justice Finlay.

In his judgment, he said that the Court of Criminal Appeal was 'satisfied that it was open to the court of trial to reach the conclusions that it did and to reach them beyond a reasonable doubt and on a review of the whole of the evidence this court cannot say that those conclusions were perverse or insupportable. The pattern emerging from this evidence was of a person who, whilst in detention, eventually decided for one reason or another to cooperate with the members of An Garda Síochána and to confess to participation in this crime.'

Nicky Kelly appealed against the decision of the Court of Criminal Appeal in the Supreme Court. In October, Chief Justice O'Higgins dismissed his appeal and stated, 'The judgment of the Court of Criminal Appeal was correct and should be upheld.'

It went on to state that 'The Supreme Court noted that Kelly had been afforded every possible opportunity of establishing that he should not have been convicted and to this end has had his appeal fully argued, heard and considered, not only by the Court of Criminal Appeal, but also by this Court. It is seldom that the appellate jurisdiction of our courts has been so fully exercised, but it is proper that it should have been so in order to satisfy the requirements of justice.' Almost immediately afterwards, the 'Free Nicky Kelly' campaign began. Meanwhile, he was back in Portlaoise prison serving the remainder of his sentence.

In March that year, I was served with a plenary summons and a statement of claim. The plaintiff was one Osgur Breathnach. The other named defendants in the case were Ireland, the Attorney General and seven other colleagues who had been involved in the case. The statement of claim alleged all manner of wrongdoing by us, including allegations of assault, wrongful arrest, false imprisonment and malicious prosecution. There followed a long, drawn-out process. We, the defendants in the action, employed the services of a well-known Dublin firm of solicitors and they represented our interests successfully in many bruising encounters both in the court and in dealings with our employer – the state. We were also fortunate to have the services of one of the finest legal minds in the country, Adrian Hardiman SC.

From the very beginning of Breathnach's civil action, we requested through the Garda authorities that we be represented by the state solicitor and his legal department in Dublin. We felt we were always acting in good faith in the discharge of our duties and at all times within the law. We were vindicated in our actions by the highest courts in the land, but were to be bitterly disappointed at the attitude of the Establishment. I and the rest of my co-defendants received correspondence from the commissioner's office informing us that the state would not represent us or indemnify us in Breathnach's civil action.

We heard nothing more on the matter for two years. Around 1984, we were informed by our solicitor that the civil action had been reactivated.

Nothing more was heard until 24 March 1988 when we were informed that the civil action would come to hearing within the next six months. In a further and welcome development for us, we were made aware that in the course of the hearing in the High Court, Mr

Justice Lardner had ruled against Breathnach's attempt to put us on trial for assault and battery against him. That judgment was delivered in July 1989. However, he was still entitled to pursue us and the state in the other matters mentioned in his statement of claim. In fairness, in that action the state solicitor took over our defence, and our costs were paid. We were truly relieved at this decision and hoped we had heard the last of Breathnach. It was wishful thinking.

After Nicky Kelly was granted a Presidential Pardon, Breathnach was on his way back to the High Court to reinstate his charges of assault and battery. In a letter dated 19 October 1992 that was sent to me and my co-defendants, we were informed by the state solicitor that because of recent developments – i.e. Nicky Kelly's pardon – we were on our own again. Our solicitor conveyed our extreme annoyance, alarm and bitter disappointment to the state solicitor at having been abandoned by them at the eleventh hour.

In 1993, this long-running saga took yet another twist. In May, Osgur Breathnach, buoyed up by the granting of a Presidential Pardon to his friend Nicky Kelly, went on *The Gay Byrne Show*. Breathnach, in highly emotional tones, poured out his heart to the nation about his experiences in Garda custody. Byrne, the famous broadcaster, encouraged Breathnach to share his sufferings with the Irish people.

In the course of the interview, Byrne suggested to Breathnach that he was entitled to huge compensation. The interview was presented in such a manner as to suggest that my co-defendants and I were not denying Breathnach's allegations and could not defend them. Our senior counsel, Adrian Hardiman, referred to the interview as 'simply horrifying to my clients in a number of respects'. My co-defendants and I instructed our solicitors to take immediate action in the High Court.

In the High Court proceedings, our senior counsel said it was 'difficult to imagine anything which could more prejudice a jury trial'. He submitted that there were four major transgressions in the interview and went on to say that there was an absolute denial of assault in any form, or of wrongful arrests or arrest with improper motives by any of the defendants in this matter.

At the end of the hearing, Mr Justice Geoghegan granted permission for the six applicants to apply on the following Monday for the jailing of Gay Byrne and the seizure of RTÉ's assets. In the subsequent High

Court action, Mr Justice Morris found that Gay Byrne was not guilty of criminal contempt. During the proceedings, Gay looked worried and upset as he faced the real prospect of a stretch in Mountjoy jail. It was a very relieved and subdued Gay Byrne that left the court that day after his ordeal in the witness box.

This entire wretched business came to a close in October 1993. On the 26th of that month, my co-defendants and I received letters from our solicitor telling us that this action had been fully and finally settled and that the action had been struck out by the High Court. Furthermore, the letter states that when the matter was being struck out by Judge Kinlan, our counsel had advised the court that whilst the matter had been settled between the state and Breathnach, neither my co-defendants nor myself or our legal advisors had any part in such settlement. As far as we were concerned, this was the end of the matter.

Meanwhile, Nicky Kelly, having exhausted all the legal avenues open to him, still remained in jail. In the early '80s, the Free Nicky Kelly campaign had reached international prominence and was supported by the Irish Council for Civil Liberties (ICCL), Amnesty International, Church leaders and troubadours like Christy Moore, who even wrote a song about him called 'Wicklow Boy'.

When Kelly failed to secure his release, on 7 June 1983 he went on a hunger strike in Portlaoise prison that lasted 38 days. The Fine Gael government of the day did not relent, despite enormous pressure to do so. As the Free Nicky Kelly campaign continued unabated, even the government lost the stomach for a fight. On Tuesday, 17 July 1984, Michael Noonan, Minister for Justice, announced to his Cabinet colleagues that he was releasing Nicky Kelly. They would later put the spin on their decision that he was freed on humanitarian grounds. The 'Wicklow Boy' was finally at liberty.

In 1991, Nicky Kelly wrote to the government and petitioned for a Presidential Pardon. The completed report on that petition was submitted to the government by the Attorney General in March 1992. The following month, the Fianna Fáil government announced that they would be recommending a pardon for Kelly. Shortly afterwards, he did receive a Presidential Pardon. The official government statement was printed in full in the *Irish Times* on Wednesday, 29 April 1992.

I found it vague and without any real substance or conclusive argument.

From reading the statement, it seems to me that the reports of the two linguistic analysts submitted by Kelly had a major influence on the government's decision to recommend a pardon. Almost half of the statement is taken up with comment on them. There is much speculation on how those experts might have influenced or affected the decision of the judges in the Special Criminal Court and the Courts of Criminal Appeal had they been available to give evidence of linguistic analysis. The statement reads:

> Following consultation with the Director of Public Prosecutions, the Attorney General has advised the government that it is likely that our court would treat the opinion of a textual analysis expert as to the statement's authorship as being admissible were a trial of Kelly to be held now, and that one cannot say that such evidence would be likely to be disregarded by a court which heard it . . .
>
> However this linguistic analysis is very much in its infancy and should be regarded as still at the experimental stage. Difficulties can be anticipated in persuading a tribunal that the technique has either a conclusive or probative value at its present stage of development. Probably, the best verdict at present on the technique is not proven.

The statement continues with the extraordinary comment, 'In the opinion of the Director of Public Prosecutions, this material, had it been available, probably would not have any effect on the original decision to prosecute.'

The linguistic analysis referred to in the statement, also known as cumulative sum stylometry, was invented by Andrew Morton, an expert on the authentication of ancient texts, but has no scientific basis whatsoever. The system was first submitted to an Irish Court in 1991 during the murder trial of Vincent Connell, which I discuss later. The linguistic expert Dr Farrington, a colleague of Morton's, appeared for the defence and using this method tried to discredit the veracity of the accused's statements. The prosecution barrister, the late Eamon Leahy, comprehensively demolished Morton's so-called scientific system, exposing it for what it was – at best, another interesting theory; at worst, meaningless mumbo-jumbo. The jury in the case rejected Morton's cumulative sum stylometry and convicted the accused of murder.

In my opinion, the introduction of linguistic analysis as new evidence was a complete red herring, a smokescreen. It did not advance the case of a pardon for Nicky Kelly by one iota. We added our voices to those of Nicky Kelly, Osgur Breathnach, the ICCL, Amnesty International and Sinn Fein in calling for a public inquiry following the pardon. My comments calling for a sworn tribunal of inquiry following the pardoning of Nicky Kelly were printed in the *Sunday World* on Sunday, 22 November 1992.

My views were not shared by the Garda Commissioner, who when asked about a public inquiry replied, as I expected, with 'No comment.' The only civil action to reach the courts was that by John Fitzpatrick taken against myself and 18 other detectives, alleging ill-treatment while in Garda custody. The case was heard in the High Court in July 1985. The jury rejected all his claims. Along with many of my colleagues, to this day I would welcome a full public inquiry into the whole affair and we firmly believe that we would be totally vindicated in such a forum.

9

ASSASSINATION

WEDNESDAY, 21 JULY 1976 STARTED OUT LIKE ANY OTHER DAY. I WAS out on routine patrol with a colleague near Dundrum in south County Dublin when we received a message on the car radio that a loud explosion had been reported close to the British Ambassador's residence in Sandyford. We rushed to investigate with sirens wailing and were at the scene within minutes. Ours was the first car to arrive. Before long, we were joined by every available Garda car in the south city.

We came upon a scene of utter devastation. The explosion had gouged out a crater 15 feet deep and 30 feet wide, completely demolishing a narrow roadway. Rocks, earth and other debris were scattered all around. One massive boulder was hurled 100 yards by the force of the blast. The ambassador's blue Jaguar was lying on its side in the crater. The four occupants seemed to be dead or unconscious. My colleague and I helped to extricate them from the tangled wreckage of the car.

Only Brian O'Driscoll, the chauffeur, and Brian Cubbon, the Permanent Under-Secretary to the Northern Ireland Office, survived. The ambassador, Christopher Ewart-Biggs, and his 26-year-old secretary, Ms Judith Cook, were killed instantly. The Special Branch officers who were providing the armed escort had had a narrow escape from death. Only the split-second precision of the bomber had saved them. The noise and flames of the massive blast had dazed and disoriented them and left them temporarily incapacitated.

The bomb had been planted under a culvert barely 300 yards away from the main gates of the ambassador's residence. The killers had lain in wait on high ground overlooking Murphystown Road and detonated the bomb by command wire as the ambassador's car passed by. The passengers had been on their way to Government Buildings for a meeting with the Minister for Foreign Affairs, Garret FitzGerald. The ambassador had only taken up his appointment in Ireland a fortnight previously.

My colleagues and I were instructed to convey Brian Cubbon back to the ambassador's residence in Glencairn as a security precaution. He was deeply traumatised and bleeding from facial injuries but was not otherwise seriously injured. On arrival at the ambassador's residence, I broke the tragic news to the ashen-faced butler and his household staff. He almost fainted at the sight of Cubbon's dishevelled and blood-spattered appearance before breaking down in tears. I tried to comfort him but he was inconsolable. He kept crying out, 'Oh, poor Mr Ewart-Biggs!' It was a truly heartrending scene in which, yet again, we had been the bearers of tragic news that had plunged the household into shock and mourning.

When we drove back to Murphystown Road, the Garda commissioner, Edmund Garvey, and the Garda chaplin, Father Clarence Daly, had arrived there with other senior officers. The full enormity of the crime was only beginning to dawn on all of us. The murders of the ambassador and Judith Cook caused shock and outrage throughout the country. It was a bitter blow to the government and they were deeply embarrassed at this appalling security blunder.

The following day, the newspapers had a field day in their condemnation of the government for its 'shambles' of a security policy, which had failed to protect the most vulnerable and obvious of targets from the death squads of the IRA. Once again, the Provisionals had shown their contempt for human life and the rule of the law: the assassination was a brazen challenge to the authority of the state. One of the biggest investigations in the history of the state got under way that evening in Dublin Castle attended by senior Garda officers, including a number of commissioners. Experienced detectives were drafted in from all over the city to assist in the investigations. I was assigned to one of the teams. A reward of £20,000 was offered by the Irish government for any information leading to the arrest of the killers.

During subsequent inquiries in the Murphystown Road area, I came upon a witness who actually saw the killers make their getaway in a Ford Cortina seconds after the explosion. He said the car appeared to be giving them trouble. He saw two men jump out of it armed with rifles. They pushed the car and it started, then they jumped back in again and drove away. He said he remembered seeing our car arrive minutes after. We probably had a lucky escape, as we were unarmed and wouldn't have stood a chance against such ruthless killers.

Despite an intense and protracted investigation involving up to 100 detectives and all the resources of the state behind us, we drew a complete blank. At one stage, there appeared to be a major breakthrough when a fingerprint was positively identified on a builder's helmet found close to the scene. It was believed the mark was that of one of the bombers. The hunt was on to arrest this suspect. There was elation in government circles at this dramatic news.

It would later emerge – in what became known as 'the Fingerprint Scandal' – that the mark on the helmet had been wrongly identified. Detective Sergeant Michael Diggin had accidentally left his own finger mark on the helmet. The print was later identified wrongly by two other experts in the Technical Bureau as being left by the main suspect in the case. Detective Sergeant Diggin and his colleague, Detective Sergeant Patrick Corless, informed the senior officers in the Fingerprint Section of their worries. The commissioner, Edmund Garvey, was also briefed on the issue.

In March 1977, Garvey called Commander G.T.C. Lambourne, the head of the Fingerprint Department in Scotland Yard, to examine the helmet. Commander Lambourne agreed with the assessment made by Detectives Diggin and Corless that the print was not left by the prime suspect in the murders. It was the worst possible outcome of the investigation and the controversy seriously undermined the credibility of the Fingerprint Section. The murders of the British Ambassador and Judith Cook still remain unsolved.

In October 1976, the IRA's relentless and bloody bombing campaign would claim the life of young Garda Michael Clerkin. He was in the prime of his life at twenty-four years of age and just starting out in a career, having only four years' service behind him.

At around one o'clock that Saturday morning, Garda Clerkin was driving with a number of colleagues down a lonely by-road close to the main Portarlington–Mountmellick road. They were followed down the laneway by an unmarked police car manned by armed detectives from Portlaoise Garda station. About 200 yards down the laneway, both cars pulled up in front of an old two-storey stone farmhouse. The house, which was situated in Garryhinch, belonged to a local farmer but was unoccupied at the time. It was in complete darkness. The officers had driven there to check out a report that there had been suspicious activities in the vicinity of the house. The origin of the report had been an anonymous telephone call to Portlaoise station shortly before midnight. The officers made a thorough search of the grounds of the house but found no evidence of any illegal activity. Using their torches, they could find no sign of broken windows or of a forced break-in.

During the anonymous call to the police station, a female caller also alluded to the threat of assassination of a prominent local Fine Gael politician. It was perhaps with that in mind that the fateful decision to gain entry to the house and check out the interior was made.

At the rear of the house, Garda Clerkin managed to enter through a ground-floor window. He walked across the floor to the front door, where he tripped a command wire that detonated a gas cylinder that had been packed with high explosives. The enormous explosion ripped the house asunder. Garda Clerkin was killed instantly, his body almost vaporised by the intensity of the blast. He would be identified only by the signet ring on his finger. His two other colleagues from Portarlington had a miraculous escape. Their injuries, though serious, were not life-threatening.

Sergeant Tom Peters and Detective Ben Thornton, the detectives from Portlaoise, were not so lucky – they had been completely buried in the rubble and debris and were barely alive when they were pulled to safety. Both men had suffered horrific injuries. Sergeant Peters would never see again and both suffered permanent loss of hearing and other neurological damage.

That Saturday morning, I was directed with other members of my unit to travel immediately to Portlaoise from Dublin to assist in the investigations. Around midday, we arrived at the scene of the explosion. Garda commissioner Edmund Garvey was already there with other senior officers. He spoke to us in a quivering voice that could scarcely contain his rage at the atrocity. It was a sombre and desolate scene. Members of the Garda Technical Bureau were going about the grim task of searching the ruins of the house and surrounding areas for body parts. Later that evening, I attended the first conference at Portlaoise Garda station.

The subsequent investigation was wide ranging, thorough and determined. Each member of the various teams had vowed not to rest until the cowardly killers of Garda Michael Clerkin were behind bars. We all worked a gruelling schedule for weeks without a break. Within hours of the bombing, intelligence reports and informants on the ground confirmed what we all believed – that the Provisional IRA was responsible for the outrage.

The levels of public outcry and revulsion at the murder of a defenceless Garda were such that the Provisional IRA issued a statement denying that they had any part in the bombing. This statement was signed by their chief of staff, the ubiquitous P. O'Neill. None of us believed their weasel words of denial.

In the following weeks in a series of early morning raids, we searched the homes and business premises of known Provisional IRA members and their supporters across the counties of Laois and Offaly. We seized guns and ammunition and made many arrests. In the course of searches and the subsequent interrogation of the suspects, we unearthed details of further deadly attacks that were to be carried out by the IRA. We discovered that plans were well advanced to assassinate a certain High Court judge whom they considered to be a thorn in their side. They also had plans to murder a prison officer who worked in Portlaoise jail because of alleged ill treatment of Republican prisoners. Booby-trap bombs were to be used on both occasions. We also uncovered evidence of widespread targeting of members of An Garda Síochána by Provisional IRA intelligence officers. As time went by, every search and arrest was bringing us closer and closer to the persons who had planted the bomb at Garryhinch.

One night in early November, I was instructed to attend a meeting in the superintendent's office in the station, which was attended by the chief superintendent, a colleague from the Central Detective Unit and three members of the Investigation Section from Garda headquarters. We were told in quite dispassionate tones by the senior officer that very reliable information had been received at the highest level that all five of us had been placed on a death list by the Provisional IRA. It was the first time my life had been threatened by that organisation – but it wasn't to be the last.

That night we travelled to Garda headquarters, where we were each handed a revolver and ammunition by an assistant commissioner. He urged us to take any measure necessary to protect ourselves in the dangerous days ahead. The godfathers and armchair generals of the Provisional IRA were obviously worried at our blitz on their members across the Midlands and the damage we were inflicting on their infrastructure, and had decided to assassinate the investigators who were causing them most damage. Our mood at the time was one of grim determination to do our duty and bring the assassins to justice regardless of the threats.

A couple of weeks into the investigation, we had built up a solid mass of evidence against one individual, a local man. He had become our prime suspect for the planting of the bomb at Garryhinch. We arrested this man on 19 October and held him for seven days under the new Emergency Powers Act, which had just days previously been signed into law by the government. He was released without charge.

We re-arrested him a fortnight later and detained him again under the provisions of the Emergency Powers Act. During this later interrogation, he made a full written statement in which he admitted to planting the bomb that killed Garda Clerkin. There was elation in Garda circles at this breakthrough but our joy was short-lived. He took a challenge to the High Court on 11 November on his arrest and detention. The High Court found that the second arrest was unlawful, as he had been arrested twice for the same crime. He was released from custody and never charged. To date, no person has ever been charged in connection with this murder.

There was much speculation at the time that the killing of Garda Clerkin was in some way connected to the enactment of the Emergency Powers Act that had been signed into law the night he had been killed. The Provisional IRA and Sinn Fein, as well as other left-wing organisations, were bitterly opposed to that Act, regarding it as oppressive and draconian. The main provision of the Act increased the powers of the Garda to detain suspects from forty-eight hours to seven days for questioning.

The most likely theory, and the one I believe, was that the intended victim that night was a detective officer who was stationed in Portlaoise Garda station but who wasn't on duty that night. The Provisional IRA detested him and accused him of harassment and of giving a hard time to visitors at Portlaoise jail when he was on duty there. In my future career, I would have the harrowing and unenviable task of investigating the killings of seven more of my comrades.

During this investigation, I witnessed an extraordinary phenomenon in the most unlikely of environs. On a Sunday night in early November, I was in the old Garda station in Kildare town. All that day, I had been interviewing a suspect who had been arrested in connection with the Garryhinch bomb. I was accompanied by a detective sergeant from the Investigation Section of the Garda Technical Bureau. At around half-seven, we decided to return our prisoner to the cell and get some food for ourselves. My colleague decided that he would drive to Newbridge, have a sandwich and meet up with some of the investigation team there to review the day's developments. I placed the prisoner in the cell and told the young Garda, who was acting as station orderly, that I would be back in half an hour.

I went out and had a sandwich and a pot of tea in a little café in the town. I returned to the station at about ten to eight. The Garda station was situated on the main street and almost opposite the Silken Thomas pub. Inside the front door and to the right was a half-glass door leading to the public office. On entering the hall, I saw an elderly man through the glass door, standing at the counter in the public office. He was no more than six feet away from me. He was a tall man, slightly stooped and appeared to be in his early 60s. His face was pale and careworn. He had a serious, sad and gentle appearance about him. He had a full head of greying black wavy hair.

He wore a beige trench coat buttoned up to his neck and stood facing the station orderly, who was seated behind a table at the other end of the room. There was a turf fire lighting in the grate. For some reason that I will never know, I went back out of the front door and walked down the side of the station. Through the side windows, I saw that the man in the trench coat was still standing at the counter. The television was on under the counter and the station orderly was deeply engrossed in what he was watching. I could see quite clearly that it was *The Riordans*, a series based on a farming community in rural Ireland. I went down to the yard and lit myself a cigar. After a few minutes, I decided to go back to the station. I again walked up to the side entrance and saw the elderly man was still standing there and the station orderly was in his position by the fire.

I walked around the corner back into the station and pushed back the glass door into the public office. There was no sign of the man in the trench coat. I asked the station orderly where the elderly man had gone. He replied that nobody had been in the station for the past 25 minutes. For reasons that I cannot explain, I realised in that instant that the visitor in the beige trench coat was not of this world.

As if I was being led by an unseen hand, I took down a Sacred Heart badge that was wedged behind a socket over the fireplace. On the reverse side of the badge, there was a photograph of the man I had seen standing at the counter for nearly ten minutes. The text under the photograph read: 'Father John Sullivan, died Sunday, February the 19th 1933'.

The photograph of the priest on the badge was identical in every respect to the man I had seen. I had no doubt then, or now, that Father John Sullivan had appeared to me that night in the flesh. I froze at the thought and experienced an emotional shock, but no fear. Although I was supposed to be a hard-bitten detective who had never been prone to a fevered imagination, something had happened to me that defied all logic and understanding.

As I was standing there clutching the photograph, a local detective who was working on the investigation walked into the public office and stood exactly on the spot where I had seen Father Sullivan. I told him what had happened. He looked at me in disbelief and told me that he had been present in his official capacity at the ceremony of exhumation of the mortal remains of Father John Sullivan on 27 September 1960 at Clongowes Wood College, County Kildare. It was the first stage in the process of canonisation for that holy man. His body lies in a lead casket in the Jesuit Church in Gardiner Street. It has become a shrine for thousands of Dubliners. I left the station shortly afterwards. I was in no mood to conduct any further interviews that night.

This strange occurrence was the final link in a chain of events that began one beautiful Saturday in June 1968. It was early morning and I had just said goodbye to my girlfriend, Kathleen, who was on her way to Scotland to see her parents. I was taking a leisurely stroll past the Green Cinema on St Stephen's Green when I felt a tug on my jacket. It was a very old man with a white beard, wearing a black overcoat. He was sitting on the granite steps outside the cinema.

I took a coin from my pocket and handed it to him. He pushed it aside and I realised he was no beggar. In a firm but gentle voice, he asked me to sit down. I sat down beside him on the steps, although feeling a little self-conscious. There was something about him that compelled me to listen to what he had to say. He told me that his name was Mr Ffrench and that he had a lifelong devotion to Father John Sullivan, the Jesuit priest. He showed me a miraculous medal and other religious items that he said Father John Sullivan had blessed and given to him.

He told me that the coat on his back was also given to him by Father Sullivan, and he asked me to touch it, which I did to humour him. He then said the country would become a sea of tears and a vale of suffering if we didn't pray for deliverance through the intercession of Father Sullivan to the Sacred Heart of Jesus. He gave me details of the saintly life that Father John Sullivan had led and his selfless devotion to the poor. He asked me to pray to him and to encourage others to do likewise, and to never forget what he had told me that morning. The sincerity and conviction in that old man's words and the air of sanctity he had about him moved me deeply.

When I walked away from him that morning, I felt some of the warmth had gone out of the day. I never again thought about that fateful meeting until my experiences in Kildare Garda station all those years later.

In the course of the Clerkin investigation, another remarkable coincidence that ties this tale together took place. During the case, it was necessary to interview the director of the Salts Textile factory in Tullamore regarding the movements of an employee who was believed to have been involved on the periphery of the crime. We were shown into a plush office, where we introduced ourselves and explained the nature and importance of this inquiry to the overall investigation.

Mr Pocock, the director, was a large, genial man with a round face and a bald head on which were deep indentations. We had finished our conversation and were about to leave his office when I noticed a framed picture of Father John Sullivan. It was identical to the one I had seen in the station. A votive lamp was lighting the photograph from underneath. I was stunned to see such a shrine and I turned to Pocock and asked him about his interest in Father Sullivan. His face became animated. He told me that Father Sullivan had been a living saint and he had devoted his life to the cause of his canonisation. He went on to tell me an incredible story.

Some years before, he had been diagnosed with inoperable tumours on his brain. The doctors had given up all hope of a recovery and, in effect, he was waiting to die. He said that he had received a visit from his wife and children, and as they left the room he knew that he would never see them again. He prepared himself for the inevitable and as he lay hovering between life and death, drifting in and out of consciousness, he heard a voice call his name. He looked and saw a man standing at the end of the bed. The man said, 'I'm Father John Sullivan, don't worry.'

When he woke up that morning, he thought at first that he had dreamt it all. He then realised with total clarity his mysterious visitor had brought him a miraculous gift. He suddenly felt physically well and experienced a peace that he had never known. He rang the bell for breakfast and got out of bed. The nurse called the doctors. He was brought for X-rays, which showed no trace of the tumours. Within three days, he was back home with his family. Doctors agreed that what had taken place was a miracle.

I told him of my encounter in the Garda station. He left his desk with tears in his eyes and, grabbing me by the hands, said that I was a very privileged person. Later, he sent me a relic of Father Sullivan and a book, both of which I treasure to this day.

There was one more fascinating twist in this strangest of tales. Before leaving Kildare, I was told a story by a retired colleague, who had been stationed in Kildare Garda station in the early '70s. He told me that one bad winter's night he was station orderly and was about to lock up when he found an old man sheltering in the little hallway inside the front door. He described him as being very old and frail with a long, white beard and wearing a heavy, black overcoat. He took pity on him, made him a cup of tea and allowed him to stay in a cell for the night. He said that the next morning he'd had to turn him out of the station before the sergeant in charge arrived or he would have got into trouble for his act of kindness. As he was leaving, the old man told him that his name was Mr Ffrench and handed him a Sacred Heart badge with the photograph of Father John Sullivan, the same one that I had discovered on the mantelpiece in the station.

All my life, I have been a spiritual person but a rather lukewarm Catholic. In November 1976, I was the last man that anybody would have imagined to have a 'road to Damascus'-type religious experience. I cannot explain what happened. It defies all logic and reason; however, I know that what my eyes saw convinced me beyond any doubt of the existence of a divine being and the certainty of life after death. I retain a deep and lasting devotion to Father John Sullivan not just because I have become familiar with his extraordinary saintly existence but most of all, despite all the horrors and inhumanity I have witnessed in my life, this encounter renewed my faith in the basic goodness of mankind.

10

STAKEOUT

THURSDAY, 9 DECEMBER 1976 WAS A COLD, MISERABLE DAY. IT HAD been raining heavily from early morning and I was soaked to the skin; even the best of raingear provides little protection from the elements after ten hours on a motorbike. The streets were slippery from the continual downpour and it took all one's concentration to avoid a spill in those treacherous driving conditions.

At five-thirty that evening, I was a relieved man to finally park up my bike. It had been a long and tiring day. I was looking forward to a couple of pints with my mates in the cosy atmosphere of the Chinaman pub around the corner from the office. Before that, I had to report off duty and complete the usual paperwork in the office. I was only inside the door when one of the sergeants on duty told me that Detective Inspector Ryan wanted to see me in his office. I got the feeling that somehow I wouldn't be seeing the Chinaman for a while yet and I was only too right.

Sitting at his desk when I went in was my lugubrious DI, the ever-present cigarette dangling from the corner of his mouth, clouds of smoke swirling around his head. When called to a meeting with Ned Ryan, I always got the uneasy feeling that I was knee-deep in trouble

– or perhaps it was just my guilty conscience. He always gave the impression of a man who was resigned to, but prepared for, life's inevitable disasters, especially to the men under his command.

On that occasion, he came straight to the point and told me he had a job on that required my assistance. He went on to tell me that earlier that day during a search of a house in St Laurence's Road in Clontarf two loaded automatic pistols, ammunition and a suitcase full of subversive material had been found. Confidential information had later been received that the flat where the guns and other items had been found had been rented by members of the INLA. The information further revealed that the guns were to be used to assassinate the leader of that organisation, Seamus Costello. As it turned out, he was gunned down shortly afterwards in his car in Fairview by one of his own men. His assassin was subsequently murdered in retaliation. The INLA was notorious for their constant internal feuding and internecine warfare, which resulted in many deaths.

The DI told me that two Special Branch officers and one man from our own unit had taken over the flat. He instructed me to join them there and arrest any callers, but to exercise extreme caution in so doing, as they were likely to be armed and highly dangerous individuals.

Shortly afterwards, I was dropped off near the house. I tapped on the front ground-floor window beside the hall door as instructed. I saw the curtains move and seconds later I was admitted through the front hall door by one of the Special Branch officers whom I recognised. He led me to a ground-floor room, the first one on the left, beside the hall door. The large, high-ceilinged room was almost in darkness, illuminated only by the orange glow of the street lamp outside the window. I whispered a greeting to my other two colleagues. They were sitting beside a window, concealed from the outside by a heavy lace curtain but with a good view of the street.

One of the Special Branch men was holding a Uzi sub-machine gun across his knees. One of them pointed out the suitcase in the middle of the room that contained the guns and ammunition. There were five other rooms rented out in the house, so there were people coming and going all evening. Every time there was a caller to the door, we went on full alert. After a few hours of false alarms, we were beginning to get nervous and jumpy. Eventually, about four hours later, there was an excited whisper from one of the lads at the window that two likely candidates, both young men, were on their way up to the front door. Seconds later, the front door opened and then closed.

We heard footsteps in the hall and the sound of a key being fitted into a lock. We waited with guns drawn, holding our breath, fearful of making the slightest sound. I was standing directly behind the door. It opened a few inches and almost immediately was pulled back out. All hell broke loose. Being the nearest, I yanked open the door and rushed out into the hallway. In the darkness, I could barely make out the figure of a person trying to open the hall door.

'Armed Gardaí – don't move!' I shouted.

'Don't shoot, don't shoot!' he started screaming.

At that instant, someone hit me hard in the head, and I felt hands around my neck and nails digging into my skin. I somehow managed to break free to turn and face my attacker, half-stunned by the blow I had received. I struggled with him and he tried to pull my gun from me. I shouted at him on several occasions to let go or I would shoot. He struggled even harder. By now he had both hands on the barrel of my gun and was trying to wrench it out of my grasp.

I knew if he succeeded he would turn the gun on me, so I had no option but to fire at him. In the narrow hallway, the gunshot was deafening and the smell of cordite filled the air. There was total confusion for that second, then the lights came on. The man I had shot at was slumped on the floor clutching his stomach, groaning, 'I'm shot, I'm shot.' My three colleagues were struggling with the other man at the front door. I got on my walkie-talkie and called the back-up teams that were circling in the vicinity for assistance. I also requested an ambulance.

I knelt down beside the wounded man and pulled open his shirt and jacket. I was mighty relieved that the bullet had only grazed his belly. All the same, it had been a close call for him and he knew it. He was white-faced and shaking with fear and shock. Minutes later, help arrived. Both prisoners were taken into custody.

An investigation was launched immediately into the shooting, and the hallway was preserved for technical examination. As per regulations, I had to hand over my revolver and ammunition for ballistic examination, and I was interviewed by a senior officer. The result of the investigation was that I was held to have acted in a lawful manner in the discharge of my weapon.

Thomas McCartan, the man whom I had shot, was subsequently jailed by the Special Criminal Court for possession of firearms with intent to endanger life. During his trial, he accused me of trying to murder him, a ridiculous claim that was totally rejected by the court.

When he was released from prison, he moved into the Crumlin area, where he became a close associate of Martin Cahill, the notorious Southside criminal known as 'the General'. McCartan would later provide Cahill with the explosive device he used in his bid to assassinate the head of the Forensic Science Laboratory, Dr James Donovan.

Thomas McCartan was involved in many other shootings and robberies before his luck finally ran out. On 22 December 1986, he was mown down in a hail of bullets on a Belfast street. Ten years earlier, his father, Jack 'Fingers' McCartan, had been gunned down by the Provisional IRA on those same streets.

I have carried a gun on and off duty for almost 24 years and although I had to draw it on many occasions, I never came so close to killing a man as I did that night. In the aftermath of that shooting, I was forced to confront the sobering and shocking truth that I was capable of taking human life in a situation of last resort. I am very thankful that I finished out my service without having to make that stomach-churning decision ever again.

In my long career, 1977 was not the most auspicious year, although it started out with great promise. In early February, we sold our house in Tallaght and were in the process of moving into a new home in Terenure. Kathleen and I were really excited at the prospect and were busy with the last-minute arrangements always involved in such a move. I was on night duty during the week in question. On Thursday night, I finished work late and afterwards got a lift from my partner to the Garda Boat Club in Islandbridge on the banks of the Liffey.

Earlier that night, we had heard on our rounds that there was a function being held there, so we decided to pay it a visit. After being stuck in a car for eight or nine hours, we were looking forward to relaxing over a few pints. When we got there, the party was in full swing. As the night wore on, I was requested by the compère to get up on the stage and sing a few songs, which I duly did, being no shrinking violet. I was always in demand as an entertainer at this kind of gathering, as I had a good singing voice and a vast repertoire of songs and ballads that I learned as a child. That night, I was in particularly good voice – singing my heart out and loving every minute of it. As usual, I was being rewarded with copious pints for my musical contributions. I think the adulation of my fan club and too much Guinness went to my head and almost caused me to end up on a slab in the city morgue.

I'm not sure at what time I left the club that morning, but instead of turning right at the main door, I turned left and walked round the corner into the River Liffey at the spot where rowing boats are launched. The water was at least 12 feet deep there. It didn't take long for me to sober up in that freezing water. I thought it was the end of me.

Somebody must have been praying for me that night because when I finally bobbed up to the surface, a pair of strong hands grabbed me and pulled me to safety. Luckily, my rescuer, who was leaving around the same time as me, had heard the splash, went to investigate and found me floundering in the water.

By this time, I was surrounded by more partygoers, who had heard all the commotion by the riverbank. I was mortified with embarrassment at my own stupidity as I stood there shivering and shaking with cold and shock. I pulled myself together and a kind colleague dropped me at home, but not before I had thanked the man who had saved my life. When I got home, I stripped myself naked in the kitchen and ran upstairs and straight into bed.

The next morning, Kathleen woke me none too tenderly demanding to know what my clothes were doing lying in the middle of the kitchen floor in a puddle of water. I told her what had happened, and was suitably contrite and apologetic about my irresponsible behaviour. Later, much later, we had a laugh about it. It was just as well that I had married a woman with a sense of humour.

Kathleen and I had now been married six years, and any illusions she may have had that life with me was going to be a bed of roses were long since dispelled. If I were to be honest, I would have to admit that at the time I was impetuous, unpredictable, hopeless with money and far too fond of the drink to have the makings of an ideal husband. Only Kathleen's innate common sense, her kind and forgiving nature, and her stoical acceptance of my many failings saved the day. Any other woman would have deservedly given me my marching orders.

The only casualty in the entire Liffey affair, apart from my dignity, was my fake leather overcoat, which I had only bought that day on account in Burtons. After immersion in the freezing water, it looked like an old rag and I never wore it again.

After barely surviving a watery end but before the month was out I was plunged yet again into a crisis. Although not life-threatening, it would have the most serious implications on my reputation and career, and on my very freedom. The incident that occurred in our unit caused embarrassment and shame, and almost wrecked the careers and good names of certain Garda officers, myself included.

Towards the end of the month, I turned up for work at Osmond House as usual around 9 a.m. It was a lovely, sunny morning. I had a spring in my step and not a care in the world as I stepped through the door of the office. I immediately suspected something was wrong. The DI was huddled in his office with the sergeants. The rest of the lads had long, solemn faces. There was none of the usual Monday-morning bonhomie and banter. When I asked what was amiss, one of them half-whispered to me that a locker had been broken into and £1,000 had been stolen out of it.

The money was the proceeds of a crime and was the subject of an impending court action. I was stunned at this awful news. I realised with a sinking feeling that I would be the prime suspect for the crime, as I had probably been the last person in the room prior to the theft. I felt sick to the stomach at the prospect of the humiliating ordeal I would surely undergo. The previous night, even though I was off duty, I had called into the office at around nine o'clock and taken one of the unit cars, as my own car had broken down and I needed to drop a relation at the airport. At around one that Monday morning, I returned to the office and dropped off the keys of the car. Not being on duty, I had no business being there that night. I realised that I would be in trouble for what is known as 'misuse of official transport' – a serious breach of Garda regulations. I was between a rock and a hard place.

I had also been logged in and out of the building the previous night by a detective on duty at the front desk. I decided that, under the circumstances, honesty was the best policy and I reported my little misdemeanour to Detective Inspector Ryan. He was sympathetic and realised my predicament but informed me that the investigation was out of his hands. Two detective superintendents had been appointed to investigate the matter, as they would any other serious crime. He was angry and very upset about what had happened and also because news of the theft would spread like wildfire in Garda circles and our unit would become the focus of much adverse publicity.

The investigating superintendents set up an incident room close to our office and experts from the Technical Bureau examined the crime scene. Due to my shenanigans the previous night, I was the first detective to be interviewed. Now I experienced what it was like to be on the receiving end of an interrogation. The first interview lasted for six hours and they didn't pull their punches in telling me that I was in serious trouble for taking the car, but that going into the office that night when I was off duty was highly suspicious and afforded me the opportunity to break into the locker and steal the money. They left me in no doubt that I was in the frame. They pointed out that I might also be strapped for cash because of moving house. As the circumstantial evidence piled up against me, I had to face the nightmare scenario that I might finish up on a charge sheet for a crime of which I was totally innocent. I made a long, detailed statement and gave the investigators access to all my private financial dealings with the bank and credit union.

As the investigation continued and each man was interviewed in turn, the tension and stress in the unit became almost unbearable. The atmosphere in the office was a poisonous mix of fear, suspicion and paranoia. The ongoing investigation was also affecting the efficiency and morale of the unit. As the pressure mounted on the two superintendents to solve the crime, there were acrimonious exchanges between different factions of the unit over the conduct of the investigation. Some men deeply resented the intrusion into their private and personal lives, and malicious gossip of half-truths, innuendos and lies whispered around the office added to our misery.

Despite a lengthy, painstaking investigation, nobody was ever charged with the crime, although the rumour machine ground on for a long while after. I was given a fool's pardon for taking out the car on personal business and let away with yet another warning.

It took most of the year before the toxic legacy of distrust and suspicion had lifted from the unit. Fences were mended and friendships were patched up and a kind of normality returned, but things would never be the same again.

It was a salutary lesson for me as I reflected afterwards what a fragile concept is the presumption of innocence. In all my future dealings with prisoners and suspects, I would err on the side of extreme caution before recommending a prosecution of any person on mere circumstantial evidence, no matter how compelling, without real proof.

11

A GODFATHER'S TALE

AT 3.20 P.M. ON 18 AUGUST 1994, I WAS DRIVING OUT OF THE SWAN Shopping Centre in Rathmines. I was on my own in an unmarked police car. At the time, I was a detective sergeant stationed in Sundrive Road in Crumlin. As I turned on the radio, I heard an excited dispatcher calling on all mobiles in the south city to go immediately to the junction of Oxford Road and Charleston Road. He repeated again and again, 'Tango One is down! Tango One is down!'

'Tango One' was the codename given to Dublin criminal Martin Cahill. I was at the scene in less than a minute. I saw Cahill's black Renault 5, which had crashed into the wrought-iron railings of number 45 Charleston Road. I ran to the car and stared in disbelief at the bullet-riddled body of Cahill himself. He was slumped sideways in his seat still strapped in by his safety belt. He had sustained massive injuries to his neck and chest, and blood was beginning to seep through his shirt. His last few strands of hair were hanging limply to one side, exposing the bald head he had made such efforts to conceal for all those years. Blood leaked from a gaping wound in his neck and was gathering in a pool on the passenger seat.

A videotape of the film *A Bronx Tale* was beside him on the seat. He was obviously on his way to Ranelagh to return it. The film is about a Bronx kid torn between affection for his honest bus-driving father and admiration for the local gang boss. Perhaps Cahill had identified with the latter character. If he had, he'd just suffered the fate of many a Mafia boss, from Alberto Anastasia, downed by a hail of bullets inside a New York barber's shop in 1957, to Paul Castellano, assassinated outside a Manhattan restaurant in 1985 on the order of arch-rival John Gotti.

Cahill's life could not be described as mundane, and his demise even less so. His end provided the very definition of a godfather's tale, one we are all used to experiencing on celluloid, but this was all too real. Cahill, an arrogant and extremely violent man, was reduced to the ultimate humiliation: he was now a lifeless heap with his blood spilling all over the interior of his modest car. Many of our encounters flashed through my mind and I remembered the times over the years he had frequently led us a merry dance as he constantly escaped the arm of the law for which he had nothing but contempt.

Despite his long and brutal reign as Ireland's leading crimelord, I felt no jubilation as I stood over him. His lifeless, blank expression, the slumped fat form and the last vestige of vanity – the wisp of hair suspended away from the bald pate – was indeed a piteous sight. I placed my hand on his chest inside his shirt to check for any sign of life. There was none.

While I was still checking his pulse, a doctor arrived beside me and pronounced him dead. By this time, the place was swarming with uniformed Gardaí and detectives, all anxious to get a glimpse of the slain gangster. A canvas sheet was placed over the car and the entire scene was taped off for technical examination. A large crowd had gathered and the incessant flashes of photographers' cameras captured the scene that would dominate the following day's front pages.

There followed angry scenes as first Christopher Cahill, Martin's youngest son, arrived on a bicycle followed by Martin junior. Christopher hurled his bicycle at a police van and shouted obscenities and accusations at all of us of complicity in his father's murder. Martin junior was more subdued. He calmed his brother down and took him away.

As I looked at his crumpled body, a part of me couldn't help but think that he had got what he deserved; after all, he had lived a life of extreme violence not hesitating to torture, shoot and bomb anybody who got in his way. Yet despite all his wickedness, I could never condone or gloat over such a brutal, cold-blooded murder and remain true to my calling and conscience.

Later, an eyewitness to the shooting would state he had seen a young man dressed as a Dublin City Corporation worker noting down the number of cars with a clipboard at the junction. He said that as the black Renault pulled up at the stop sign on Oxford Road, the man dropped the clipboard, ran around to the driver's door and shot the person inside at point-blank range through the closed window. The black Renault then went out of control, skidded across the road and crashed into the railings. The gunman followed the car across the road and fired three or four more shots at the driver. The witness described how the gunman smiled and laughed before escaping on the pillion seat of a waiting motorbike.

Before leaving the scene that day, I telephoned Dr Jim Donovan, who had himself escaped death at the hands of the General, and informed him of Martin Cahill's assassination.

Within hours of the killing, a number of subversive organisations claimed credit for the murder. The INLA was the first to issue a statement of claim but later retracted same. The Provisional IRA then issued a very detailed statement outlining their reasons for killing him. These included his alleged involvement with pro-British death squads and especially his involvement with the Portadown UVF, which, they alleged, was responsible for the gun-and-bomb attack on the Widow Scallans pub on Pearse Street in Dublin, in which a Sinn Fein member had been shot dead.

There is little doubt that the Provisional IRA was responsible for Cahill's murder. He had always been a thorn in their side and had never backed down in any confrontations with them. After Cahill had pulled off the massive O'Connor's jewellers robbery in July 1983, the IRA had approached him and demanded half of the proceeds. His response was: 'Fuck off and rob your own gold.' The Provisional IRA had signed Cahill's death warrant ten years previously in 1984. That year, Tommy Gaffney, a lifelong friend of Cahill's, had been kidnapped by the Provos and held for 12 days. During that time, they interrogated and tortured him to gain information about Cahill and the whereabouts of the loot from the O'Connor's robbery. Before they released him, they told him to convey the message to his friend that they would not kidnap him but 'stiff him on the street'. They made good on their threat and murdered him before declaring a ceasefire in September 1994.

Martin Cahill was born on 23 May 1949 to decent working-class parents. In the grinding poverty of post-war Dublin, the family was forced to live in the run-down inner-city slums of Grenville Street just north of the River Liffey. The slums of Dublin were among the worst in Europe at that time, with entire families living in dank, filthy and overcrowded conditions, many without water or sanitation. In those slums, Cahill suffered hunger and want and, as he grew older, his sense of rejection and alienation irrevocably jaundiced his views against society.

In 1960, the fortunes of the family appeared to take a turn for the better when the Dublin Corporation moved them into a new house on Captain's Road in Crumlin in Dublin's south city. It was a vast improvement on their previous lodgings, but unfortunately, and inevitably, poverty, hunger and deprivation followed them there, casting their cold shadow and blighting all hopes and aspirations for a better life. In their straitened circumstances, the sprawling, soulless housing estate where they were now living only increased their sense of isolation and social exclusion, and added to their misery. At least in the overcrowded slums they had left they had experienced a sense of community, close friendships and a sharing of troubles that only the poor and downtrodden know. At times, when his parents had no food in the house and no money to buy it, Martin and his brothers were reduced to stealing to feed themselves.

In 1961, the young Martin was convicted in the Metropolitan Children's Court for simple larceny. He was given the benefit of the Probation of Offenders Act and released. He was 12 years old. Over the next two years he was again convicted in the Children's Court for larcenies and burglaries. On one of these occasions, he was sentenced to 12 months' detention, which was suspended. However, later in 1963, he was convicted yet again and sentenced to one month's detention. This was the first time Martin Cahill was to be locked up.

When he was sixteen, Martin was convicted for committing a burglary and sentenced to two years' detention in the industrial school in Daingean, County Offaly, down in the Midlands. While incarcerated in that institution, he was subjected to a harsh and brutal regime of physical violence that was endemic in the culture of those so-called reformatory schools. Only now, 50 years later, is the full extent and the horrifying nature of the criminal abuse – mental, physical and sexual – that was inflicted on innocent defenceless children being fully revealed.

I remember as a young boy being caught in the local sweet shop helping myself to a few toffees. The angry owner threatened to have me sent to St Joseph's industrial school in Tralee for my crime. The fear and terror that prospect conjured up in me gave me nightmares for days afterwards. The very name of the place filled me with dread. I can only imagine what Martin Cahill and thousands of other children endured in those hellholes.

After his ordeal in Daingean, the last vestiges of hope that he could lead a normal life were gone. His heart had hardened to stone. His already jaundiced view of society had mutated into a cold, unforgiving fury fuelled by an implacable hatred and contempt for the Establishment that he despised. He would later wage an unrelenting criminal campaign of bank robberies, kidnappings and shootings, and commit some of the most high-profile crimes in the history of the state.

I first met Martin Cahill when I was attached to the Crime Task Force in 1972. I had followed a suspect car into Hollyfield Buildings in Rathmines and when I checked out the driver, he gave his name as Martin Cahill. He became insulting and abusive when I insisted on searching his car. Afterwards, he told me he wouldn't forget me and to be careful around Rathmines on dark nights. It was to be the first of many confrontations with him over the course of my career.

Six months later, I met his trusted henchman, Martin Foley, during a very violent encounter at the Mont Clare Hotel in Merrion Square. I had pulled him in for dangerous driving. Suddenly, he and another friend of Cahill's attacked me with a golf putter and the exhaust pipe of a motorbike. During the altercation, they broke the window of the squad car and hammered in the roof with their weapons; however, when back-up arrived, we managed to overpower them and they both ended up in the cells that night.

After joining the Central Detective Unit in 1975, I renewed my relationship with Cahill and his cronies. During the mid-'70s, there was a dramatic escalation in armed crime in the country. Although Dublin city suffered the brunt of it, quiet country towns were also targets for marauding gangs. The authorities had channelled the lion's share of men and resources into combating paramilitary activity, believing that to be the greatest threat to the security of the state. Units like ours that dealt with so-called ordinary, decent criminals were being continually starved of manpower and funds.

Because of the ongoing Troubles in the North, high-powered weaponry was being acquired by an emerging new breed of more vicious and ruthless gangster who recognised the benefits of operating in tight-knit groups. These gangs, who emulated the exploits of the paramilitaries and copied their methods, heralded the arrival of organised crime in this country. From around 1975 onwards, about five of these highly organised gangs were operating in the city.

The outfit led by Martin Cahill was the most prolific, audacious and dangerous of them all. Detective Inspector Ned Ryan was the first senior officer to recognise the awesome ability, cunning, and fanatical hatred of authority that Cahill possessed – all traits that would mark him out as a fearsome and formidable enemy of the state. Both men had detested each other since their first confrontation. In the following years, DI Ryan would utilise all his legendary qualities of patience, energy and determination in his pursuit of Cahill and become his most implacable foe.

Regardless of our other commitments, Ryan insisted and ordered that at least one car crew concentrate their activities each day on Martin Cahill and his associates. Martin was a wily old fox who knew every laneway and shortcut in South Dublin like the back of his hand. He had a tape recorder installed on the dashboard of his car and activated it every time he was stopped. He would speak into it and record the time, date, place and names of the Gardaí involved in the stop-and-search. On every occasion, he would blame Ryan for his troubles, and rant and rave about the harassment the inspector was causing him.

Despite our best efforts, Cahill and the gang were still getting away with major armed robberies. In 1976, Cahill and his gang robbed the Werburgh Street employment exchange, a stone's throw from our offices and Special Branch headquarters in nearby Dublin Castle, and got away with over £100,000. He was really rubbing our noses in it. He and his gang pulled off several other armed robberies that year. The following year, he carried out an armed robbery at the Semperit tyre factory in Ballyfermot and made off with £53,000 in cash.

About a month after that robbery, one of our units tailed Cahill to the car park in Killiney Hill, a well-known beauty spot in south County Dublin. They watched him climb the hill but remained in the car park, where they had his car under observation. They called for assistance and were later joined by Ryan and another detective. One man stayed in the car park while Ryan and the other two decided to climb the hill and see what he was up to. When they were halfway up the hill, they met Cahill on his way down. Darkness was falling.

While yet some distance away, the DI spoke to him and asked him if he was picking up the Semperit money. At that, Cahill turned around and ran back up the hill. DI Ryan and the others raced after him. In a frantic attempt to escape, he jumped down a steep cliff at the top of the hill and disappeared into the undergrowth. They searched for him in the gathering darkness but to no avail; however, they found the jacket he had discarded in his headlong flight. In it were the keys of his car. He turned up the next day, battered and bruised from his ordeal.

He later made a statement to a solicitor that Ryan had been armed with a rifle the night before on Killiney Hill and had threatened him with it. The subsequent inquiry found that there wasn't a shred of truth in his bizarre story. Ned had only had his walking stick with him. These wild and untrue allegations were always part of Martin Cahill's armoury. His philosophy always was, 'If you throw enough mud, some of it is bound to stick.' He would later carry out another vendetta on DI Dick Murphy, Ned's successor, writing all manner of insulting graffiti about him on walls and shop fronts in the Rathmines area.

Shortly after the incident on Killiney Hill, I was involved in a surveillance operation on another notorious Southside gang who had carried out a string of bank robberies right across the city. The gang was led by Anthony 'the Boss' Duff and included a number of hardened criminals from the north inner city. During an early-morning swoop, we arrested five of the gang, including the Boss, and recovered guns and money from a recent raid.

At one of the gang member's flats, a young English woman was arrested. She had been working in a brothel in the city centre, where she had met up with the gang member in question. She was a very pretty and friendly young woman, who had left her home in London because of conflict with her stepfather. I explained to her that she was going to get into serious trouble hanging around with bank robbers. We chatted for a while and I gained her confidence. The more we spoke, the more frightened she seemed to get. Then she made the startling revelation that she had a bottle of strychnine poison hidden in her flat in Rathmines. When I asked her for what purpose she had it, she broke down and cried. She told me that the gang member she was living with had given it to her to hide. He told her he was keeping it for Martin Cahill. When I pressed her about how much more she knew, she told me that the poison was going to be used by Martin Cahill to kill Inspector Ryan. She told me that the plan was to inject it into milk bottles on DI Ryan's doorstep.

Later that day, I recovered the bottle of poison from where she had concealed it – up the chimney in her apartment. I immediately informed Ned of Cahill's murderous plot. The young English woman's life was now in danger, as she had divulged details of the plan and handed over the poison. DI Ryan instructed me to stay with her and protect her round the clock until we got her out of the country. The devilish plot that we had so luckily uncovered demonstrated the cunning, evil and vengeful personality that made Cahill such a dangerous enemy to all who crossed him.

I myself had a narrow escape from accidental poisoning in a bizarre incident that occurred some years later. That morning I had gone to a house in Ballybrack with a number of other detectives and arrested a young man who had burgled a pharmacy shop in Rathdrum, County Wicklow, stealing £1,000 worth of drugs and jewellery. Included in the haul was a quantity of strychnine, which the burglar had mistaken for heroin. He had unwittingly sold several fixes of the poison to drug addicts. One person was already dead and others were in a serious condition in Jervis Street Hospital, having injected themselves with the deadly substance.

During the course of the search of the house, I found drugs and a large sum of money – some of the proceeds of the robbery. I arrested the man and lodged him in Bridewell Garda station. A short while later, I was about to tuck into breakfast in Bewleys café in Georges Street when two detectives burst in the door and asked me if I had eaten anything using my hands. They told me that the money I had counted had been contaminated with the lethal strychnine poison.

I was rushed to Jervis Street Hospital and kept under observation for several hours. I was scared out of my wits until I got the all-clear. The young criminal who had caused such death and suffering was subsequently convicted and received a prison sentence.

In 1977, the Hollyfield complex where Cahill lived was a run-down, filthy slum. Most of the other flats were vacant or vandalised; pools of stagnant water gathered in deep craters in front of the building; piles of refuse and rubble littered the entire site; raw sewage erupted from broken pipes and ran down the outside walls. Amidst all that chaos and decay, Martin would park his Mercedes 500 and his Harley-Davidson. It made for an incongruous scene.

He had also erected a flagpole and placed a battery of loudspeakers on the roof of his block. When he was in residence, he would hoist up the tricolour and blast out rebel songs in defiance at any intrusion into his fiefdom by the police.

I followed him numerous times into the flats, and stopped and searched him. Apart from exchanging mutual insults, he rarely, if ever, became physically aggressive. That just wasn't his style. Although on one occasion I approached him as he was getting out of his car and, for no reason, he ran away screaming, 'Don't shoot! Don't shoot!' At times, he did act deranged but that's what it was – just an act.

Another strange incident occurred on a sunny Sunday afternoon in the summer of 1977. I was riding my motorcycle along Aungier Street when I saw Martin coming out of the door of Whitefriar Street Church. Although it was scorching hot, he was wearing a heavy anorak with the hood fastened tightly around his face. I pulled up alongside him and said hello. I was going to ask him what he was doing in the church, but when he saw me he broke into a little trot. I stayed with him all the way as he ran the mile and a half to Hollyfield Buildings. A few times, I told him to take it easy or he would have a heart attack, but he looked straight through me and spoke not a word in response.

When he got to the flats, his face was as red as a beetroot, and he was lathered in sweat and struggling to get his breath. He looked on the point of exhaustion, but he had kept going rather than show any weakness in front of me.

That Sunday, I realised what a strange and complex individual he was. I never did find out what he was doing in the church that day. But I don't think he was in there for quiet contemplation on the great mysteries of his faith!

Shortly after that incident, his luck finally ran out. He was arrested along with his brother Eddie as they picked up a stolen car that they had stashed away for another robbery. On 24 November 1977, he received a four-year prison sentence. Two years later, his brothers, John and Eddie, both members of his gang, were jailed for ten years for an armed raid on Smurfit's Packaging in Clonskeagh in the south of the city. His brother, Anthony, later died in the Curragh Military Prison of a drug overdose.

Martin Cahill got out of prison in 1980 and in November that year I got a special promotion to the rank of detective sergeant and was transferred to the Investigation Section at Garda headquarters in the Phoenix Park. In my new position, I spent a great deal of my time investigating murders and serious crime throughout the country, especially along the border county of Monaghan. At that time, a County Monaghan man, James Lynagh, a member of the Provisional IRA, was leaving a trail of death and destruction all along the border.

I had been involved in the investigation into three of his victims, all retired members of the 'B' Special Constabulary and the Ulster Defence Regiment. He led the most evil band of mindless, homicidal psychopaths that the Troubles had so far spawned. We were successful in solving almost all those murders. We convicted several key members, but Lynagh continued his violent, murderous career until May 1987, when he was gunned down in a fusillade of bullets along with seven members of his East Tyrone Brigade of the Provisional IRA at Loughgall. They had been on their way to the police station there to plant a 200-lb bomb when they were ambushed by the SAS. There were no tears shed by the police on either side of the border when the news broke. James Lynagh had been the top assassin for the Provisional IRA.

Despite busy and turbulent times on the murder squad, I had kept a watchful eye on the ongoing career of my old adversary Martin Cahill. In January 1981, there was an armed robbery at the offices of Quentin Flynn Limited, a computer wholesaler in Clondalkin. The two robbers, who were wearing motorcycle helmets, got away with over £6,000 in cash. Later that morning, Cahill and his close friend and associate Christy Dutton were arrested in Terenure in connection with the robbery. The money from the robbery was later recovered in waste ground beside the River Dodder close to the village.

Both men were interviewed at Bridewell Garda station, where they were detained. On 31 January 1981, Martin Cahill and Christy Dutton were charged with the robbery. Dutton, a Ballyfermot man, was one of Cahill's most trusted friends and criminal associates, with a long list of previous convictions. That afternoon, I went down to the District Court to see them make their appearance and to hear the evidence of arrest charge and caution. Neither of them made any reply. I thought Martin had got a lot older and plumper, and he was almost bald. One thing that had not changed was his voracious appetite for armed crime.

Sometime after midnight on 2 September of that same year a group of heavily armed men broke in to the private quarters of the Funland amusement arcade on Patrick's Street in Limerick through the upstairs rear window. On gaining entry, they terrorised and tied up the occupants – the owner, his wife and teenage children. One of the intruders put a gun to the proprietor's head and threatened to kill him if he didn't open the safe on the premises. The injured party would later describe the raiders as extremely abusive and vicious. He said he feared for his life and his family. As he was about to open the safe, he saw another member of the gang climb through the window. At that moment, there was a loud bang and he saw one of the raiders almost lifted off his feet and fall to the floor. He saw blood pumping from the man's chest as he lay motionless. The other gang members were roaring and shouting and were in a terrible panic. They ran from the building, leaving their dead friend behind.

The owner cut himself loose and telephoned for the Garda. A doctor was sent for and pronounced the raider dead. He was later identified as Joseph Skerrett, an armed robber and member of Martin Cahill's gang. Within twenty-four hours of the shooting, we received confidential information that Cahill and four of his gang had carried out the robbery. Further information revealed that John Skerrett, brother to Joseph, was another member of the gang and it was he who had fired the shot by an accidental discharge of his shotgun. Along with colleagues of mine from the Investigation Section and members of the CDU, we arrested John Skerrett and took him into custody. After a number of hours, he told us the whole story and described how he had shot his brother dead. He said Joseph had pushed a sawn-off shotgun out of the window for him to grab on to, as he was having difficulty getting in. In the course of that manoeuvre, the shotgun went off, hitting his brother in the chest and killing him instantly. In his own words, he described in chilling detail the gruesome event.

'I haven't slept since. I keep seeing his face, the force of the blast lifted Joe across the room, the blood spurted out like a tap turned full on. I'll never again handle a gun, not after seeing my brother blown in two. I'm happy now that I've told the truth, you would have to be.'

John Skerrett was subsequently convicted of the manslaughter of his brother. Martin Cahill was never arrested in connection with that crime despite masterminding the entire operation. Later, through an informant, I heard that he was very upset at having to leave the body of his friend, Joe, behind. It had been his first and only foray into Limerick and it had been a disaster. He would stick much closer to home for his next infamous exploit.

I did not see him again until the following year when he was in custody in Ballyfermot Garda station following the assassination attempt on the forensic scientist Dr James Donovan. Dr Donovan was driving to work on 6 January 1982 when a bomb exploded under the driver's seat of his car as he passed near Newlands Cross on the outskirts of Dublin. The bomb caused massive and permanent injuries to Dr Donovan's legs and feet. He was lucky to survive, as the device had been designed to kill him.

A couple of months earlier, Donovan had survive another assassination attempt when a petrol bomb had exploded under his car at around the same location. He was not injured on that occasion. Cahill was also responsible for that attack.

Following the bombing, a major investigation got under way at Ballyfermot Garda station headed by Chief Superintendent Dan Murphy and Detective Superintendent John Courtney of the Investigation Section. Every available detective in the city was drafted in on the inquiry.

The attack on Dr Donovan caused outrage and consternation throughout the country. The government was alarmed at this blatant challenge to the state, believing it to be the work of the Provisional IRA or another subversive organisation. The paramilitaries denied all involvement. As the investigation continued, confidential information was received that Martin Cahill was behind the attack. He had tried to murder Dr Donovan to prevent him from giving vital forensic evidence against his brother, Eddie, and his accomplice, Harry Melia, in a kidnapping case that was still before the courts. In early February 1982, we arrested Cahill in connection with the attempted murder of Dr Donovan.

During his 48 hours in custody under the Offences against the State Act, he ranted and raved and was completely uncooperative. He rocked back and forth in the chair like a disturbed child throughout the interviews. He covered his face with his hands, repeating his well-known mantra ad nauseam: 'I have nothing to say to youse men.' At one point when I was interviewing him, he looked at me through his fingers and said, 'I know where you live,' and 'You have a black Labrador.' He was right about the dog. Martin was just letting me know that I could also be a target.

We had a most difficult task when we tried to take his fingerprints. It took about ten of us before we eventually succeeded. Immediately afterwards, before we could wash off the ink, he smeared it all over his face to frustrate the taking of his mugshot. We made no headway with him while he was in custody and he was released without charge.

In the course of my own inquiries, I learned that the bomb had been supplied to Cahill by INLA member Thomas McCartan, who had been introduced to him by Martin Foley. This was the same Thomas McCartan whom I had shot on St Laurence Road in Clontarf in 1977.

Despite the arrest and interview of almost 50 suspects and a prolonged and intensive investigation, nobody was charged in connection with the bombing. Dr Donovan went on to testify against Eddie Cahill and Harry Melia for the kidnapping of Ambrose Sheridan in December 1978 although he was still suffering from physical and mental trauma. Cahill's murderous plan had failed utterly. He had underestimated the resilience, determination and courage of Donovan.

On Wednesday, 27 July 1983, Martin Cahill and his gang carried out one of Ireland's biggest and most audacious robberies. The target was O'Connor's jewellers on Harold's Cross Road in Dublin, a manufacturing facility that employed almost 100 people. Other Dublin gangs and even paramilitary organisations had contemplated a raid on the premises but had been put off by its state-of-the-art security systems; however, Cahill had an inside man on board to help bypass the sophisticated alarm and the raid was painstakingly planned down to the last detail. It was for his meticulous, military-style planning and ruthless, clinical execution of this raid that Cahill was nicknamed the General.

Hours before the raid, Cahill held a meeting in the Dropping Well pub in Milltown with his nine-man gang to brief them on all the last-minute details. The men were carrying the tools of their particular trade – pistols, revolvers, smoke bombs, balaclavas, walkie-talkies and gloves – concealed in sports bags. At closing time, the gang piled into a waiting blue Hiace van that was parked nearby and drove to a laneway beside the premises. Three members of the gang scaled the high walls around the factory and entered the yard, where they hid themselves in an unlocked boiler house.

At around 7.50 in the morning, the factory manager arrived for work. He held the keys and the codes to the alarm system. He opened the main gates and deactivated the perimeter alarms. He then opened up the main factory and switched off the alarm there. At eight o'clock, the managing director arrived for work and went straight to the main office, where the strong room was situated. Within minutes, he was joined by the factory manager and at exactly that instant the gang members burst in on them with their guns drawn.

Others in the gang took each of the staff members as they arrived at work to the toilets and held them there at gunpoint. In the main office, the others had already forced the managing director to open the safe that contained a fortune in gold and precious gems. All through the raid, Cahill remained on the roadway outside on his motorbike, directing the operation with his walkie-talkie, on the alert for trouble. Meanwhile inside, the gang were loading up the blue van with gold bars, thousands of gold rings and precious gems that included diamonds, emeralds and rubies. The entire haul weighed about half a ton.

Before leaving the premises, the gang exploded a smoke bomb to cover their escape. They sped off in the van, turning right onto Harold's Cross Road and after a short distance disappearing off to the left along Kimmage Road. Almost immediately after the alarm was raised, a massive manhunt began for the raiders. Dozens of detectives and uniformed police officers fanned out across the city searching lock-up garages and the haunts of well-known criminals. Warrants were obtained and a large number of suspects' houses were raided.

A special search was coordinated throughout the city for the blue Hiace van but nothing turned up. There had not been a single sighting of it. News bulletins throughout the day were calling it the biggest robbery ever to have taken place in the country. Early estimates put the haul at over £2 million. Over the next couple of weeks, there followed the usual arrests and detentions of known armed robbers, but there was no breakthrough in the investigations. Almost from the very first hours after the robbery, Martin Cahill and his gang were the prime suspects.

Most of his gang were arrested and interrogated in relation to the robbery, but they had to be released due to the lack of evidence. In our legal system, the DPP requires that the evidence against an individual be watertight before directing a prosecution. The professional criminals we were dealing with covered their tracks and usually had cast-iron alibis prepared in advance. Cahill himself was not taken in, as it was thought to be a waste of time without any solid evidence linking him to the heist. Nothing of any evidential value had been found in O'Connor's following the forensic technical examination there. Cahill had left nothing to chance.

Apart from a small quantity of diamonds found in Mount Jerome Cemetery some weeks later, not so much as a ring was ever recovered.

We later received information that Cahill had sold most of the haul to a west London gangster and top fence by the name of Les Beavis and the rest to the notorious Quality Street Gang in Manchester. In a strange twist of fate, almost four years later I would discover answers to many of the baffling questions that had intrigued me and members of the original investigation team involved in that robbery.

I was in my office at Sundrive Road Garda station one evening in January 1987 when I was told that a woman was waiting to see me at the front desk. I went down and introduced myself. She was an attractive, well-dressed woman in her mid-40s but appeared nervous, even a little frightened. I escorted her upstairs to my office and she told me her name was Eileen Egan, and that she was a nurse. She asked me if I was the Detective Gerry O'Carroll who had been involved in the Kerry Babies case, which I confirmed. She seemed to relax a little and sat down. I sat at the table beside her. She told me that I was probably not going to believe what she was about to say but that she would tell me anyway. I tried to put her at her ease and asked her to tell me her story. I said that I would make up my own mind about the truth or otherwise of it.

She then blurted out that every bar of gold, every ring, every diamond and precious gem from the O'Connor's robbery had been weighed, counted and wrapped in the sitting room of her home at Sundrive Road, Kimmage. She went on to say that her husband, Michael Egan, had allowed his workshop to be used by the gang following the heist to hide the blue van containing all the gold and jewellery. She had seen the robbers in the workshop later that morning. They were all wearing balaclavas and were armed with handguns.

She had brought them down tea and jam sandwiches, which, to her surprise, they ate without removing their masks, leaving breadcrumbs and jam all around their mouths. She said her husband had agreed to help the gang and provide his premises to them because he needed cash as his business was going down the tubes. He was in the aluminium-window business and his workshop was located to the rear of the house. Mrs Egan said that the gang had remained in the workshop all that day sorting out the jewellery, and later that night had moved into her sitting room, where they weighed and bagged it. The gang then left in two cars, taking everything with them.

She said she could no longer cope with the shame of her husband's involvement in the crime. The tension and strain caused by their criminal association had caused the irretrievable breakdown of their marriage and she was now in the process of a particularly painful separation. I could barely believe my ears: this quietly spoken, middle-class, professional woman and her businessman husband had been an integral part of the huge jewellery robbery. It was clear to me from her demeanour that she had acted under duress in the whole affair.

I took a lengthy written statement from her that took almost four hours to record. I dropped Mrs Egan off at home and tried to convince her that she had done the right thing. Although she had been an accessory to a serious crime, her coming forward with this evidence would be taken into account when deciding her fate.

Eileen Egan was never charged with any offence in connection with the O'Connor's raid. Her husband, Michael Egan, had no idea that she was going to spill the beans that night and bring his world crashing down around his head. The following morning, I met with my boss Detective Inspector Michael Canavan and handed him Eileen Egan's statement. Having read it, he believed, as I did, that at last we might have found the weak link: Cahill's 'Achilles heel', which might finally lead to his arrest and conviction for the O'Connor's job.

A few days later, accompanied by DI Canavan and a team of detectives, I arrested Michael Egan under Section 30 of the Offences against the State Act in connection with the robbery. Whilst in custody, he made and signed a full written confession of his involvement. In it he states:

'I am self-employed, and supply and fit aluminium windows for a living. I have a large workshop at the back of the house where I make up the windows. I remember that Sunday evening, the 24th of July 1983. I received a phone call at my home made by a male caller requesting permission from me to leave a van in my workshop the following morning. He said he was a friend of an acquaintance of mine. I now know the name of this man who was on the phone on that occasion, but I don't want to say it.

'He told me that there was a small stroke coming off and that he would want me to be at my garage door in the back lane at nine o'clock on Wednesday morning, the 27th July 1983, to open the door to allow the van to come in. That Wednesday morning, after leaving my children [at] school, I came back to the house. I went into the garage at 8.50 a.m. I opened the door a bit and at nine o'clock on the dot the van came up the lane, and I opened the door fully. It was a blue Hiace van and there were at least four or five masked men in the van. The van was reversed into the garage, and once inside, they all got out.

'As far as I know, they all had what looked like .38 revolvers in their hands. When I saw this, I got frightened and realised this stroke was an armed robbery, which if I had known I would have had no wish to take any part in it.'

His statement went on to describe how one member of the gang had pointed a revolver at his head and warned him to keep his mouth shut. In another part of the statement, he described in chilling detail an incident that happened when the masked gang were sorting out the 14 bags of gold and gems in the workshop. He said about two o'clock that day there was loud banging on the door of the garage and when he peered out he saw two detectives and a uniformed Garda outside in the laneway.

He said that the robbers grabbed their revolvers and pointed them at the doors and one of them whispered to him that they would shoot the Gardaí. He said he was terrified and really believed that they would have carried out their threat if he had opened the door. He said that after a while the Gardaí left and walked back down the laneway. He went on to say that they were lucky to be alive. Hearing about that incident really brought home to us that Cahill and his gang were prepared to shoot down members of the Garda in cold blood if they felt it necessary to save their own skins.

I charged Michael Egan in connection with the O'Connor's robbery for the theft of items amounting to the value of £1,300,000 and receiving the same. Later at the Circuit Criminal Court, he was sentenced to seven years' imprisonment for his involvement in the crime. Yet again, despite our best efforts, we had only caught the minnow; the big fish had eluded us. Michael Egan was the only person ever charged or convicted of the robbery. His paltry reward for the role he played in the crime was a small bag of gold rings. The loss of his freedom was a high price to pay.

12

TANGO ONE

DURING THE EARLY HOURS OF 21 MAY 1986, CAHILL AND HIS GANG
entered Russborough House, near Blessington, County Wicklow. It was
the home of Sir Alfred Beit, a South African diamond magnate well
known for owning one of the finest private art collections in the world.
They had neutralised the alarm system before entering. In less than ten
minutes, they had removed eighteen paintings and left in two jeeps
heading for the Blessington Lakes. At Manor Kilbride in County
Wicklow, they abandoned seven of the least valuable paintings. They
held on to eleven others, including a Vermeer, a Goya, two Metsus, two
by Rubens, a Gainsborough and a view of the Grand Canal in Venice by
Guardi. The entire haul was considered to be worth more than £100
million.

Initially, it was thought that paramilitaries were involved in the
theft, as they had robbed some of these very paintings 12 years
previously during an armed raid on the house. But eventually, through
intelligence reports and the word on the street, it was indicated that
Martin Cahill and his crew were responsible for the theft.

Cahill hid the paintings in the Dublin mountains in a specially
prepared bunker. Over the following years, various police operations

169

and stings were tried to recover the paintings but with no success. The nearest we came to nabbing Cahill and the paintings was on 28 September 1987 in an operation codenamed Killakee. Earlier that year, a Dutch fraudster named Kee Van Scoaik met with an associate of the General in the Dutch town of Arnhem and negotiated a £10,000 deal for *View of the Grand Canal, Venice*, one of the paintings from Russborough House.

Van Scoaik travelled over to Dublin, where he picked up the painting. He was persuaded by Dutch detectives and the promise of a £50,000 reward from this state to help us recover the remainder of the paintings. From the moment he arrived in Dublin, things started to go horribly wrong.

Van Scoaik was a flamboyant character and spent the £2,000 pocket money he'd received on champagne and girls in Leeson Street nightclubs. A colleague of mine who was very much involved in the operation said he had to borrow £1,000 from a publican friend of his to give to Van Scoaik, as he was threatening to call the whole thing off. In the end, the whole operation turned into an embarrassing debacle. There were claims and counterclaims and bitter recriminations between the different state agencies and amongst the Dutch and Irish police and Interpol, who protested that their agent's life was being put at risk.

In the subsequent post-mortem, the blame was placed on the failure of the surveillance units to make contact with the heavily armed snatch squads who were to arrest Cahill and the other gang members with the paintings. The radio equipment and walkie-talkies failed to work because of so-called 'black spots' in the mountains.

Cahill had once again carried off another of his Houdini-like escapes. After the disaster in the mountains, he was on such an ego trip that he began to think of himself as invincible. The authorities were furious that Cahill had outwitted and publicly humiliated them again. In an ever more direct challenge to the rule of law, Cahill had, one month earlier, broken into the offices of the DPP in St Stephen's Green in Dublin and stolen many sensitive files. He had also broken into an office in the Four Courts, causing thousands of pounds' worth of damage. They were acts of brazen defiance to the authority of the state and it was apparent that something would have to be done about him before he made a complete laughing stock of every agency in the country.

On 1 December 1987, Cahill pulled off another major robbery. The previous night, he and his gang had kidnapped Anne Gallagher, the postmistress of Kilnamanagh post office in Tallaght, County Dublin, from her home in Inchicore. She was taken to another house where the occupant and his eight-year-old daughter were also being held captive by the gang. It was the beginning of a terrifying ordeal for them.

The next morning, they forced Ms Gallagher, along with the man and his daughter, to call at the post office in Kilnamanagh and withdraw £30,000 in cash. Cahill had tied a radio-operated bomb around the man's chest and threatened to detonate it if he didn't carry out his instructions. This demonstrated yet again Cahill's callous disregard for human life.

Superintendent Ryan had been warning his superiors for years about the growing menace posed by Cahill to the rule of law in the city of Dublin and the effect his depredations were having on the morale of the force. On many occasions, I had sat in his office with DI Canavan and other detectives discussing the worsening situation. After a few of these crisis meetings, Superintendent Ryan finally had his voice heard.

That same December, a high-powered meeting was held in Garda headquarters. Present were the five chief superintendents commanding the five city divisions and the chief superintendent of the CDU. It was decided at the meeting that Martin Cahill and his gang had to be stopped. A further meeting was held where it was decided that each of the chief superintendents would supply 15 men from their divisions to form a new unit whose sole purpose would be to target Martin Cahill and his gang in a system of open surveillance. Five days later, almost a hundred officers attended a meeting at City Headquarters in Harcourt Square. The chief superintendent in charge of the unit explained that the role and ultimate aim of the unit was to put Cahill and his gang behind bars. The new unit was called the Special Surveillance Unit, later to be known as the Tango Unit.

It was the first time that such a novel approach had ever been tried to control organised crime, and we were in uncharted waters. Each of the gang members to be targeted was to be given a codename. It was then that Martin Cahill was first given his sobriquet Tango One. I was one of the five detective sergeants assigned to the new unit. We were intimately acquainted with Cahill and his gang, their associates, their haunts, their idiosyncrasies and their habits. Every member of the special unit also had to undergo intensive firearms training and a tactical driving course before they were sent out onto the streets. Each member carried laminated cards with maps and a coded index of every street and laneway in Dublin to confuse Cahill and his associates should they be listening in on Garda radio frequencies.

On the first day of the New Year 1988, the operation really got under way. The Tango Squad had begun their own war of attrition against the criminal whom the media had christened the General. Cahill had not anticipated nor was he prepared for this type of open surveillance that targeted his every move and those of his mob. Their houses were placed under 24-hour guard. We followed them from the time they left their homes in the morning until they went to bed at night. We followed them when they went shopping, and sat down beside them when they went for a pint in their local pub with their family and friends. In a few short weeks, we turned their lives upside down.

The bizarre spectacle of a cavalcade of police cars following Cahill and his gang became a familiar sight on the streets of Dublin, provoking much media comment. At first, Cahill put on a show of bravado, pretending that he couldn't care less, and laughing and jeering at his tormentors. In reality, he was becoming a bag of nerves and was behaving in an increasingly erratic and deranged way. On one occasion in early February, he was caught trying to slip back into his newly acquired residence in Cowper Downs after shaking off his Garda shadows. It was a freezing cold night and a light scattering of snow lay on the ground. One of the surveillance team saw something moving near the wall of the house. He shone his torch and saw Cahill crawling along the ground.

As soon as he was picked up in the glare of the torchlight, Cahill stopped moving. For the next six hours, he remained motionless on the frozen ground and, despite persistent taunting and goading by the surveillance team, never moved or opened his mouth. At daylight, he just jumped up, climbed over the wall and into his house. For the first time in his long criminal career, Cahill began to panic and buckle under the intense, sustained actions of the surveillance teams.

As the pressure increased, he became a frightened and dangerous man who would use all methods, break all rules, even resort to murder, if necessary, to evade justice. Anonymous death threats were telephoned to the homes of members of the surveillance teams. There were spates of tyre-slashing, and mysterious outbreaks of fire in the Cowper Downs Estate where he lived, intended to embarrass us and turn the neighbours against us. When he was being followed by the surveillance teams, he would drive to the homes of members of the teams, park outside their front doors and switch on his warning lights. On one occasion he drove into the housing estate in Rathfarnham where I lived, parked outside my house and did the usual. I was at home reading the morning newspapers when I looked out of my sitting-room window and saw him grinning at me. His visit didn't come as any surprise to me.

I went out to confront him. He appeared upset and agitated, and pointed at the surveillance cars parked behind him. He said, 'Can youse do anything about these men, Gerry? Me civil rights are being violated.' I told him to fuck off.

When the strange convoy had driven away, some of my neighbours who had witnessed the scene approached me on the road and asked me what was going on. I told them I had been speaking to Martin Cahill and he was enquiring about buying a house in the estate. There were a number of houses up for sale at that time.

Sometime around the end of January reliable information was received by a member of one of the teams that Cahill was planning to have Detective Superintendent Ryan shot. Cahill had harboured an intense, bitter hatred for Ned Ryan for many years and blamed him for setting up the surveillance operation that was causing him so much grief. Years before, of course, we had uncovered his plot to poison Ned Ryan. Cahill had also organised a protest meeting outside Crumlin Garda station in 1980 when Ned Ryan was appointed Detective Superintendent there. The threat was taken seriously and an armed Special Branch detective was assigned to protect Ryan's home.

A detective inspector had been given information from a reliable source that confirmed our worst fears. The informant told him that a few nights earlier armed men had been at Superintendent Ryan's house to carry out the hit. They waited for him to return home and after Ned entered the house, they had crept and peered in through the Venetian blinds and were shocked to see a machine gun sitting on the table. They had then realised that Superintendent Ryan was under armed protection. They panicked, fled the scene and called the whole thing off. The following day, the two would-be assassins returned to London from where they had been recruited for the job.

Ryan later told me that when he got home that night the Special Branch officer had left the Uzi sub-machine gun on the sitting-room table while he was having a sandwich and a cup of tea in the kitchen. Following further inquiries, neighbours came forward to state that they had seen two men acting suspiciously in the vicinity of Ned's house that night. Detective Superintendent Ryan, although shocked by these dramatic revelations, was only concerned about the safety of his wife and children.

A couple of days later, I was summoned to a meeting at Garda headquarters by the chief in charge of the Tango Squad. At that meeting, he told me that Superintendent Ryan had been allocated around-the-clock armed protection by the commissioner and had requested that I be assigned to the job. I readily accepted and told the chief that I would consider it a privilege to accept that role. Later that day, I packed my bags and for the next two months I remained at Ned's side until the crisis had blown over. We reminisced about old times and played cards to while away those long nights. Despite the seriousness of the threat to Ned's life, he put up a brave appearance in order to help his wife and children survive the harrowing ordeal.

During my absence, the surveillance operation continued uninterrupted. The unrelenting pressure being applied by the squads was finally beginning to pay dividends as, one after another, Cahill's gang began to make mistakes. At the end of February, Seamus 'Shavo' Hogan and John Foy, Cahill's brother-in-law, both hardened criminals, were arrested on the Naas dual carriageway by two uniformed Gardaí from Crumlin station following a high-speed car chase. In a desperate bid to evade capture, Hogan fired up to eight shots at the unarmed officers before ending up beneath the wheels of their van.

They had planned to rob a security van at the Walkinstown roundabout as it was making deliveries to the local bank. Cahill himself was on the job that day in one of his many disguises, but he had escaped before the detectives pounced. Hogan and Foy were later charged before the Special Criminal Court with serious firearms offences.

Martin's brother, John Cahill, was eventually also arrested and charged in connection with a £107,000 raid on the Employment Exchange on Navan Road in West Dublin. Eddie, his other brother, and Harry Melia were arrested and charged around the same time in possession of £50,000 of heroin. Eamon Daly, another trusted lieutenant, was sentenced to 12 years' imprisonment for the attempted armed robbery at the Atlantic Homecare store in Sandyford. The following week, Daly and Michael 'Styky' Cahill were sentenced to five years for an armed robbery they committed in College Green in 1985. Martin Foley, another gang member, would be sentenced to two years' imprisonment for a serious assault on a member of the surveillance squad.

The godfather's world was crumbling around him, but characteristically he refused to recognise the signs that would eventually lead to his own demise. The loss of so many experienced and loyal acolytes was a major setback and severely limited his ability to carry out other, even more spectacular, plans that were in gestation. We believed that one of his future plans included the theft of the Book of Kells from the library in Trinity College in Dublin. The Book of Kells is one of the most revered, irreplaceable and priceless manuscripts in the world and one of the greatest treasures of our nation. Although Cahill was now more isolated and vulnerable than he had ever been, he remained a deadly menace and was still the undisputed godfather of the criminal underworld.

After I finished my stint with Ned Ryan, I returned to Sundrive Road station and played no further role in the Special Surveillance Unit. Meanwhile, Cahill continued his crime rampage unhindered and was apparently unstoppable. In May, Cahill and his crew kidnapped Brian Purcell, a senior civil servant with the Department of Social Welfare, from his home in Santry, North Dublin. In front of his terrified pregnant wife, he was beaten up before being dragged away by the masked men. Two hours later, he was shot in both legs and left lying in a pool of his own blood close to the railway line in Sandymount. Cahill carried out the shooting himself as a reprisal against Purcell, who had taken the decision to cut off his unemployment benefit that January. The dogs on the street knew Cahill and his gang were responsible for the atrocity. Some of the gang were arrested and interviewed in connection with it but were released without charge.

Despite irrefutable knowledge of his involvement, Cahill was not arrested or interviewed about this crime. Senior Garda officers had once more acted against the advice of detectives in the Tango Squad and refused to sanction the arrest and detention of Cahill, considering it to be a waste of time. Many of us believed that the real reasons behind this disastrous and defeatist policy was the negative publicity that inevitably followed the orgy of tyre-slashing and fires in the Rathmines area every time Cahill was arrested. This reluctance to tackle him head on was interpreted by Cahill as a sign of weakness, which fuelled his arrogance and contempt for the forces of law and order and increased his belief in his own invincibility. This attitude would in time be his own undoing, but in the interim he perceived himself to be the Dublin equivalent of the infamous New York Mafia boss John Gotti, known as the Teflon Don because of his evasion of FBI surveillance.

In November 1992, a teenage girl in the Crumlin area reported to her grandmother that her father had raped her in a bedroom of the family home. The teenager's mother had died years previously. Her father, the alleged culprit, was a notorious thug, who was involved in armed crime and protection rackets, and was a lifelong friend and associate of Cahill. The grandmother took the teenage girl to the hospital, where she was examined and her worst fears confirmed. She later reported the crime at Crumlin Garda station. DI Michael Canavan took charge of the case.

A few days later, the suspect was arrested and taken into custody. On arrival at Sundrive station, he became very violent and aggressive, and punched his fist through a window. He also assaulted a number of detectives, biting one of them on the arm. After a fierce struggle, we subdued and handcuffed him. We then took him to an interview room. After he had calmed down and given us his word that he would behave himself, we took the cuffs off. Because of his previous violent behaviour, DI Canavan and I remained in the room.

The DI read his daughter's statement to him. After he had listened

In front of the rick of turf, 1950: (left to right) Grandma, Dad, Mam (holding Louis),
Tom, Tony, Bob, Vincent, Dinny, Liam, Dympna, Ella, Gene, Michael, Joe,
me, Anne and Philip.

Louis, Ella, Mam and Dad at
the Lakes of Killarney, 1959.

Philip, Nell Fitzmaurice and brother
Louis at the Soldiers' Houses
circa 1957.

Tony's ordination in Freiburg, Switzerland, circa 1960.

Garda Training College. I'm in the middle row on the far right.

Our wedding day, October 1971, Edinburgh.

Our five children:
(clockwise from left)
Brian, Conor, Philip,
Margaret and Eleanor.

Crime Task Force, September 1971. I'm in the middle row, fifth from right.

The team involved in the Kerry Babies case, including Dept. Supt. John Courtney, head of the Murder Squad (front row, second from left, with a woman on his knee). I'm in the middle row, second from the right.

With my 'Kerry Babies' colleagues on the White Strand, Cahirciveen, in 1984, close to where the 'Cahirciveen baby' was found.

The Hayes family arrive at Tralee courthouse in January 1985. From left: Ned, Michael, Kathleen, mother Mary and Joanne. (Independent Newspapers)

Me, Pat Culhane and Dan Murphy at the Wailing Wall in Jerusalem, 1983, during our trip to the Middle East to investigate the shootings at Tibnin Bridge.

The pencil sketch by Private McAleavy drawn the year before he shot three of his colleagues in Lebanon.

Being presented with a security diploma by Government Minister
Michael Woods (left) and General Commissioner Patrick Byrne from
the Security Institute of Ireland (second from right).

Martin Cahill's black Renault 5 on Charleston Road,
where he was shot dead on 18 August 1994.

With An Taoiseach Bertie Ahern, Prime Minister of
the Republic of Ireland (left) and his driver.

On the set of *The General* with Jon Voight and my wife Kathleen.

With American actress Joan Allen on the set of *When the Sky Falls*,
a film about the murder of journalist Veronica Guerin.

My retirement: (left to right) Me, Kathleen, Assistant Commissioner
Tony Hickey, and daughters Eleanor and Margaret.

to the long catalogue of stomach-churning, horrific allegations made against him, he started to shake his head. He then said that if he was guilty of those crimes against his daughter, he would kill himself and he would kill anyone else who did such things to her. He refused to cooperate any further or to supply a sample of blood for analysis. He said that he had a serious alcohol problem. That same day, he was charged before the Dublin District Court with incest, sexual assault and rape.

On hearing the bad news about his friend, Cahill immediately began a campaign of harassment and intimidation against the teenager's family in a desperate bid to get them to drop all the charges. Cahill's interest was not altogether altruistic, as both he and the accused, who was now the subject of serious criminal charges, had been planning a major crime that was now being jeopardised by these events.

Initially, Cahill confronted the teenager, offering her £20,000 to drop the charges against her father. He later upped the offer to £35,000, but she refused to budge. She was terrified by his sly, sinister approaches and the implied menace that she should accept his offer for her own good or else. She had known Cahill since she was a child and was well aware of the danger he posed to her and her family.

Cahill then turned to her uncle and offered him a large sum of money if he persuaded his niece to withdraw her allegations. This uncle, who was no angel himself, told him to 'fuck off with his blood money'. Cahill was incensed at the uncle's defiance, and threatened to kill him and his niece if the trial went ahead. Even the teenager's grandmother was not immune from Cahill's vicious campaign of intimidation. One morning, at her request, I called to her home. She was a woman in her late 50s, who had raised a large family herself under very difficult circumstances and had suffered more than her fair share of personal tragedies. She was not a woman who was easily frightened and was fiercely protective of her granddaughter at the centre of the storm, who had moved in with her after the attacks by her father. She told me that on the previous evening as it was getting dark, she was taking in her washing in the backyard, when she was startled by a man who suddenly came up behind her. She turned around and saw a figure in black clothes wearing a full-face black balaclava. He was holding a revolver in his hand. He pointed the gun to her head and said he would shoot her and her granddaughter if the case against his friend wasn't dropped. She replied, 'I know you, Martin Cahill, and I'm not afraid of you. I've known you since you were in nappies; your mother and I were good friends. Now get out of my sight.' The masked man left without saying another word.

She refused to make a written statement or press charges against him, which I fully understood; nevertheless, I had the utmost respect for that brave woman in standing up to Cahill and I told her so. I also reassured her that we would do everything in our power to protect her granddaughter until the court case was over.

The case dragged on, and when Cahill had failed in all his attempts to intimidate the family, he decided on a more drastic course of action. In January 1994, he sent two men to the home of the alleged rapist. They burst in through the front door and shot him in the leg. He suffered only superficial injuries since the shooting had been pre-arranged with Cahill to prevent the trial going ahead three days later.

Despite Cahill's attempts to pervert the course of justice, his friend was convicted on all counts on the indictment and was sentenced to ten years' imprisonment for his depraved crimes. The conviction of Cahill's friend had been another significant victory against the empire of crime and one that had been long overdue. But still the godfather, like his New York cousin, appeared to be untouchable by the considerable forces of the law. Like the Mafia, some of the best lieutenants had gone down, but none of them were going to deliver the boss. The General, it seemed, would march on despite his recent defeats.

Our war with Martin Cahill ended on that sunny afternoon in August 1994. After the post-mortem, Cahill's body was brought to Massey's funeral parlour on Crumlin Road. I was present there when Michael 'Styky' Cahill was brought in handcuffs from Mountjoy Prison to say his final farewell to his brother. For a few minutes after he left, I was alone in the room with my old adversary. In the heavy silence, I mused on the turbulent life and violent death of the country's most infamous villain. Like many a godfather, power had made him immune to the thought that anyone could permanently settle a score with him. No one would dare mess with the undisputed king of Irish criminals and armed robbers – except the assassin with the clipboard, who did not even bother to wear a disguise and who dispatched the General with a terrifying *coup de grâce*.

His invincibility finally stripped from him, Cahill looked uncharacteristically peaceful in death. The face he had tried so hard to hide beneath masks, hoods and his own hands was now an open book. I stayed until the undertaker sealed the coffin. I said a little prayer for his soul and left. Death, for all of us, is the great leveller.

In 1997, the famous film director John Boorman made a film in Dublin about the life and times of the General, Martin Cahill, starring a number of leading Irish actors, including Brendan Gleeson, who took on the role of Cahill, and American Oscar-winner Jon Voight. It was one of three films made about Cahill and was based on the bestselling book *The General* by Paul Williams, author and crime editor of the *Sunday World* newspaper. I met Jon on the set and over the course of the following weeks we became friends and remain so to this day. On many a night out, I helped him to master his Irish brogue and assisted with his portrayal of Inspector Ned Kenny, Cahill's nemesis in the film. Although one of Hollywood's greatest actors, I found Jon to be self-effacing, friendly and humorous, without the slightest trace of arrogance or pomposity.

The film, which was shot in black and white, gained critical acclaim at the Cannes Film Festival in 1998, when Boorman received the award of Best Director. In an interview about *The General* for San Francisco's *San Jose Mercury News* in 1997, Jon paid me the following undeserved and gracious compliment: 'I went to school on him. I said, "How can Jon Voight, with my body, my voice, my mannerisms, represent the sturdiness of this character?" When I met Gerry O'Carroll, I said, "There he is."'

13

THE LIGHT-BULB MURDER

ONE OF THE MOST FASCINATING CASES OF MURDER THAT I EVER helped to investigate was the murder of Nan Mulqueen at her home in Rosbrien in Limerick in October 1983. She was 80 years old and lived alone. She had retired after a long and distinguished nursing career and was enjoying her twilight years in this quiet rural setting. Her house, although only two miles from Limerick city, was rather isolated: her nearest neighbours lived about 200 yards away. The railway line from Limerick to Patrickswell ran close by.

Nan was a sprightly old lady whose energy belied her age. She was in good health with a sharp mind and had devoted the remaining years of her life to her grandnephews and grandnieces, who lived in the area.

On the evening of Friday, 7 October, Nan called to see her nephew, Jeffery McDonnell, who owned a workshop close to her home. He was not there, so she spoke to one of his employees. She left a message with him that he was to tell Jeffery on his return to call and see her at the house because she needed a light bulb changed over her cooker in the kitchen. Sometime later, Jeffery returned to the workshop but he did not receive the message about his aunt's visit. A short time later, he left again to attend business in Limerick.

At about five o'clock as he was returning to the workshop, he met this same employee driving past him on the road. Both men stopped their cars and had a chat. Once again, the employee forgot to tell him about Nan's visit to the workshop. This failure to convey a seemingly trivial request would have tragic and far-reaching consequences before the day was out.

Around eight o'clock that night, Nan telephoned Jeffery and asked him to call by the house the following morning, as she needed him to tax her car and to please change the light bulb in the kitchen. Jeffery would later confirm that his aunt sounded upset because he had not called as she had requested. He said that he apologised to her and explained that he had not received her message, and that he would call the following day and sort it out. After that telephone call, she phoned her niece in England, who would later confirm that her elderly aunt had been in good form but had mentioned about the broken light bulb over the cooker in her kitchen. Her niece could tell she was slightly annoyed at her nephew for not calling in and fixing it that day.

The following day, Jeffery tried to telephone his aunt a number of times but got no reply. Towards the evening, he telephoned her neighbours. He told them that he could not get a reply on his aunt's telephone and asked the husband to check on her, as he was getting worried. The neighbour went to Nan's bungalow at around 6.45 p.m. to see if everything was all right. He knocked on her front door and rang the bell but got no reply.

He went round to the rear of the house and looked through the blinds in the bedroom window. He was shocked at what he saw. Nan lay across the bed with her feet still on the bedroom floor. He said he banged on the window but even as he did so, he knew something terrible had happened to her. His first reaction was that she might have suffered a stroke.

He said he gained entry through the kitchen door, which was closed but not locked. The light was on in the bedroom. There was a serving tray on the table beside her bed with biscuits and a full cup of tea. He noted that her clothes were ripped down the middle and there was blood on her lips. There was a white cloth tied around her neck, which seemed to be knotted. He said he realised immediately that she was dead.

He ran from the house and raised the alarm. He also phoned Jeffery and gave him the grim news. He then returned to the house and waited there until Sergeant Kenny and a number of officers from Edward Street Garda station arrived. Nan's family doctor was called and pronounced her dead at the scene. Her body was later removed to the regional hospital in Limerick, where Professor Harbison, the state pathologist, carried out a post-mortem examination on her. Dr Harbison found defensive injuries to the back of both her hands and minor injuries to her head.

He said he found no evidence of sexual assault, although there was evidence of a violent struggle. Dr Harbison suggested that her assailant must have been powerfully built because of the force used in tearing so many layers of clothing in half. He concluded that she had died from asphyxia due to strangulation by ligature. Part of her clothing had been used by her assailant to strangle her. The scene at the house was preserved for technical examination pending the arrival of the forensic team from Garda headquarters.

That Saturday, Detective Inspector Culhane, Detective Jim Butler and I travelled to Limerick to assist in the investigations. The following morning, we had our first conference in the incident room that had been set up at Edward Street station. It was chaired by the district officer and was attended by detectives from all over Limerick city. The brutal murder of a defenceless old woman had instilled fear in many elderly people who were living alone in that isolated neighbourhood.

It would turn out to be a protracted and painstaking investigation. Teams of detectives were instructed to carry out house-to-house inquiries in the area, while other teams were sent to take statements from any possible witnesses and every family member. Roadblocks were set up in the vicinity of the house, and every motorist was spoken to and asked to fill in a questionnaire form. DI Culhane and I went to the murder scene to consult with the fingerprint experts, detective sergeants Hogan and Fitzgerald, who were carrying out an examination of the house.

At the house, we spoke to Nan's nephew Jeffery and her niece, Vivienne, who had flown over from England for the funeral. We discussed the conversations that they'd had with their aunt on the

Friday night and how she had told them that the bulb over the cooker in the kitchen was broken. During their examination, the fingerprint experts found the bulb over the cooker was working perfectly. In a plastic bag in the kitchen, they found two used light bulbs with fresh fingerprints on them. It was obvious that someone had changed the bulb for Nan. We were convinced that whoever changed the bulb was responsible for the sickening murder of that old lady. When the fingerprint experts removed the bulb from over the cooker, they found fresh fingerprints on it of a high quality, which were easily identifiable. Now all we had to do was find the person who had left those prints. The actual technique involved in removing the fingerprints intact from the bulb was a delicate and highly skilled task that was eventually accomplished successfully.

The most baffling aspect of the case was the apparent absence of any real motive. The victim had not been sexually assaulted or interfered with in any way, and the only property missing from the house was a gold sovereign ring, and it was possible that it might have been mislaid earlier.

A couple of weeks into the investigation, we made an important breakthrough when we established that Nan had spoken to her grandnephew about a caller to her house earlier that month. Nan had told him that a young man wearing a tracksuit had called to her on two occasions. Once, he had asked for a drink of water and the other time, two weeks later, he asked to use the toilet. She told her grandnephew that the young man was polite and friendly and had thanked her for her help. This new information gave a much-needed impetus to the investigation. Teams of detectives were sent out to make discreet inquiries about possible suspects in the local sports clubs and fitness centres. Members of the local rugby club and golf clubs were approached and interviewed.

Every male over 18 who was interviewed was asked to supply his fingerprints at Edward Street Garda station, where a special office had been set up manned by local scene-of-crime personnel and fingerprint experts. This office was kept open around the clock. We got almost 100 per cent cooperation during that exercise. There were some who objected in principle to giving their prints, but when we explained our reasons to them they eventually consented. Later, we extended the dragnet and fingerprinted all males over 18 years within a mile radius of the murder scene.

We also acquired the fingerprints of every male who had been convicted of committing a sexual offence in the Munster area. The Fingerprint Section in Garda headquarters in the Phoenix Park was also checking out known sexual offenders throughout the Republic. It was a mammoth operation and was one of the few times it was carried out in the course of a murder investigation. Despite the vast scale of our investigation, we still had not made the breakthrough we had hoped for. After almost two months in Limerick, DI Culhane, Detective Butler and I headed back to our unit at Garda headquarters. The investigation was still very much alive and in the capable hands of the district officer and his team.

Four months later in February 1984, a young girl was on her way home from a disco during the early hours of the morning when she was subjected to a minor sexual assault by a man on a Limerick street. A Garda car that was circulating in the vicinity was alerted and came to her assistance. They took her into the patrol car and drove her around to see if she could identify her assailant. She picked him out a few streets away. He was arrested and charged with sexual assault, and a month later was convicted before Limerick District Court, where he was fined and ordered to pay compensation to the victim.

Five days later, Detective Fitzgerald of the Fingerprint Section received the set of fingerprints taken in Limerick belonging to the assailant. The prints were compared with those left behind on the light bulb at the murder scene and were found to be identical in every respect. When Inspector Culhane and the rest of the detectives heard this news, we had a quiet little celebration in our local. We knew we had our man. His name was Anthony Massey and he was a native of Limerick.

Shortly after receiving the report of this dramatic breakthrough, Inspector Culhane and I headed back to Limerick. The next morning, accompanied by two local detectives, I drove to the bakery in Limerick city where Massey was employed. One of the detectives went inside and a few minutes later he and Massey emerged. He was a tall, slightly built young man with a pale, pasty complexion and a worried expression on his face. I asked him to accompany me to the Garda station to answer a few questions. He agreed and said he was only too happy to help us. We drove back to the station and I took him into an interview room.

I asked him about his movements on Friday, 7 October 1983 between 8 p.m. and 10 p.m. He replied that he had stayed at home all that night. I then asked him if he had jogged out to Rosbrien Road in September or October 1983. He replied that he had. I asked him if on those occasions he had called to a house where an old lady lived asking for a drink of water or to use the toilet.

He paused for a few minutes. 'I'm thinking about death, I'm thinking about murder,' he said. I asked him what he meant. His whole body began to tremble and he started sobbing. Then he blurted out, 'I killed the old lady. Charge me with murder.'

I observed the legal requirements before asking him if he wanted to make a written statement, to which he consented. He then began to cry uncontrollably.

'What will my father say?' he wailed. 'I'll tell ye the whole story, God help me!'

I took down the statement as he dictated to me.

'My name is Anthony Massey. I was born on the 13th June 1965. I live in Ballinacurra Weston in Limerick. I work as a slicer in Keane's bakery. I remember Friday, the 7th October 1983. I finished work at the bakery that day at around 10.30 a.m. I then went straight home and went to bed. I got up out of the bed at 6 p.m. I had my tea and then watched the television until about 8 p.m. At 8.30 p.m, I decided to go jogging out by Rosbrien, towards the golf club, and back into the city by Rosbrien.

'I changed into a grey tracksuit and left my house. I then jogged out by the Greenfields, the Sandy Stream and past the Old Crescent Rugby Club. I then decided to call into a bungalow on the right-hand side past the rugby club. I had called to this house on two previous occasions. The first was about one month earlier when I called for a drink of water, and the second time was two weeks prior to this third visit. On the second time, I had called to use the toilet. There was an old lady living alone in this house.

'On the night in question, the 7th October 1983, I decided to call at this house again to steal a few pounds. It was roughly about ten minutes to nine when I called to the house. I went around the side entrance and I knocked on the door. The old lady opened the door and asked what I wanted. I just said that I wanted a drop of water. The old lady handed me a drink of water. I was still standing outside the door. I finished the water and then the lady asked me would I change a light bulb for her.

'I came in to the kitchen and she handed me a bulb and asked me to change the light bulb over the cooker. I took out the old one and put in the new one. I then asked the old lady if I could use the toilet. I didn't really need to go to the toilet, I just wanted to look around and see if I could steal a few pounds. On my way to the toilet, I saw a bedroom door open and I noticed a handbag down on the floor at the end of the bed. I looked around and couldn't see the old woman, so I went into the bedroom and opened the handbag.

'I saw about six or eight pounds lying loose in the handbag. I also took a flat, gold ring that was lying on a locker beside the bed. Just then, the old lady came into the bedroom and saw me with my hand in the handbag. She grabbed me by the back and turned me around to face her and she said, "I'll remember your face. Go away, you little thief!"

'I then pushed her on the bed by her shoulders and she fell on to it, hitting the side of her head off the end board. I was still holding her by the shoulders on the bed and she was struggling and kicking like mad.

'I turned around and said, "I'm not trying to hurt you, lady," and the old woman replied, "You are trying to murder me!" and she started screaming at the top of her voice. With this, I grabbed a white vest which was hanging over her shoulder and I put it around her neck and tightened it with a knot. As I was tightening the knot, she stopped screaming and struggling and lay quiet. During the struggle, I remember ripping the front of her clothes down the middle.

'As the old lady lay there after I had tightened the vest around her neck, I put her legs together and pulled the two sides of her clothes together. When there was no move out of her, I jumped up and ran out of the bedroom and left the house the same way I had come in. This was by the door leading to the kitchen and was the only door I knew.

I came out onto the roadway and turned left to run back home. After I had run about 150 yards, I threw the flat gold ring that I had taken off the bedside locker over a ditch to a field on the left-hand side of the road. Then I got onto the railway line and ran home. When I got home, I was terrified, as I had seen no signs of life in the woman when I left the house. I did not try to sexually assault the old lady. I am very sorry for killing her. I lost my head!'

When he had finished the statement and signed it, I took him back out to Rosbrien to point out the spot where he had thrown the gold ring. I then brought him back to the station. We never found the ring, despite an extensive search. Before he was formally charged, his father, Patrick Massey, called to see him. When he saw his father, he started to weep bitterly.

'Did you kill that old lady, Anthony? Tell the truth,' his father asked him.

'I did, but I did not sexually assault her. It wouldn't have happened if she hadn't asked me to change the bulb.'

His father broke down in tears and left the room. Later that day, Anthony Massey was charged with the murder of Nan Mulqueen and was remanded in custody. On 25 June 1985, he pleaded guilty to murder at the Central Criminal Court in Dublin and was sentenced to life imprisonment.

Nan Mulqueen had trained as a young woman in St Vincent's Hospital in Dublin. During the Second World War, she joined the Queen Alexandra Royal Nursing Corps. She saw active service throughout the North African campaign and was promoted to the rank of captain. She had accompanied the allied army in the Anzio landings and was among the first allied troops that entered Rome in 1945. It was a tragic irony that having survived all the trials and dangers of that dreadful and bloody conflict, she would meet a brutal death in the tranquil setting of Rosbrien, County Limerick.

14

THE KERRY BABIES CASE

AT 8.30 P.M. ON SATURDAY, 14 APRIL 1984, JOHN GRIFFIN, A FARMER from Kimego West, Cahirciveen, County Kerry, was out jogging at the White Strand when he found the body of a male infant wedged between two rocks. Griffin went for help to a local man, Brendan O'Shea, and shortly afterwards both men returned and stayed at the scene. At 9.25 p.m., Sergeant Reidy and Garda Collins arrived at the scene. They saw a naked, newly born male infant with cut marks on the neck and chest. The body of the infant was later removed to Currnane's funeral parlour in Cahirciveen.

On 15 April 1984, the body was removed to Killarney hospital for the purpose of carrying out a post-mortem examination. At midday, Dr John Harbison, the state pathologist, carried out the post-mortem on the unnamed infant and reported the following injuries:

1) Fracture and dislocation of neck
2) Stab wounds, four in number, up to ³⁄₁₆" long into the right ventricle
3) Bruising in right side of back over the 8th to the 11th ribs at angle
4) Full term normally developed male infant with fresh umbilical stump. Appearance of lungs suggest separate existence achieved

Dr Harbison also recorded further minor injuries to the infant. Following his examination, a full-scale murder hunt commenced. Superintendent J.P. Sullivan from Cahirciveen led the investigation from the outset.

On Thursday, 26 April 1984, I travelled to Cahirciveen to assist in the investigations and teamed up with detectives Shelly and Harrington from the Investigation Section in the Garda Technical Bureau, who were already working on the case. As a result of investigations carried out in hospitals in County Kerry, 25-year-old Joanne Hayes, a single mother of Drumcunnig Lower, Abbeydorney, County Kerry, became the prime suspect in the case.

In light of this development, Detective Superintendent John Courtney and Detective P.J. Browne travelled to Kerry on Sunday, 29 April 1984. The following evening, I attended a conference in Tralee Garda station chaired by Superintendent Courtney. There I learned that confidential inquiries carried out at the regional hospital in Tralee had revealed that Joanne Hayes gave birth to a full-term infant that was now missing. When Joanne Hayes had been confronted at the hospital by the resident obstetrician as to what she had done with the baby, she replied: 'I had no baby. Do you not think I would know the difference between a 26-week miscarriage and a full-term baby?' The examination had been carried out by the obstetrician on 16 April 1984.

These inquiries also revealed that Joanne had been examined on the evening of 13 April by her own doctor at his surgery. On this occasion, she also lied about her condition, telling her doctor that she was threatening to miscarry when she had already delivered a baby. Other detectives at the meeting also confirmed that Joanne Hayes had been in the advanced stages of pregnancy, but there was no baby reported at the Hayes family homestead. Joanne had also told her friends and staff at the sports complex in Tralee, where she worked, that she had miscarried.

Towards the end of that conference, it was decided to ask Joanne Hayes and members of her family to the Tralee Garda station to assist us in our inquiries. The following day, shortly after noon, a number of local detectives called to the sports complex and asked her if she would go along with them to Tralee station. She agreed and left with them. A couple of other detectives spoke to Jeremiah Locke, the groundsman, and asked him to go along as well. He also agreed to be questioned at the station. Shortly afterwards, Mike and Ned Hayes, Joanne's brothers and her aunt, Bridie Fuller, were conveyed to the station and sometime later in the afternoon Kathleen Hayes, Joanne's only sister, was also taken there.

As I saw some members of the Hayes family and Bridie Fuller arriving at the station, I felt a real sense of compassion for them. Members of the family would only have been inside a Garda station to have some legal forms or driving-licence applications filled in. They looked uncomfortable and nervous in their ill-fitting workday clothes. They appeared to me to be a decent, hard-working farming family, much like those I had known all my life in North Kerry.

The Hayes farm in Abbeydorney comprised sixty acres of moderately good land, and was situated about a mile and a half from the village and six miles from Tralee town. They kept a herd of sixteen milch cows. The milk they supplied to the local creamery provided the family with a steady, if small, income. There are two houses on the family farm: one is a fairly modern county-council cottage, the other a much older farmhouse situated about 200 yards in from the main road. Mrs Mary Hayes, Kathleen and Ned occupied the council house, whilst Mike, Joanne, her daughter Yvonne and their aunt Bridie lived in the old farmhouse. At least, those were the sleeping arrangements that pertained on the night of the alleged events.

Jeremiah Locke, a married man with two young children, had begun an affair in October 1981 with Joanne, who had borne him a daughter two years later in May 1983. The child was christened Yvonne and was brought up by Joanne at the family farm. This affair, which caused much anxiety and distress to both families, finally ended in December 1983.

I spoke to Joanne for the first time at about two o'clock on 1 May in Tralee Garda station. I was accompanied by my colleague from the Investigation Section, a fellow Listowel man, Detective Browne. I introduced myself and my colleagues to her. She was a petite, dark-haired young woman. She looked composed, but nervous and pale-faced. We had a pleasant conversation with her about herself and her family. She spoke freely about her job in the sports complex and about her little daughter, Yvonne, and her relationship with Jeremiah Locke. She was at pains to point out that her affair with him had ended.

I then asked her about her recent pregnancy and the whereabouts of her baby. She denied that she had ever given birth, saying that she had a miscarriage at her family home and had flushed the foetus down the toilet. I said we would drain the septic tank and find out if she was telling the truth. She became upset and started crying. We explained to her that we had carried out exhaustive inquiries and were satisfied beyond any doubt that she had given birth to a full-term child. At this, she began to sob uncontrollably. The interview had been going on for two hours by this stage. 'I'm a murderess,' she cried out. 'I killed my baby.'

We comforted her, as she looked so distraught and pitiful. After I had administered the legal caution to her, P.J. Browne asked her if it was a boy or a girl.

'A boy. I was going to call him Shane,' she replied.

We asked her to tell us what had happened on the night she had the baby. Joanne replied that she did not go to work on Thursday, 12 April 1984. She said:

'Around midnight, I felt very hot and flushed and started getting labour pains. I went out to the back of the house and after a while I delivered my baby. The head came out first, and I pulled it by the neck by putting my two hands around its throat. I pulled the umbilical cord and broke it. The baby cried and I caught it by the throat and held it until the baby stopped crying. I laid it on the ground and covered it up with some old hay. I then went back inside the house and cleaned myself up in the bathroom. While I was outside, my sister Kathleen came out and called to me and asked me if I was all right. I told her that I was and that I would be back in a minute.

'I then changed my nightdress and put the old one in the rubbish barrel outside the back door. I then asked Kathleen if she had any sanitary towels as I was having a heavy period, but she said she hadn't any. When Kathleen went into the kitchen, I went up to bed. I got up the next morning at around 5 a.m. and went out to where I had left my baby. I carried out two bags: one was a brown paper bag, and the other was a white plastic bag from O'Carroll's chemist in Tralee.

'I picked up the baby and it was cold. I then put it into the brown paper bag, and then I put it in the white plastic bag and I tied the bag at the top by the handles. I then took the body and dropped it into a pond of water near a river about 100 yards from the house. I then returned to the house and went back to bed. I felt very bad all day on Friday, 13th April 1984. I was so sick that I got my neighbours, Elsie Moore and Mary Shanaghan, to bring me to Dr Daly's clinic in Tralee that night. I told him that I had had a miscarriage but he told me that I was still pregnant and was gone about 16 weeks.

'Dr Daly gave me a note for St Catherine's hospital in Tralee, but I told him that I would go the following day, as I wanted to spend that night at home with my daughter, Yvonne. On the following day, I went to St Catherine's hospital. My brother, Ned, took me there in his car. I was admitted to the hospital by a lady doctor, who told me I was [still pregnant]. I was examined on Monday, the 16th of April by Dr Creedon, the obstetrician, and he told me that the scan revealed that I had just given birth to a full-term baby. He asked me what I had done with the baby, but I only told him lies. While I was in the hospital, I got a couple of blood transfusions. I was released from the hospital on the 21st of April.'

She seemed to be more relaxed after she had told us all about it. We asked her for more detailed information about where on the family's land she had hidden her baby. I left the interview room satisfied that Joanne was telling the truth and informed DS Courtney of that fact. I gave him the details of where the baby's body was and he told me he would send out a team immediately to search for it. I then returned to the interview room.

From the description she had given us, I was very optimistic that the body would be found without any difficulty. Yet after three searches by different teams of detectives and uniformed personnel nothing was found. From her demeanour, I was absolutely satisfied that Joanne had being telling the truth about how she had killed her baby and the location on the farm where she had concealed it. That evening, I left the interview a number of times and spoke to Superintendent Courtney. I told him that I was completely satisfied that the body of the infant was at the location as described by Joanne. I further said to him that I intended to take her out to the farm to point out the exact spot herself. He refused point-blank to countenance such a move and told me in no uncertain terms that I was mistaken and that he did not believe the story. I protested vehemently at his adamant refusal, but he was my superior officer and I didn't force the issue as I should have, a decision I have bitterly regretted ever since.

I returned to the interview room and again told Joanne that we had failed to find the baby. She begged and pleaded with us to be taken out to the farm to find the baby, but I told her that was not possible. She stuck to her story, repeating again and again that her baby was in the place she told us about. When we told her that despite all the searches the baby's body had not been found, she broke down in tears and cried out 'I'm a murderess. I killed my baby, I must be insane.' When local Garda Liam Moloney came into the room at eight o'clock and spoke to her, she repeated to him the same account she had given to us all that day, including where she had thrown the baby into the pond.

Shortly after eight o'clock, two local detectives, Smith and Coote, came into the interview room where P.J. Browne and I were still interviewing Joanne. They showed her a brown wooden-handled carving knife, a white bath brush and a large grey bag. At the sight of these objects, Joanne broke down in tears. 'That carving knife with the timber handle is the one I stabbed my baby to death with. I hit my baby with that white bath brush, and that grey bag is similar to the one my family used to take the baby away.'

At this stage, Detective Browne and I took a written statement from Joanne.

'I am cautioned that I am not obliged to say anything unless I wish to do so, but anything that I do say will be taken down and used in writing and may be given in evidence.

'I started to go out with Jeremiah Locke, who worked in the sports centre in Tralee with me as a groundsman. I knew he was married. It [was] exactly the 26th of October 1981 I first started to go out with him. He told me he wasn't getting on with his wife. I fell deeply in love with him, and we were very intimate from the beginning.

'Around May 1982, I became pregnant by Jeremiah but around the bank holiday in June, I think it was the Sunday, I lost the baby. I wanted to be pregnant. I thought from the beginning that

Jeremiah Locke would go away with me and we would live happy ever after.

'I remained going out with Jeremiah and on the 19th May 1983, I had a baby girl in St Catherine's hospital in Tralee. I called the baby Yvonne. I still thought that Jeremiah would go away with me, especially after having the baby for him. Jeremiah only saw Yvonne twice and that also upset me. I stayed going out with Jeremiah, and I still loved him, and he said he loved me and that he might go away with me eventually.

'I became pregnant again for him last year and I had my last period in August 1983. My mother and all the lads at home were upset about the first baby, but they accepted it and decided to help me rear it. They were all very upset when I became pregnant again, and I was thoroughly and absolutely ashamed of myself and I tried to hide it. I wore tight clothes and I tried not to let it show. On 12th/13th April 1984, I was at home in the farmhouse in my own room, the baby Yvonne was in the cot. Sometime during the night, I started to go into labour and a baby boy was born. I was in my own bed in my own room in the old farmhouse. My auntie, Bridie Fuller, was present at the birth and delivered the baby. Michael, my brother, was in the house at the time.

'The baby was alive and crying, and my auntie Bridie placed him at the end of the bed. She left the room to make a pot of tea, and I went to the toilet. On the way back to the bedroom, I picked up the white bath brush, and I went to the cabinet in the kitchen and picked up the carving knife with the brown timber handle. These are the items i.e. the white bath brush and the brown timber-handled carving knife I have been shown here today by Detective Garda Smith and Coote. I went back to the bedroom and I hit the baby on the head with the bath brush. I had to kill him because of the shame it was going to bring on the family and because Jeremiah Locke would not run away and live with me.

'The baby cried when I hit it, and I stabbed it with the carving knife on the chest and all over the body. I turned the baby over and I also stabbed him in the back. The baby stopped crying after I stabbed it. There was blood everywhere on the bed, and there was also blood on the floor. I then threw the knife on the floor. My mother, Auntie

Bridie, Kathleen, and my two brothers Ned and Mike ran into the bedroom. I was crying and so was my mother, my sister Kathleen and my auntie Bridie. I told them that I would have to get rid of the body of the baby, and then my two brothers said they would bury it. I told them to take away the baby from the farmyard and they said they would. Everyone was panicking at this stage. The boys then brought in a white plastic bag, and they put the baby into it and then they put this bag into a turf bag similar to the one Detective Smith and Coote showed me earlier on this evening at the station.

'The boys then left in our car with the baby. I heard the car leaving the backyard. I was feeling sick and depressed and soon afterwards the afterbirth came and I put it into a brown bucket beside the bed. I then changed the sheets and I put the bloody sheets on the floor until the following day. I then took my baby Yvonne into my bed and Bridie remained on in the house. All the others left and went to our cottage about 100 yards away. I got up around 5 a.m. and I took the brown bucket with the afterbirth in it and I went out the front and I put the afterbirth into the old hay beside the wall. I went back up to the house and I went to bed again.

'I woke up at about 7.30 a.m. and my brother, Michael, was back in the house again. I started to clear up my bedroom after that. I gathered up all the sheets that had blood on them, and the brown-handled carving knife and the white bath brush. I washed the knife and the brush and put them back in their proper place. I then washed the sheets. All day Friday I was bleeding heavily and feeling bad, and my sister Kathleen went up for two neighbours, a Mrs Mary Shanaghan and Elsie Moore, who is a nurse. I was then taken to Dr Daly's surgery in Elsie Moore's car along with Mary Shanaghan. I told the two neighbours that I had a miscarriage. I told Dr Daly that I had a miscarriage.

'Dr Daly examined me and told me that I hadn't lost the child and that I was four months pregnant. He gave me a letter for St Catherine's hospital, Tralee, to go in as soon as possible. I didn't go into hospital that night, as I did not want to leave Yvonne. On the next day, Saturday, the 14th April 1984, my brother Ned took me to St Catherine's hospital. I was examined by a doctor, a lady doctor, a tall, very thin lady with black hair. This lady doctor told me after examining me that I was pregnant. She didn't say for how long. I told her that I thought I had had a miscarriage. I was kept in the hospital until the following Saturday, when I was discharged. Since the night that I killed the baby, there was never any talk of it in the house.

'When the body of the baby was found at Cahirciveen, I knew deep down it was my baby. I was going to call him Shane. I am awful sorry for what happened, may God forgive me.'

When the statement had been completed and signed, two other Garda officers took over from us.

I was absolutely convinced of the truth of her written statement. P.J. Browne and I had been very kind and understanding with Joanne, and I treated her the same way as I would have treated my own daughter. We sympathised with her predicament, and felt sorry for her family and the trouble she had brought on them. During that day, Ned Hayes, his brother Michael and sister Kathleen, and his aunt Bridie Fuller all made statements that Joanne had given birth in the farmhouse to a baby boy and had killed him by stabbing him with a carving knife and hitting him on the head with a bath brush. Mary Hayes, Joanne's mother, who had been interviewed by detectives in her own house, also confirmed that Joanne had given birth to a baby boy in the bedroom in the farmhouse and had killed it.

There were many irreconcilable discrepancies in the family's versions of events of that fateful night. Hereunder, I will deal with some but not all of them, as it is almost impossible to separate the truth from the statements, even now. The total conflict of evidence in the statements furnished by the Hayes family and Bridie Fuller to the police – and indeed when giving their testimony under oath during the ensuing tribunal – is inexplicable. I believe that no satisfactory explanation has ever been found to explain the vast inconsistencies.

The five members of the family could not even agree on the day or date that Joanne gave birth to her baby. Joanne, Ned and Kathleen all agree and made statements that the baby was born on Friday morning, 13 April, at around 2 a.m. Mary Hayes and her son, Michael, state that the baby was born on Wednesday morning, 11 April, at around 2.30 a.m. The aunt, Bridie Fuller, stated that she thought the baby was born on Tuesday, 7 April, or in the early hours of Wednesday, 8 April.

There are also glaring contradictions in all their statements about who supplied the murder weapons. Joanne said she herself got out of bed and took the bath brush and the timber-handled carving knife from the bathroom and kitchen. Kathleen Hayes makes no mention of the bath brush but states that she herself procured the carving knife from a drawer in the kitchen at Joanne's request. Michael Hayes confirms Kathleen's account of the knife but not of the bath brush. Ned Hayes, when he arrived at the scene, did not see any knife or bath brush. Mary Hayes stated that she had seen her daughter Joanne hit her baby with a white bath brush but makes no mention of a knife or of stabbing. Bridie Fuller, who claimed she delivered the baby, stated that she was not in the room when the baby was killed and saw neither bath brush nor knife.

The most serious and inexplicable conflict in their statements about the events of that night is their versions of the disposal of the body of the infant. Joanne just states that the boys (Ned and Mike) put the baby in a plastic bag, which they in turn put in a turf bag: '. . . the boys then left in our own car with the baby. That was the last I saw of it.'

Kathleen Hayes states:

'I went to the drawer under the television and got a white plastic bag and Ned put the dead baby into it. Ned then put the white plastic bag containing the baby into a turf bag. The bag containing the baby was then brought out to the back kitchen by Ned and Mike, who tied it with a piece of twine. Ned then took out the bag and put it in the boot of our car. Ned, Mike and I left our house at about 3.50 a.m. in our car, a blue Ford Fiesta. We drove through Tralee and on to Dingle town for about six miles, and we stopped at a place where the road runs beside the sea and Ned, who was driving, got out and opened the boot of the car, and took out the bag containing the baby and threw it into the sea. It was about 5.30 a.m. on Friday, the 13th April when Ned threw the bag into the sea.

'You could see the water from the road where we were parked, and when the bag was thrown in, it sank and resurfaced and floated on the water. We arrived home at 7 a.m. Ned was the driver that morning, I was in the front passenger seat and Mike was sitting in the

back seat. We told my mother, Joanne and Bridie that we had thrown the baby into the sea back around Dingle.'

Ned's account of what happened was as follows:

'I saw the body of a newly born infant at the foot of the bed. The infant was lying face-downwards naked on the bed. I said to my sister, "Why in fuck's name did you do it?" My mother suggested that we would have to get rid of it. We talked for about three-quarters of an hour about getting rid of it. I was in favour of burying it on the land, but my mother and Auntie Bridie weren't. Auntie Bridie was in favour of throwing it in the sea. My brother and I went outside to get a plastic bag. My brother picked up a fertiliser bag from the gable end of the house. We went back inside the kitchen and up to Joanne's room.

'We caught a leg each of the infant and put it head first into a brown shopping bag. As we lifted the dead infant, I could see blood on its little chest. It had been stabbed in the chest. I couldn't see how many wounds were in the chest. When we had placed the dead infant in the brown plastic bag, Joanne asked to be left alone in the room with the child for a few minutes. Both of us went back into the kitchen and left her alone for about ten minutes.

'We laid the bag containing the infant on the floor beside the bed. When we returned to the room, she was on the bed turned towards the wall. The brown bag had been rolled closed, so that the infant was not visible. We opened the grey fertiliser bag . . . and each caught an end of the brown bag and put it into the grey bag. Joanne asked again to be left alone with the infant. We again left it on the floor for about two minutes. When we returned, she was in a similar position, facing the wall, and the top of the grey bag was tied with a string. I took hold of the top of the bag and Michael took hold of the bottom of it. We took it through to the kitchen.

'My sister, Kathleen, had the door of the car open as I had already asked her. Kathleen had the keys of the car and she handed me [them] afterwards. I placed the bag on the floor of the car behind the driver's seat. Our car is a Ford Fiesta, blue colour. I went back into the house and brought a road map with me. I went back into the kitchen and told my mother and aunt that I was leaving. My sister, Kathleen, had gone down into Joanne's room, where she was sleeping on a mattress. I drove the car and my brother accompanied [me] in the front passenger seat of the car. We brought a shovel with us in case we might get a quiet place to bury it.

'We had fully intended when we left the house that we would go to the sea with the bag, and the further away the better. I drove the car into Tralee on to Blennerville out the Dingle Road. At Camp Cross, I stopped and took out the map to decide which way to go. We decided to go by the Connor Pass, as we thought it would be the quietest. Going up the Connor Pass, we stopped for about three minutes and looked at the map again to decide what way we would go. We went on into Dingle and went out on the Ventry Road. We stopped this side of Ventry and looked at the map again. It was then we decided to go to Slea Head. I am familiar with Ventry and Slea Head, as I have been there on a number of occasions. When I got to the spot that I thought was the most suitable place, I got out of the car and took out the bag containing the baby.

'I asked my brother to keep a watchout and I went in over a stone ditch, walked about 20 yards to the edge of the cliff and I flung the bag from the cliff into the sea. I would say there was a drop of about ten feet, and I watched the bag fall directly into the water. I returned to the car and drove back the same way we had come. We arrived back in Abbeydorney at about 10 a.m. The mother and the sister met us outside the door and I told them where I had disposed of the bags and their contents. We milked the cows and had breakfast.'

Ned makes no mention in his statement of Kathleen accompanying them. In Mike's statement, he said as follows:

'Joanne stabbed the baby on the chest three times. The bedspread was all blood. The baby's face was towards the ceiling and his feet were facing the bottom of the bed. I saw Joanne catch hold of the toilet brush in her hand, and she hit the child a number of times on the face and body. The baby was on the floor at this stage, as it had fallen out of the bed when Joanne was getting out of the bed. Joanne then took the baby and put it back on the bed. The baby was dead at this stage.

My mother said we would bury the baby on the land, and the rest of us said we would throw it into the sea.

'Myself and Ned went out into the backyard. We got a manure bag. We got a big stone in the yard, which we dug up and put into the bag. Ned came out into the back kitchen with Kathleen and they had the baby wrapped in newspaper and a clear plastic bag and a brown shopping bag similar to the two bags shown to me by the detectives.

'I held the manure bag, and Ned put the baby's body, which I saw was a baby boy, into the manure bag. I got a piece of baling twine off a bale of hay in the shed and I tied the top of the bag. Ned put the bag into the boot of our Ford Fiesta car. Ned drove the car and I sat in the front passenger seat. We didn't know where we would go at that time. It was about 4.30 a.m. on Wednesday morning we drove into Tralee. We went down by Dingle Bridge outside Tralee. We stopped after passing the bridge and Ned took out a map. We decided to drive down to Dingle.

'We went over the mountain road. When we got into Dingle, we turned right and we continued straight on until we came to a bridge about a mile from town. We continued on straight for about another seven or eight miles. We were near the sea, and Ned took the bag with the body in it and he crossed over a field, and I saw him throwing the bag containing the baby's body into the sea. The sun was just rising in the sky then. I had no watch and I don't know what time it was then. We came back to Tralee by the same road. We got petrol in Tralee at Horan's Garage; we drove home then. I had my breakfast and milked the cows and went to the creamery. We tried to keep it all quiet and it looks like we didn't succeed.'

Mike Hayes said this trip took place on Wednesday morning, 11 April, and so is obviously mistaken in his dates. His account of the bagging of the infant's body is also at variance with the account given by Ned and Kathleen. In his statement, he also contradicts his mother when he says that she wanted the baby buried on their land. In her statement, Mary said the exact opposite. She states as follows:

'I said to Joanne, "You will have to bury the child," and Mike or Kathleen said, "We will bury the child on the land." I said, "The child cannot be buried on the land."

'Ned and Mike went to the back kitchen, where they got a turf bag, and they put the child in the bag. I told Ned and Mike that they would have to bury the child. They left with the child in the bag and drove out of the yard at about 5 a.m. They returned at about 7 a.m. and said they had buried the child. I did not ask them where.'

Mary Hayes makes no mention at all about Slea Head or the child's body being thrown into the sea; however, she agrees with her daughter Kathleen that it was 7 a.m. when the car returned from the heartless mission. Ned contradicts both his mother and his sister by stating that it was 10 a.m. when he and Mike returned to the house. Mike was unable to help either way, as he had no watch.

Bridie Fuller's statement read as follows:

'Kathleen and Mary came down to our house and I told them that Joanne was in labour. It was about 2.30 a.m. in the morning and Joanne was at an advanced stage. We went up to see her and I helped her break her waters. The baby was born and I did the best I could to help her. It was a baby boy. I saw it move. It was bubbling with mucus. I was not in the room when the baby died. I think I was making tea in the kitchen.

'After this, I don't know what happened, but I remember that it was light before I got back to bed and Michael milked the cows at around 7 a.m. that morning. Joanne was alone in the bed and Michael went to the creamery. Kathleen came down while they were milking to the farmhouse. Joanne got up late, and I don't know what happened to the baby.'

Despite the discrepancies and the glaring anomalies, and the differing accounts of what transpired in the Hayes' farmhouse on the night of 12/13 April, the decision was taken to charge them with the various crimes committed.

At around 11 p.m. on 1 May, a Special Court was convened in Tralee Garda station that was presided over by a local peace commissioner. Joanne Hayes was arrested by Detective Sergeant Dillon and charged with the murder of an unnamed infant at Drumcunnig, Abbeydorney, between 11 and 14 April 1984. In answer to the charge, she replied that she was guilty.

She later appeared before the Special Court, where DS Dillon gave evidence of arrest, charge and caution. She was remanded in custody to appear at Tralee District Court the following day, 2 May. Joanne spent that night in the cells at Tralee station. Four members of her family – Ned, Mike, Kathleen and Bridie Fuller – all appeared before the Special Court and each of them was charged 'that between the 11th and 14th day of April, 1984, at Drumcunnig Lower, Abbeydorney, County Kerry, within the court area of Tralee, you did endeavour to conceal the birth of an unnamed male infant, born to Joanne Mary Hayes, by secretly disposing of the dead body of the child contrary to Section 60 of the Offences Against the Person Act, 1861'.

On being charged with that offence, Mike Hayes replied, 'I helped conceal the child.'

Kathleen Hayes replied, 'I didn't conceal the child.'

'No, no!' said Ned Hayes.

Bridie Fuller replied, 'I have nothing to say.'

Mrs Mary Hayes was not charged with any offence. Ned, Mike, Kathleen and Bridie Fuller were all released on bail to appear at the Tralee District Court the following day. The four then left the station and went home. The following morning, I left Tralee to attend the Circuit Criminal Court in Dublin.

I returned to Tralee later that day to the dramatic news that a male infant had been found on the Hayes' farm in Abbeydorney. I attended a meeting in the station to discuss this development. At the sitting of the Tralee District Court on 2 May, Joanne Hayes was remanded in custody to Limerick prison. Just before she was taken away, she called her sister Kathleen and told her the location on the farm where she had concealed her dead baby. When Kathleen, Ned and Mike returned home from the court, they went down the land sometime shortly after 2 p.m. to search for the body of their sister's baby. They found the body approximately 200 yards from their dwelling house in a drain at the corner of the field. They didn't touch it. They said later they did not want to leave their fingerprints on the bag.

The three of them just left the baby where it was and drove to the office of their solicitor, Mr Mann, in Tralee, where they had an appointment at 4.30 p.m. They informed him of the discovery of the body of the infant on their farm. The solicitor instructed them that they must report the matter to Garda Moloney immediately. At about 6 p.m. they drove to Abbeydorney Garda station and informed Garda Liam Moloney. At 7 p.m., a team of detectives from Tralee Garda station accompanied Garda Moloney on to the Hayes farm and removed the plastic bag from the drain. On opening it, they saw it contained the body of a baby. From then on, this baby was referred to as the Tralee baby, whereas the corpse found on the beach earlier was known as the Cahirciveen baby.

The body was removed to the mortuary in Tralee general hospital. The body was in a white plastic shopping bag. The bag had O'Carroll's Pharmacy stamped in blue on the front. The following day, along with almost all the other detectives on the investigation, I attended the post-mortem on the Tralee baby. This was carried out by Dr John Harbison, whose report read as follows:

> . . . I then commenced opening these packages. The outermost layer comprised two clear plastic bags, one open and one tied with string. These, I was informed by Gardaí, had been placed over the original plastic bag as found. The original plastic bag inside these clear bags was of opaque white plastic and printed with 'O'Carroll's Pharmacy, Tralee'. This bag was knotted using the plastic handles. Beside the knot, the bag had been torn open, and inspection of the tear revealed the body of an infant. I placed the chemist's bag, the remains of a brown paper bag inside it and a quantity of vegetation consisting of grass, leaves and other debris. I then washed the body of the infant.
>
> It was that of a fully developed normal male infant. There was a 36 cm long length of umbilical cord still attached at the abdomen. The end of the cord appeared to have been cut diagonally. *Vernix caseosa* or cheesy material was still present on the skin, in the groin, armpits and in the ears, indicating a new-born infant. There was no evidence of obvious injury on the body. There was no external injury or bone injury. Apart from the dark area on the left side of the neck, there was no sign of skin injury to suggest strangulation of the neck. Dissection of

the face showed no signs of injury. The lungs showed areas of non-expansion.

Summary and conclusions:

This male infant was normally developed full-term and new born.

No firm opinion can be expressed concerning the achievement of a separate existence, because of the presence of putrefactive gases in the lungs. The impression, however, is that full expansion of the lungs had not taken place, and therefore breathing had not been properly established.

Dark discolouration of the skin on the left-hand side of the neck and of the underlying left lateral spinal muscles could have been bruising. If so, it would suggest the neck had been compressed either deliberately or as part of an attempt at self-delivery. As the possible neck injury did not involve the larynx or trachea, and as no sign of asphyxia was seen, strangulation cannot be inferred as a cause of death.

No other marks suggestive of injury were found on the body.

Cause of Death – Unascertainable.

After the post-mortem was finished, we all adjourned to a local hostelry to discuss these new, extraordinary developments in the case. We were a much more thoughtful and subdued bunch that night, as we contemplated the likely repercussions from our own authorities and from the offices of the Director of Public Prosecutions. My deepest regret that night was my failure to convince DS Courtney that Joanne Hayes should have been allowed out on to the farm herself to locate her baby. If the baby had been found on 1 May, we would all have been spared the subsequent nightmare and the catastrophic consequences for all our lives and careers.

* * *

I returned to my unit in Garda headquarters the following day, Friday, 4 May, and had no further involvement with the investigation. But the case rumbled on. Blood tests carried out on the body of the Tralee baby by Dr Louise McKenna of the Garda Forensic Science Laboratory confirmed that the baby was blood group O. It was also established that the alleged father of the Tralee baby, Jeremiah Locke, and the mother, Joanne Hayes, were also blood group O. Serologists and scientists at the laboratory concluded that Joanne could not have given birth to the Cahirciveen baby, who was blood group A, assuming that Jeremiah Locke was the father. Events moved fairly fast after that.

On 8 May 1984, the state solicitor, Donal Browne, forwarded a preliminary file to the DPP's office. Between that date and 26 July 1984 there was much correspondence and numerous telephone calls between Brown in Tralee and the DPP. On 26 July 1984, the Garda file, now completed, was forwarded to the office of the DPP minus the report from Dr Harbison. On 16 August, Dr Harbison's report was in the hands of the DPP. On 4 September, the DPP decided not to prosecute any members of the Hayes family. However, he decided that he would not issue those instructions until he'd had a consultation with DS Courtney.

On 20 September, a very stormy meeting was held in the offices of the DPP on St Stephen's Green. DS Courtney and Detective Garda P.J. Browne, who had been instrumental in the preparation of the Garda file on the case, represented the Garda side. There were no punches pulled at this meeting. After a heated and sometimes acrimonious debate, the Director informed Superintendent Courtney and Detective Browne that he was sending instructions to the state solicitor in Tralee forthwith to withdraw all charges against the Hayes family.

Courtney and Browne knew they were rowing against the tide but put up a spirited defence of their recommendations in the case, which was included in the Garda report. In the report, which was signed by Superintendent John Courtney, the case for the prosecution of the Hayes family was set out as follows:

> At paragraph 450 within the file there is, I submit, evidence adduced to show that Joanne Hayes gave birth to twins, secretly hid the first born on her mother's farm, having killed it, and after some hours gave birth to a second baby, which she, with the cooperation of some of her family murdered and with the further full cooperation of the entire family and live-in aunt secretly disposed of the second infant's body to prevent its finding.
>
> *(see Appendix I for extracts from the Garda report)*

The contents of that report and the conclusions were argued strenuously by Superintendent Courtney and Sergeant Browne at that meeting with the DPP and his staff on 20 September, but to no avail. After they left the office, Simon O'Leary, senior legal assistant in the office of the DPP, wrote the following letter to Donal Browne:

> Dear Sir,
> This amazing case had been carefully studied and a consultation was held today with Chief Superintendent John Courtney, Detective Sergeant Browne, the director and the writer. The accused stand charged in respect of a baby, which on the evidence, was not the baby of Joanne Hayes. Even if she were charged in respect of a baby unknown, you could not possibly run a prosecution on this evidence. All charges should be withdrawn at first opportunity.
> Simon O'Leary,
> Senior Legal Assistant

On Wednesday, 10 October 1984, Donal Browne had all charges against the Hayes family struck out at Tralee District Court. He stated, 'It would not be proper to put persons through the ordeal of a trial when there simply [is] not evidence to justify the charges.' The media frenzy was about to begin.

On 14 October, the *Sunday Independent* newspaper published extracts of the statements made by the Hayes family at Tralee Garda station on 1 May. The statements had been taken from the official Garda report and leaked to the newspapers. It was a serious breach of the Official Secrets Act and a despicable act of betrayal, which, as the report found, could only have come from the offices of the DPP or the Gardaí. This important factor is a matter that I will discuss in greater detail at a later stage.

On 23 and 24 October 1984, Joanne, Kathleen, Ned, Mike and Mary Hayes called to the offices of their family solicitor, Patrick Mann, in Tralee. They made detailed statements of complaint to him against members of the investigating Gardaí who had interviewed them at Tralee station on 1 May. In the case of Mary Hayes, the complaints were made against the two detectives who interviewed her in her home in Abbeydorney. In their statements, all the family except Mary made allegations of assault of varying degrees of force against named members of the team involved in their questioning. All five also alleged that they were forced by those detectives to make incriminating statements, which they were then coerced into signing. In layman's terms, we were accused of stitching them up.

Radio Telefís Éireann's *Today Tonight* programme was broadcast on 25 October and dealt exclusively with the treatment of the Hayes family and An Garda Síochána's conduct of the entire investigation. Members of the Hayes family were interviewed, as was Patrick Mann. Through their solicitor, the family made serious allegations of misconduct against the Gardaí on the investigation. Certain politicians under privilege of Dáil Éireann started calling for an inquiry into the whole affair.

The Minister for Justice, a prominent Fine Gael politician, came out with what I and many of my colleagues considered to be insulting and intemperate comments, of course under Dáil privilege: 'I will root out those rotten apples and I will show them no mercy.' The basic tenet of our judicial system had been turned on its head. We were now guilty until proven innocent. Shortly afterwards, the commissioner of the day, Lawrence Wren, ordered an internal inquiry to investigate the allegations of assault and ill-treatment made by the Hayes family and Bridie Fuller. After that decision was taken, I was confined to office duties on the unit.

The Hayes family refused to be interviewed by the two chief superintendents who were appointed to head up that inquiry; instead, they submitted the statements of their allegations of assault and ill-treatment against us through their solicitor. I was interviewed by the two chief superintendents, as well as every other member of the investigation team. I welcomed the opportunity to clear my name of the false allegations and cooperated fully with the inquiry, which was in the end deemed futile and rejected by all sides as inconclusive and unsatisfactory.

Dáil Éireann and Seanad Éireann passed identical resolutions on the establishment of a tribunal on 11 December and 12 December respectively. It was called the Tribunal of Enquiry into the Kerry Babies case. After the failure of the internal investigation, I viewed the setting up of the tribunal as the only forum where my colleagues and I would have the opportunity to clear our names and restore our reputations and put an end to the torrent of vile allegations circulating about us in the media.

During this period, I was forbidden by senior management to carry out any of my normal duties. Despite numerous requests, no explanation was ever offered to me as to why I had been singled out for such humiliating treatment. After the dramatic revelations of the Hayes family in the newspapers and television, the investigation unit was awash with rumour and counter-rumour, and dire predictions were being whispered about the fate of those who had had the misfortune to be caught up in the sorry saga. The wagons were circling and the sacrificial lambs were already being staked out for the kill.

I believe that I was singled out and given the cold-shoulder treatment by senior management because it had come to their attention that I was vociferous and outspoken in my condemnation of the disgraceful conduct of certain individuals of high legal standing who leaked the Garda report on the Kerry Babies case to the print media. My public rebuke to the Minister for Justice for his rash outburst in the 'bad apples' speech and his threats in Dáil Éireann that some of the allegations, if substantiated, might lead to criminal proceedings did nothing to endear me to my politically aware bosses and undoubtedly contributed further to my ostracism.

These sanctions also affected me financially, as I was no longer in receipt of overtime, subsistence or mileage, additions to my salary that I had come to depend on. More importantly, Kathleen and my older children were upset and concerned about the growing criticism of the Garda's handling of the case as published in the print media and broadcast on radio and television on a daily basis. The allegations of assault and misconduct levelled against us by the Hayes family hung over all our heads like a black pall. As the public clamour grew and calls for a judicial inquiry into the case became ever more strident and intemperate, I realised that not only had my career been well and truly derailed but that my job itself was also on the line. These were worrying times indeed.

The fallout from one incident that occurred in December that year brought home to me – as if I needed proof – how far I had fallen from grace. It happened that the inspector on my unit was directed by the detective chief superintendent to address a meeting of the Irish Medical Organisation (IMO) at their headquarters in Fitzwilliam Place with the title 'Sexual violence against Women – a Garda Perspective'. On the Saturday morning that he was due to deliver his speech, he developed a throat infection and became very hoarse. He telephoned me and in a whispered croak explained his predicament and asked me to give the talk to the IMO on his behalf. I readily agreed but reminded him of the embargo I had been placed under by the detective chief superintendent in our section. He brushed away my concerns and told me he would deal with any problems that might arise as a result of my appearance there. I joined him later in Fitzwilliam Place and gave the talk, which was very well received by all the delegates.

The event was covered by an RTÉ television crew and journalists from most of the national newspapers. I later gave a short press briefing to a number of those journalists. From 1 p.m. that day, RTÉ television news and most of the radio stations reported excerpts of my address to the meeting in all their news bulletins. As I had expected, my appearance on the national airwaves caused a furore in Garda headquarters. When I turned up for duty the following Monday morning, my inspector and I were immediately summoned to a meeting with our chief superintendent. The chief looked like he hadn't had a wink of sleep for a couple of nights. He stamped around the office almost incandescent with rage, threatening all kinds of retribution for my blatant insubordination. The inspector didn't escape a tongue-lashing either. He was warned that his involvement with me in this matter wouldn't exactly enhance his prospects for promotion.

In the chief superintendent's subsequent report to the commissioner on that matter, of which I obtained a copy, he states, 'In the past, I found Detective Inspector Culhane to be reliable and conscientious' – apart from saying that I acted without authority, he found nothing in my past to recommend or praise me in his report. It was obvious that I had become the bête noire of the Investigation Section in the eyes of my superiors. Despite all the favourable publicity generated by my lecture, the authorities only saw fit to berate and threaten me. It was an early indication of the unjust and vindictive treatment that would be meted out to me in the coming months and years.

On Monday, 7 January 1985, I attended the first sitting of the Kerry Babies Tribunal in the Urban District Council offices in Tralee, County Kerry, under the chairmanship of Mr Justice Kevin Lynch. The three superintendents involved were represented by Martin Kennedy SC and a junior counsel, and the rest of us were represented by Anthony Kennedy, likewise SC and a junior counsel. The chairman had his own legal teams, as had the DPP and the Attorney General. The Hayes family was represented by Dermot McCarthy SC and his junior Brian Curtin. The terms of reference of the tribunal were as follows:

> The facts and circumstances leading to preferment on the 1st May, 1984 of criminal charges against certain members of the Hayes family
>
> Related allegations made by members of the Hayes family, and any matters connected with or relevant to the matters aforesaid which the tribunal considers it necessary to investigate in connection with the inquiries into the matters mentioned in 1) and 2)

In the following pages, I only intend to write a concise and abbreviated account of events in the tribunal sittings. The tribunal report itself runs to almost 300 pages and is a highly interesting and controversial account of the whole affair.

Members of the Hayes family were among the first witnesses to be called to give evidence. There was a media circus in Tralee during Joanne's presence in the witness box. She received a gruelling and merciless cross-examination from our barristers; the most intimate secrets of her private and personal life, including her sex life, were exposed and dissected, and she was asked to describe her first miscarriage in 1982. Every aspect of her affair with Jeremiah Locke, the father of her daughter Yvonne, was examined in the most minute detail, sometimes in a brutal and insensitive way. Joanne broke down many times during the cross-examination and at one stage had to be sedated. On those occasions, she looked so frail and vulnerable. I was almost sick to my stomach witnessing her ordeal and had to leave the hearings.

Although I believed that a full, searching and thorough cross-examination was vital, I still had the utmost sympathy for Joanne.

But our barristers had a job to do: to clear our names and restore our reputations in the teeth of the Hayes family's allegations. In our adversarial system, the only means open to our lawyers to succeed was to discredit and undermine our lying accusers. I'm quite sure that our legal representation found the ordeal distasteful and upsetting also.

Despite all the pressure and the obvious distress she was suffering, Joanne stuck to her guns, insisting that she gave birth to a baby out in the field. She also refused to withdraw her allegations of ill-treatment against us. Her treatment at the tribunal generated much adverse comment in the media. Women's groups all over Ireland were incensed at what they perceived as the persecution of a young single mother. Every day, hundreds of bouquets of flowers, cards and letters arrived at the tribunal for Joanne from women's groups all over the country.

The people of Abbeydorney would protest outside the offices of the tribunal. On one occasion, in the biting cold and bitter wind, they held a silent vigil, carrying placards supporting Joanne and her family. It was a dignified and peaceful protest. The following day, though, another protest was not as peaceful. This time Mna na h-Éireann, a widely based national feminist movement, arrived in force. The protest was organised by the Women's Centre on Dame Street, Dublin. The group was joined outside the tribunal building by a couple of hundred like-minded women from the surrounding counties. One coachload had come from Belfast. It was a noisy, raucous protest. As the Gardaí and barristers emerged from the building, we were greeted with taunts and jeers of 'Bastards! Bastards!'

When Judge Lynch emerged, he was also verbally abused. Fearing for his safety, a number of detectives, including myself, escorted him to his hotel. Later that evening, the protesters marched on the Garda station and held a noisy demonstration there. I was in the station and could hear the angry voices of the mob. They were howling out the names of Superintendent Courtney and Martin Kennedy and shouting, 'Burn the pigs out!' After venting their anger for about an hour, they dispersed. It was an ugly scene and for a while it looked like things could have got out of hand.

The following Monday morning, the chairman, Mr Justice Lynch, issued a stern warning that he would imprison anyone who, in his opinion, insulted or obstructed the workings of the tribunal. He described the protesters as 'raucous, ignorant urban dwellers'. The judge's warning had the desired effect and no further protests occurred.

What appeared to me to be the first chink in the Hayes case occurred on Monday, 4 February during the testimony of Mike Hayes. Mike was a rather simple young man, quiet and soft-spoken and very suggestible. He was socially and emotionally reserved and his only interest lay in working on his family farm. Up to this juncture, the family had maintained through thick and thin that there was only one baby born out on the land that night with no assistance from any other members of the family. Under cross-examination from James Duggan, counsel for the tribunal, Mike sensationally admitted that his sister Joanne had given birth to a baby boy in her room that night. Mike's dramatic admission sent shock waves around the courtroom and ruptured beyond repair the unity of the family's stance in the whole affair.

After Mike Hayes had completed giving his evidence at the courthouse in Tralee, the tribunal moved lock, stock and barrel to Tralee General Hospital to receive the evidence of Bridie Fuller, who was recovering there from the effects of two major strokes, which she suffered in the autumn of 1984. Certain members of the Hayes family had attempted on more than one occasion, without success, to have her certified by a number of doctors as unfit to give evidence because of her illness. They were terrified of what she might say concerning the events at the farmhouse on the night Joanne gave birth. The family also became concerned and annoyed when their aunt refused to make a statement to the family solicitor alleging abuse against the detectives who had interviewed her in Tralee on 1 May 1984.

From her sick bed, Bridie Fuller gave evidence under oath to the tribunal. She confirmed that her niece Joanne had indeed given birth to a baby boy in her bedroom in the old farmhouse on the morning of 13 April 1984. She agreed with counsel that she helped to deliver the baby. She states:

'It was now about half past two and Joanne was at an advanced stage. We went up to see her and I helped her break her waters. The baby was born and I did the best I could to help her, it was a baby boy; I saw it move and it was covered with mucus. I was not in the room when the baby died.'

After the dramatic admissions to the Tribunal by Mike Hayes and Bridie Fuller, the Hayes family story of what went on that fateful night began to unravel. We were relieved at this turn of events and were more confident that we would be cleared of any improprieties. After six weeks, the tribunal finished its work in Tralee and moved to Dublin Castle, where it reconvened in February 1985.

I spent five days there giving evidence and found it a gruelling and emotionally draining ordeal. Each day, I had to make my way through a battery of journalists and photographers. The media interest was intense; the story took up acres of space in the national newspapers. I informed the tribunal that I believed that Joanne Hayes had given birth to twin boys on the morning of 13 April 1984. I told Judge Lynch that I believed Joanne had given birth to her firstborn at around 12.30 a.m. in the field outside her house, left it in the hay and then returned to the house, believing that her ordeal was over. I believed that around 2.30 a.m. she went into labour and gave birth in her bedroom to a second baby boy, which was delivered by her aunt, Bridie Fuller, and subsequently murdered by Joanne. It was then taken to Slea Head and thrown into the sea by her brother Ned. I gave my reasons for believing that she had had twins to the tribunal and how their bodies were disposed of.

After a total of 77 days, in which 109 witnesses were heard and 61,000 questions asked, the tribunal concluded the taking of evidence and adjourned pending publication of the findings. I returned to my enforced confinement at Garda headquarters to await my fate.

The tribunal report was published in October that year. In its penultimate chapter, 'The Summary', Mr Justice Lynch made 43 separate findings in the case. The important conclusions for myself and the other Gardaí involved were contained in that chapter. 'There was no assault or physical abuse of any member of the Hayes family or Bridie Fuller by any member of the Garda,' it said. It also states:

> The confessions of Joanne Hayes, Kathleen Hayes, Ned Hayes
> and Mike Hayes . . . contain a large element of what happened

to the Tralee baby transposed to the Cahirciveen baby, with additions as to stabbing and a journey to fit involvement with the Cahirciveen baby . . .

The Tralee baby cried and Joanne Hayes put her hands on the baby's throat to stop it crying by choking it, as a result of which it died . . . Joanne Hayes also hit the Tralee baby with the bath brush in the presence of Mrs Mary Hayes and Kathleen Hayes.

Although Judge Lynch in his report completely exonerated us of any form of physical abuse on the Hayes family, he was scathing of our attitudes, procedures and actions in other parts of his summary. At various points, he states:

The Cahirciveen baby is not the child of Joanne Hayes and Jeremiah Locke . . . The Cahirciveen baby is not the child of Joanne Hayes . . . Joanne Hayes gave birth to one baby only in April 1984, namely the Tralee baby . . . The obvious belief of the Gardaí in the involvement of the Hayes family and Bridie Fuller with the Cahirciveen baby gave rise to pressure on the Hayes family and Bridie Fuller to confess such involvement.

His most critical comments on the Garda are in the following paragraphs:

The Gardaí were so convinced of the involvement of the Hayes family and Bridie Fuller with the Cahirciveen baby that on the finding of the Tralee baby on the evening of the 2nd of May 1984, they concluded that Joanne Hayes had had twins and they did not carry out a proper appraisal of the case.

Joanne Hayes' belief that she was held in custody was increased by the refusal of the Gardaí to take her out to the Hayes farm so that she might point out to the Gardaí the place where she had hidden the Tralee baby. This refusal was completely unjustified.

The Garda searches for the Tralee baby on the 1st of May 1984 were deplorably inadequate and the failure to find the Tralee baby on that date is inexcusable. This failure to find the Tralee baby put further pressure on Joanne Hayes to confess that her baby was not on the land and therefore must be the Cahirciveen baby.

Judge Lynch also found that elements of the original investigation into the murder of the Cahirciveen baby were slipshod. He was particularly critical regarding the markings for identification purposes and the custody of the three plastic bags found on the rocks beside where the Cahirciveen baby was found. The bags, which were listed as important exhibits, were later lost. He was also highly critical of the methodology of the members of the Gardaí who were involved in the investigations following the discovery of the Cahirciveen baby. It emerged that for the first ten days, no notes had been kept of conferences held regarding the murder.

Judge Lynch's report was greeted with much negative publicity. Many journalists rejected the judge's findings and questioned the way in which he used the evidence given at the tribunal to reach conclusions that the evidence did not support. He was bitterly criticised by many sections of the media for failing to answer the central question in the whole affair, namely: why did the Hayes family make confessions to a crime which they did not commit?

The November edition of *Magill* magazine was exceptionally critical of the report. Its cover carried a caption: 'Kerry Babies: We Say the Judge Got It Wrong'. The report written by Gene Kerrigan so incensed Judge Lynch that he sent a lengthy written statement on his conduct of the Kerry Babies inquiry and the subsequent media treatment of the issue to *Magill* magazine, which they published in full. It was an unprecedented response from a member of the judiciary and indicated that the chorus of hostile comment had deeply upset him.

Public opinion was also divided on the issue. For my part, I felt that I had been completely exonerated by Judge Lynch for my actions during the investigation. He did not hold me responsible for any of the defects listed in his report. In the chapter entitled 'Searches', he states:

> In fact, Joanne Hayes pinpointed the position of the Tralee baby exactly when she said to Detective Sergeant O'Carroll that it was about two fields away on the Abbeydorney side and about 200 yards away from the house in the Abbeydorney direction

and down the river. 'A' marked on the map as indicating where the Tralee baby was actually found on the evening of the 2nd of May 1984 is exactly correct when measured from the back door of the Hayes farmhouse.

I gave evidence to the tribunal that I passed on those exact directions to Detective Superintendent Courtney. I also gave evidence to the tribunal that I informed DS Courtney on a number of occasions that Joanne Hayes was very anxious and willing to go to the farm and point out the body of her baby to me.

In his report, Judge Lynch pointed out that the description I had passed on to DS Courtney was the exact spot where the dead infant was eventually found. He went on to absolve me of any blame in the subsequent deplorable and inadequate search when he stated, 'Detective Sergeant O'Carroll returned for the interview in the belief that a full and thorough search was under way utilising eight or nine men.'

For the record, I submit that I acted in a responsible and professional manner and cannot ever be held liable for either the failure to take Joanne Hayes out to her farm or the failure to locate the dead infant on the farm. I think that I performed my duties that day to the best of my ability and experience, and I was not guilty of any act of commission or omission that I will ever regret or reproach myself about. In the evidence to the tribunal, DS Courtney said that he could not remember my conversation with him regarding these vital matters. I will comment no further on that but to say my recollection of those meetings is clear and precise, and I gave true evidence to the tribunal regarding them.

15

THE FALLOUT

MY COLLEAGUES AND I HAD WAITED EXPECTANTLY FOR PUBLICATION OF the tribunal report and welcomed the findings that exonerated us of any involvement in a frame-up or assaults on the Hayes family. In my evidence to the tribunal, I gave the reasons why I believed that Joanne Hayes had given birth to twins on the morning of 13 April 1984. I said that I believed that Joanne gave birth to a baby boy out in the field shortly after midnight and within two hours gave birth to another baby boy in her bedroom in the farmhouse. I do not accept all the findings of the Lynch tribunal and feel that the evidence taken during the hearings supports the twins theory.

Throughout the tribunal report, Judge Lynch sets out the events at the Hayes house as if seen by an observer. Conversations between the Hayes family members, which were constructed and outlined in the report, were, in my opinion, speculation. A glaring example is illustrated in the chapter of the report entitled 'What will we do?' It states:

> It was then agreed that it was Joanne Hayes' responsibility to
> get rid of the body. The other members of the family and Bridie

Fuller pointed out that she ignored everybody's advice to give up Jeremiah Locke and [that] she had brought about this whole tragedy. It was therefore up to her to dispose of the body of the baby without involving any other members of the Hayes family or Bridie Fuller. She was told that she could hide the baby temporarily somewhere out on the land, but she was to arrange with Jeremiah Locke to get rid of the body off the land altogether, and the sooner the better.

There was not a shred of evidence produced to substantiate such a conversation. In fact, the opposite was said, as was shown in the statements of the family when they argued bitterly as to what was to become of the baby born in the bedroom. Some of the family said they wanted it buried on the land; others, like Mary Hayes and Bridie Fuller, wanted it taken away. There was never a mention in any of these statements that Jeremiah Locke should have a hand or play a part in the disposal of the baby born in the bedroom.

In Chapter 8, entitled 'Cover Up', the report makes an assertion without any back-up evidence: 'All the other members of the Hayes family assumed that Joanne had taken steps to dispose permanently of the baby with the help of Jeremiah Locke.' It states on page 92:

When the finding of the Cahirciveen baby was published, including a short description of his injuries, Kathleen Hayes had an uneasy feeling that the baby might have been Joanne's baby transported by Jeremiah Locke to Cahirciveen, although the presence of the wounds as described in 'The Kerryman' of the 29th of April was somewhat puzzling.

It goes on to state on page 98: 'In the days following this dreadful night, Ned Hayes believed the Tralee baby had been removed from the land by Joanne Hayes with assistance of Jeremiah Locke and permanently and safely disposed of.' Again, there was no evidence given at the tribunal hearing or unearthed during the Garda investigation in support of these theories. Indeed, there had never been a question that Locke had been involved in any way in the disposal of

Joanne's baby; in fact, no evidence has ever been produced that he was even aware that she had given birth.

There was never even a suggestion nor did any member of the investigation team believe that Locke had anything to do with the concealment of the dead infant. There was no way that Locke could have driven onto the Hayes farm, searched for the body and removed it without the knowledge of the Hayes family. If his car had been seen around the farm, their neighbours would have told them, or they would have seen it themselves. Further in that paragraph, the report makes a finding that is difficult, if not impossible, to reconcile with the facts:

> Nevertheless, since the publicity about the findings of the Cahirciveen baby, some members of the Hayes family had an uneasy suspicion that it might be Joanne Hayes' baby that she had stabbed after death in a frenzy. However, none of them spoke about these worries.

The Hayes family could not have harboured these suspicions. The Cahirciveen baby was found on Saturday, 14 April 1984. Joanne Hayes was admitted to Tralee General Hospital that same day at noon. The previous day, Joanne was at home all day in a very frail condition until the neighbours took her to the doctor that evening. Joanne Hayes had no opportunity to get rid of that body, and the family knew this because she was confined to the house all that day, getting steadily weaker through loss of blood.

I believe that Ned and Mike Hayes were telling the truth in their statement about the trip to Slea Head with the body of the infant that was born in the bedroom. Bridie Fuller said that she cut the cord and washed the baby and that it cried and was bubbling with mucus. In her statement, Joanne said she stabbed the baby and hit it with a bath brush. It is my belief that they were describing the death of the Cahirciveen baby.

On the morning of 2 May 1984, Joanne told Kathleen about the baby's body on the farm. I am absolutely convinced that up to then no member of the Hayes family was aware of the existence of that baby. Even after Joanne told them of the baby on the farm, it was nearly four hours later before the baby was eventually found. Judge Lynch states on page 100 of his report:

> The delay between Joanne Hayes telling Kathleen Hayes shortly after 11 a.m. on Wednesday, the 2nd May, 1984, where she had hidden the Tralee baby and the time when Kathleen, Ned and Mike went down the field to search for it sometime after 2 p.m. on that day is incomprehensible. The baby was found between 2 p.m. and 2.30 p.m. and the delay between finding the baby and notifying the Garda is also incomprehensible.

I believed that lack of action after almost four hours is further proof that the Hayes family did not believe that Joanne had concealed a baby out on the land, as they had taken her baby away as described in their statements. In my opinion, they did not believe Joanne when she made this startling revelation. Their inordinate delay in searching for the baby displayed a total lack of belief on their part of the story that Joanne had told them. If the Hayes family had known that Joanne's baby was out on the farm, one of them would certainly have told the investigating team on 1 May in Tralee Garda station. Why would they all have made such detailed and incriminatory statements about carving knives and bath brushes and a trip to Slea Head if they could have given up to the Garda a little baby's body without a mark of violence on it? They didn't because they knew nothing of the baby out on the land.

Bridie Fuller said she washed the baby that was born in the house. The Cahirciveen baby had been washed; the Tralee baby had not been. The baby boy born in the house had cried and was bubbling with mucus, and the evidence of Bridie Fuller was that it may have lived for at least an hour or more. The Cahirciveen baby had achieved a separate existence, and the lungs had been inflated according to Dr Harbison; however, the Tralee baby had not achieved separate existence, as the lungs had not been expanded and breathing had not been established. During his evidence to the tribunal, Dr Harbison stated, 'If I were to be asked, looking at the two lungs of the two babies, which survived six hours and which did not, I would deduce the Cahirciveen baby had survived for six hours.'

We also had evidence from the Hayes family that Joanne had stabbed her baby in the bedroom with a knife and hit it with a bath brush. Dr Harbison states that the causes of death in the Cahirciveen baby were shock and haemorrhage, stab wounds to the heart, fractured cervical spine and subdural haemorrhage. The baby Joanne admitted to having out on the land had slight bruising consistent with the account she gave Detective Browne and me as to how she delivered herself of that baby. Dr Harbison stated in his post-mortem of the Tralee baby:

> Dark discolouration of the skin on the left-hand side of the neck and of the underlying left lateral spinal muscles could have been bruising. If so, it would suggest the neck had been compressed either deliberately or as part of an attempt at self-delivery. As the possible neck injury did not involve the larynx or trachea, and no sign of asphyxia was seen, strangulation cannot be inferred as a cause of death.

Judge Lynch states, 'Joanne Hayes also hit the Tralee baby with the bath brush in the presence of Mrs Hayes or Kathleen Hayes.' Nowhere in Dr Harbison's report does he suggest that the baby received a blunt-injury trauma, such as from a bath brush. He states the bruise was 'consistent with either deliberately or as part of an attempt at self-delivery'. No other injury was found on the body.

In fact, during his evidence to the tribunal, Dr Harbison, in reply to a question by Mr Kennedy, senior counsel, stated that he believed that if either of the babies had been forcibly hit with a bath brush, he would have expected that the blows would have fractured their skulls.

Despite the medical evidence of Dr Harbison, our most distinguished pathologist, stating that the cause of death was unascertainable, Judge Lynch came to a different conclusion. In summary in the tribunal he states in relation to the Tralee baby, 'Joanne Hayes put her hands onto the baby's throat to stop it crying by choking it and as a result of which it died.'

Another element that would add credence to the twins theory regarded the weights of the two babies. Dr Harbison carried out the post-mortem of the Cahirciveen baby in Killarney. He did not have the assistance of the members of the Garda Technical Bureau. He did not take a sample of blood from the baby or even weigh it, as there were no weighing scales available. However, he stated at the tribunal that from detailed measurements he had taken he would conclude that the baby weighed about 5 lb. He gave evidence that the Tralee baby weighed 5 lb also. Yvonne, Joanne Hayes' first baby, weighed at birth 8.062 lb. Medically, it is highly unusual and unlikely that if Joanne Hayes had given birth to only one baby, it would weigh almost 3 lb less than her first child. It also answers those sceptics who say that because of Joanne's small stature she could not be the mother of twins. The two small baby boys in question together weighed approximately 10 lb, not much more than her first baby.

The Hayes family, when testifying, swore under oath that their first statements to the Garda were a tissue of lies manufactured at the whim of various experienced Gardaí, but the burning question that they can never escape from is: 'Where is the baby that Joanne was delivered of in the house?' They cannot say it was the baby found on the farm – they had had the chance to say something but because they did not know of its existence they could not. They did know she had a baby that she could not deliver up for inspection because they had witnessed its destruction and eventual disposal.

I gave evidence to the tribunal in this extraordinary, unprecedented case, probably unique to the annals of criminal investigations in Ireland, that Joanne Hayes was the mother of the Tralee baby and the Cahirciveen baby. To put this issue beyond doubt, I have called in the past for the exhumation of the bodies of both of these babies for the purpose of DNA analysis. To add further impetus to the argument that the matter be settled through such analysis, I refer to the disagreement that emerged between Dr Harbison and Martin Kennedy SC during the taking of evidence at the tribunal about samples of tissue taken from the Cahirciveen baby by Dr Harbison. Below is a transcript of this exchange:

> MK: Dr McKinnon says she received only one jar labelled frozen
> tissue and yet you said you sent a lung or portion of a lung and
> a piece of muscle to the Forensic Science Laboratory. Did I take
> it down correctly on that – that is the Cahirciveen baby?
> JH: It was one of the other counsels who raised the issue of the

muscle. I had not a record of the muscle, but I gave the reason why I must have taken it, which was to have tissue from the body other than the lung for diotom examination, but I had to be reminded of it by counsel. I did not have a record of keeping the back muscle for the simple reasons that these were samples which I would not have anticipated going to another laboratory, and therefore did not need the individual document.

Before moving on, I feel I must comment on the role played by the office of the DPP in this matter. I do so reluctantly, but I consider what transpired to be a matter of such fundamental importance as to outweigh any other qualms I might have about going public on the issue.

The office of the DPP was established in 1974 and replaced the office of the Attorney General as the sole prosecuting agency in the state. The Attorney General was a political appointment, whereas the DPP is a totally autonomous and independent role. The DPP is sent Garda reports on all major crimes where suspects have been nominated and recommendations have been made that certain individuals be prosecuted. The Director himself, or his staff of legal assistants, after examining the report decide whether a prosecution goes ahead or not. At times, especially in the more complex cases, he would have a consultation in his office with the senior Garda officers involved before making a decision to prosecute, or to explain reasons why a prosecution should not go ahead. Some of these meetings could be quite confrontational and heated, as each side sought to convince the other of the validity of their respective arguments. At the end of the day, the Director's word was final and binding in all cases. I attended a number of these consultations with senior Garda officers from the Investigation Section almost always in connection with a murder case. On a number of occasions, the decision of the Director not to prosecute was a source of bitter disappointment to us but, of course, we had to accept his decisions no matter how unpalatable. Some senior officers resented what they considered the imperious and dismissive attitudes of a number of senior legal assistants in his office during some of these conferences, but overall we enjoyed a good working relationship with the Director and his staff.

Eamon Barnes, now retired, was the first Director in that office and was a man I admired and respected, even though I didn't always agree with his decisions. I had many meetings with him in the course of my career and always found him to be polite and courteous, and he possessed a brilliant legal mind. It was with some surprise then, in August 1981, that I learned from a member of the legal profession, a close friend of mine, that certain staff in the DPP's office were highly critical of my section. This friend told me that at a recent function he had attended one legal assistant spoke disparagingly of one of the senior officers in the unit and commented that this senior Garda would 'dispense with the services of this department if he had his way'. The staff member also voiced concerns at our methods of work and our lack of respect for his office. After this meeting, I had a discreet word with the superintendent in question back in headquarters and we discussed the serious implications of what I had been told. He was startled by my revelations and could not comprehend why he had been singled out for such criticism.

Two years later, the Investigation Section was scattered to the four winds. The Garda file on the Kerry Babies case was leaked to Don Buckley, a freelance journalist, some days prior to the dropping of charges against the Hayes family on 10 October 1984. In his book *Lost Innocence*, Barry O'Halloran states that Don Buckley visited an office where he was handed the Garda report on the Kerry Babies case. O'Halloran states that the official who handed over the report had been discussing Garda reports with Buckley and commenting on the merits or otherwise of individual files. In describing the files, the official said, 'Some of them [are] excellent, most of them were adequate and there were a few that contained some incredible rubbish.'

O'Halloran states that the official had then pulled out the Kerry Babies report and pointed out the more colourful and contradictory passages in it. He told the reporter that the charges against the Hayes family were about to be dropped before handing him over the Garda report.

Later that month, the *Sunday Independent* carried a very detailed report on the whole case, which included the publication of large tracts from the statements made by the Hayes family and Bridie Fuller to the Garda on 1 May 1984. Following that publication, many people were convinced we had pressurised or beaten the Hayes family into making those incriminating confessions. At the time, we had no way of defending ourselves from these untrue allegations. The publication of the statements also seriously damaged the reputation of the Hayes family in the little tight-knit community in Abbeydorney. No investigation was ever carried out to find the official who leaked the Garda report, although it was a breach of the Official Secrets Act, which is a criminal offence. It is obvious from the report in O'Halloran's book that the leak did not emanate from any Garda source.

After I left the force, I was given copies of the internal memos that were attached to the Garda report on the Kerry Babies case, the original of which was stolen by Martin Cahill during a burglary at the DPP's office in August 1987. Part of the copied report appeared to have sustained some water damage but most of it is still perfectly legible. A number of typed and handwritten internal memos are contained in the foreword to the report. In one handwritten memo, the writer refers to the Garda report in a scathing and sarcastic manner and calls it 'a hysterical attempt to cover up a GUBU'. This is an acronym for Grotesque, Unbelievable, Bizarre and Unprecedented. The legal assistant refers to other parts of the Garda report as lies and makes reference to the writer being mad.

The typed memo dated 19 October 1984 deals with the leak of the Garda report and contains some astonishing and disturbing passages (see Appendix III). It is quite apparent from reading the memo that the author, a very senior DPP official, was deeply disturbed and embarrassed by the observation in Judge Lynch's tribunal report. He stated that the source of the leak had to have come from either the Garda or the office of the DPP. The author writes, 'To make matters worse, one of the rash of books on the babies, *Lost Innocence* by Barry O'Halloran, contains the passage which I showed you, which, if true or substantially true, describes a source which does not read like a Garda source.'

In this same memo, it is stated:

> Leaving aside again the unfortunate deceased infants, when the
> dust settles on the Kerry Babies case and report the integrity of

the Garda and of this office must survive. To that end, there should be some kind of inquiry or investigation into the leak.

I suggest you have a statutory consultation with the Attorney General about the matter. It would be better if the initiative came from within than from without.

The writer has his own suspicions about the source of the leak and it is quite obvious that he did not believe the Garda was responsible for it.

There should now, despite the passage of years, be an investigation to expose the individual responsible. He should be made to pay the price for the serious damage he inflicted on the integrity and honour of his office, and the embarrassment and hurt the leaking of the report caused to the Hayes family and ourselves.

The Kerry Babies case was a cathartic event in all our lives. It was a uniquely Irish crime: clandestine, pathetic and redolent of centuries of sexual repression. Irish society had a mirror into which it looked and saw its reflection; it didn't like what it saw. The case led to an outbreak of moral schizophrenia throughout the country. The unedifying spectacle of Joanne Hayes being quizzed about her sexual proclivities at the tribunal caused alarm and dismay amongst the conservative establishment and, of course, Holy Mother Church. The cracks had appeared and widened, and the whole rotten edifice of that carefully constructed house of cards that was the hidden Ireland came down in ruins. Despite the passage of time, there is still widespread interest in this extraordinary, complex and tragic case.

Sometimes we forget, amidst all the controversy, that the real victims were the two little, innocent babies whose lives were so cruelly ended. They, at least, should always deserve our remembrance and our prayers.

16
......

MY DARKEST HOUR

I EXPECTED, FOLLOWING THE PUBLICATION OF THE REPORT, THAT I would soon be back at my old job. However, as the days went by I heard rumours from friends in the media and whispers from colleagues that I was facing the chop. This news was further confirmed by an article in the *Irish Times*, which stated: 'The Garda Commissioner, Mr Wren, is expected to transfer two of the Garda in the Kerry Babies investigation shortly. It is understood that he will move to transfer Detective Sergeant Gerard O'Carroll and Detective Sergeant Joseph Shelly.'

After this, I saw the writing on the wall and prepared for the worst. I decided to pre-empt the decision by writing an impassioned report directly to Commissioner Wren, appealing for justice and reminding him that I had been exonerated of all the wrongdoing and inefficiency in the investigation. In my report, I also drew his attention to my enforced idleness from 11 October 1984 to that date without just cause or reason. I also reminded the commissioner of the effect this degrading treatment was having on my morale, and the severe psychological and financial strain it was having on my family.

I also informed him that I believed we had already been judged guilty by the Minister for Justice in remarks he had made from the sanctuary of Dáil Éireann. These comments were widely reported in the media and were peremptory and prejudicial to the interests of fair play and justice, and constituted trial by public opinion.

I pointed out it would appear that myself and another sergeant had been singled out from the 28 other officers involved in the case in a vindictive way, and had been subjected by implication and innuendo to an attack on our integrity. In the final paragraph, I wrote:

> To conclude, I feel that a savage and unjust attack has been made on my honour and integrity as a human being, and as a member of An Garda Síochána. I believe that if I do not fight to clear my name and right this injustice, I could not remain, nor would I be fit to serve as a member of An Garda Síochána.
>
> During my career, in which I was promoted to Detective Sergeant on special meritorious grounds, I have never been the subject of any serious disciplinary proceedings within An Garda Síochána or the courts.
>
> I consider that my career, which could have been fairly promising, has suffered grievously as a result of allegations made against me, which were totally groundless, over which I had no control and of which I have been completely exonerated. I will exhaust every financial, political and legal means available to end this victimisation, clear my name and to ensure the tenets of fair play and natural justice apply to each and every member of An Garda Síochána.

My entreaties fell on deaf ears.

On the morning of 23 October, along with two other colleagues, I was reverted from detective duties and transferred to uniformed duties in the computer section of Garda headquarters in the Phoenix Park. On the same day, I forwarded a further written appeal to Commissioner Wren against the decision to revert me to uniform duties and my transfer to the computer section. I also brought to his attention my sense of outrage that the Minister for Justice should have made an announcement that same day of our transfers from the Investigation Section to other duties.

The Minister for Justice had stated in the Dáil that we were being transferred to other duties, and that our moves were not disciplinary but done in the best interests of the force in a policy of reallocating personnel from specialised units to other duties. I reminded the commissioner in my report that I regarded the Minister's statement as hollow and unconvincing. I also pointed out that the vast majority of the people of the country and the force, because of the ambiguous and self-contradictory nature of the Minister's statement, would see my reversion to uniform and transfer as disciplinary, a punishment for wrongs committed and a demotion for me. I reminded him that articles in certain newspapers were already referring to our transfers as demotion.

I finally requested a personal interview with Commissioner Wren. Both appeals were turned down, and later that day, I reported for duty to my new section. I subsequently appealed to the commissioner to review his decision but that was also turned down. I have included the entire affidavit of that appeal, as it sums up my personal feelings and sense of injustice at my treatment (see Appendix II).

On 26 October that year, exasperated by the lack of any meaningful response from the authorities, I spoke to the inspector in charge of the public relations office at his private residence accompanied by colleague P.J. Browne, who had also been involved in the case and was facing sanctions. I asked this inspector to convey a personal message to Commissioner Wren that unless we were given justice, I would use every means at my disposal, including a media and letter campaign to every politician, trade unionist and church leader, even the president. From that night on, we mounted a blitz to secure some recognition and backing for our cause. That same night, I gave my first interview to a journalist for the *Sunday Tribune*. The following day in banner headlines read the caption on the front page: 'Kerry Babies Gardaí say "We are scapegoats."' I did interviews with journalists from all the leading newspapers, and every chance I got I appeared on radio stations and in magazines. Liam Skelly, Fine Gael TD, took up our cause and lobbied for us among his colleagues in Dáil Éireann, and had questions tabled from the floor of the house about our treatment.

One of our most unlikely champions in the media was journalist Gene Kerrigan of *Magill* magazine. Although highly critical of the tribunal report and indeed of the Garda's handling of the Kerry Babies case, he nevertheless highlighted our disgraceful treatment in a major article in that magazine. In this, he states that we were made the scapegoats in the whole affair, and he outlined our unjust and inhumane treatment at the hands of the Garda authorities. I also went to Dáil Éireann and personally lobbied members of the government and the opposition. I went to the home of former Fine Gael Minister for Justice, Paddy Cooney, who received me graciously and listened to my tale of woe.

He appreciated our dilemma and, although he was unable to provide any material assistance, was morally supportive of our stand. I spoke to Cooney because as Minister for Justice he had earned the respect and admiration of the entire force. I also met Senator Jimmy Deenihan of Fine Gael, a distant relation, on a number of occasions and enlisted his help. Each time, I was accompanied by one or more of my colleagues who were in the same boat. We met Jimmy Deenihan on a number of occasions in Buswells Hotel and once in the Members' Bar in Dáil Éireann on the invitation of Michael Noonan.

At that meeting, we were told that Minister Noonan now realised that we had been placed in unsuitable positions after our transfers and if we stopped the agitation, we would be restored to our former duties in Detective Branch. Nothing came of this so-called deal and our struggle continued. During this time our wives were no less active. My wife, Kathleen, and Anne Browne and Dolores Shelly (the wives of P.J. Browne and Joe Shelly) issued a joint statement in all the national newspapers on Sunday, 3 November 1985. In this statement, they accused the commissioner of making scapegoats of their husbands (for full statement, see Appendix IV).

They mounted an amazing campaign, bombarding every TD and Minister in Dáil Éireann with a copy of a letter signed by all three of them. They also sent a copy of it to all the provincial newspapers and to every Catholic bishop and archbishop, and to the leaders of every other religious denomination in the country. They regularly issued press releases on the progress of their campaign, as well as giving interviews to radio and other media organisations. They received hundreds of letters of support, which greatly encouraged us and kept up our hopes.

It came to pass that hardly a day went by that our 'Campaign for Justice' did not get a mention in some newspaper or magazine, or on a provincial radio station. We also went down the legal route and had solicitors' letters dispatched to the Minister for Justice, the Attorney General and the Garda commissioner, outlining possible legal action over what we perceived as our unjust treatment. The central theme of these letters was that by transferring us in a blaze of publicity, we had been exposed to odium, ridicule and contempt on an unprecedented scale. Our campaign was further highlighted at the annual conference of the Association of Garda Sergeants and Inspectors (AGSI) in April 1986. I was a delegate from the Garda headquarters.

I had selected to speak on a motion 'that the Conference discuss the unfair treatment to AGSI members meted out as a result of the Kerry Babies case'. Before I left Garda headquarters, I was advised by one very high-ranking officer that if I addressed the conference on that issue, I would be finished in the Gardaí for all time. On that day, 8 April, I was warned by several members of the media of rumours that I would in some way be prevented from delivering my address. In case something untoward should happen to me, the night before I delivered copies of my speech to all the members of the media who were covering the conference. But I did finally make it to the podium.

'We were sacrificed on the altar of expedience to appease the blood lust of the liberal wolves,' I said. I then went on to point out the unjust treatment I had endured, the false promises to restore my colleagues and me to our former posts, and how the Minister for Justice Michael Noonan's comments had fanned the flames of hostility raging against us in the media. At the end of my speech, I asked those listening to 'support us in our efforts to win a reprieve from this intolerable burden of injustice and shame that has blighted our lives and our careers since October 1984'.

The conference unanimously passed the motion and gave me a standing ovation. The invited delegate from the British Police Federation also promised that his association would support us all the way, financially or otherwise, if necessary, to the European Court of Justice. Now that I had the support of my association, I really believed that we were coming to the end of a long road and our ordeal would soon be over.

When I arrived back at Garda headquarters the following day, I was approached by colleagues from all sections and warmly congratulated on my speech to the conference. Naturally, my appearance there did not go down well in the commissioner's office. I had become a thorn in their side that would not go away. On 22 April, there were heated exchanges in Dáil Éireann between Deputy Liam Skelly, Dr Michael Woods of Fianna Fáil and the Minister for Justice Alan Dukes regarding our transfers and reversion to uniformed duties. Serious allegations were made by Skelly and Dr Woods about the whole sorry affair and how we had been treated by our authorities.

Around May 1986, after all the publicity generated in Dáil Éireann, my appearance at the AGSI conference and the ongoing campaign from our wives, we got word that the authorities were sick to death of the negative publicity surrounding our case and were in a conciliatory mood. At this stage, only Sergeant P.J. Browne and I were left out in the cold. My other two colleagues had accepted positions and were no longer in dispute with the authorities. I was approached by a uniformed inspector, who informed me that he had been appointed as a mediator between us and the commissioner's office. Thus began a day of shuttle diplomacy to try to resolve the crisis. Our protest had by now become a highly publicised affair and was a source of great embarrassment for the then Minister for Justice. Our tireless quest had become a cause célèbre. What I think really alarmed them was the realisation that we were close to getting an important resolution passed in the prestigious all-party Dáil committee on 'Crime, Vandalism and Lawlessness' that would have major repercussions for at least one party involved in the dispute. This long day ended without any resolution being found.

Later that month, another major effort got under way; this time the go-between was a chief superintendent. He was a most amicable man and told me that the time had come to settle this issue. He told me that I was a victim of the system and that I could not expect City Hall to say it was wrong. We could not roll back the years or expect the commissioner to apologise to me. He told me that a solution to my problem would be found before the day was out. Nothing came from these negotiations. This horse trading went on into the next month, when all the talks broke down.

During these parleys, I was made the extraordinary offer that I could have the station of my choosing in any part of the country, whether a vacancy existed or not, at public expense, provided I accepted a uniformed posting. I refused, stating that, as always, I would accept nothing less than to be restored to my original rank of detective sergeant. I have kept detailed notes from these negotiations, during which there were many angry and heated exchanges.

My struggle eventually came to an end when I received a telephone call in August from the assistant commissioner's office that I was being restored to detective sergeant. P.J. Browne, who had stood beside me through thick and thin and who had also figured in the recent negotiations, was also restored to the duty of his choice.

It had been a long, bitter and hard-fought battle that at times seemed hopeless. I felt no sense of elation when I got the good news. All I wanted was to put the past behind me and get on with life and career.

17

AN UNLIKELY KILLER

AT 7 P.M. ON FRIDAY, 29 DECEMBER 1981, THE GARDAÍ WERE CALLED
to the scene of a fatal accident near Coolnafeeragh Bog on the
Monasterevin to Portarlington road. When the Gardaí arrived at the
scene, they saw a yellow Datsun saloon had left the main road, rolled
down a steep embankment and crashed into a fence. On investigation,
they found the driver, a woman in her 30s, dead behind the wheel. She
was the only occupant of the car and there appeared to be no other
vehicle involved in the collision. It was apparent that she had died
from massive head injuries, which were plainly visible. There was
blood all over the driver's seat and dashboard. The victim was
identified as Anne Holmes, a married woman with three children and
pregnant with her fourth.

Anne had married Henry Holmes on 3 August 1967 and they lived
in a large detached house on Togher Road, Monasterevin, County
Kildare. To the investigating Gardaí, she was just another tragic victim
of the ever-increasing and appalling carnage on our nation's roads. To
their neighbours, family and friends, she and Harry appeared a united
and loving couple, devoted to each other and their three children.

As inquiries were continuing into the cause of the accident, Harry

Holmes was in his textile factory in Ballybrittas, County Laois, with two customers. At around nine o'clock, this meeting was interrupted by the arrival of Sergeant Halloran from Monasterevin. The sergeant, who had the unenviable task of breaking the tragic news, took Holmes gently by the arm and steered him towards an office where Father O'Sullivan, the parish priest of Monasterevin, was waiting. Henry Holmes, who suspected something terrible had happened, blurted out, 'Is it my father?' Father Sullivan then told him the heartbreaking news that his wife, Anne, had been killed in a traffic accident earlier that evening.

On hearing the shocking news, Harry Holmes broke down in tears and became inconsolable. The sergeant and Father Sullivan tried to comfort him as best they could before driving him to the scene of the fatal crash. Harry Holmes said he was too upset and distressed to drive himself. At the scene, Father Sullivan asked Holmes if he wished to see his wife's body, but he refused, saying, 'I cannot stand the sight of blood.' Sergeant Halloran showed him a lump hammer that had been found in the car, which Holmes identified as his property. Everybody there had the utmost sympathy for him, as he appeared to be on the point of collapse from grief and shock.

Later that evening, the body of Anne Holmes was removed to Portlaoise General Hospital. Dr Declan Gilsenan, the pathologist, carried out the post-mortem examination and concluded that her injuries were not consistent with having been sustained in a car crash. After further detailed examination and tests, he found that Anne Holmes had died as a result of blunt-trauma injury to the head. He later conveyed these findings to Superintendent Flynn, the district officer in Kildare town, who immediately initiated a murder investigation.

The following morning I travelled to Kildare to assist in the inquiry with a team of detectives from the Investigation Section from Garda headquarters led by DS John Courtney. The incident room had already been set up in the new Garda station in the town. After our first conference, teams of detectives and local officers were assigned to the various tasks that are an essential part of every murder investigation. While the overall charge of the investigation remained in the hands of the local superintendent, the actual conduct of the inquiry was the responsibility of DS Courtney – he directed the activities of the various house-to-house inquiries and the questionnaire teams. In the incident room, other senior personnel pored over completed questionnaire forms and engaged in detailed statement analysis, searching for that vital piece of information that often meant the difference between success and failure.

Having sifted and examined all the available evidence, the most experienced detectives were given the crucial role of nominating a suspect or suspects for the crime. In this case, Harry Holmes was nominated as our main and only suspect. I was detailed to interview Harry at his home on the morning of 31 December.

Harry was a rotund, little man in his early 30s with rounded, stooping shoulders. His face was pale and drawn, and his eyes were puffy and red, as if he hadn't slept for several days. He became very emotional and sobbed uncontrollably at various times when I was with him. He looked like the type of individual who wouldn't hurt a fly. After the full horror of what he had done came to light, I was reminded very forcibly of the old adage, 'Beware the wolf in sheep's clothing.'

I took a detailed statement from Holmes, going into all aspects of his life, especially the relationship he had with his wife. I found him self-assured, articulate and extremely polite. He was a highly successful businessman, who had worked in England and Germany in textile production. However, for a man who had just lost his wife in such appalling circumstances, I found his demeanour disconcerting and suspicious. He was curiously detached and unemotional, and exhibited few signs of a normal grieving husband.

In one part of his statement, he came out with an extraordinary comment. 'I was told my wife might have committed suicide or have been murdered, and I remember thinking "I hope to God it was murder for the children's sake."'

During the taking of the statement, I took a very detailed account of his movements on the day his wife had died. The account he gave me of his activities would have been enacted by thousands of other fathers all over the country: dropping off and collecting children, going to the shops for last-minute purchases and doing little odd jobs around the house in preparation for the New Year festivities. Yet all the similarities ended there. Harry Holmes may have appeared a normal, loving father and husband as he went about his chores, yet before the day was out he would reveal himself as a heartless monster.

When the statement was completed, I reported back to DS Courtney and the rest of the team, and we discussed our next move. It was decided that we would formally invite Harry to Kildare Garda station for interview after he had attended the removal of his wife's body to the church that evening.

At around nine o'clock that same night, I again spoke to Harry in an interview room in Kildare station along with DS Tom Connolly. I told him that we had found certain discrepancies in various accounts he had given about his movements on the day of Anne's death. I also told him that our technical experts, during their examination of his house, had found bloodstains on the skirting board and on the floor of the kitchen, and blood spatters on a radiator. I told him that they had also found bloodstained clothing belonging to his wife and a bloodstained hammer in a shed at the rear of the house.

We went on tell him that we believed he had murdered his wife in the kitchen of his house and subsequently placed her lifeless body in the passenger seat of the car and then had driven out the Monasterevin to Portarlington road. We put it to him that near the Coolnafeeragh Bog he had stopped, transferred the body to the driver's seat and pushed the car down the embankment to make it look as if Anne had been killed in a tragic accident.

Throughout the interview, Holmes put on an air of righteous indignation and protested in shock and outrage that we could even have suspected him of having committed such a monstrous crime. To all our accusations and questions, he replied time and time again that he was an innocent man who loved his wife and wouldn't hurt a hair on her head. He told us that we should be out looking for the real killer of his wife and not accusing a grief-stricken father and husband. He told us that another man must have broken into the house after he had left for his factory and killed his wife. After every outburst, he would cry his heart out. I must confess he was a very convincing actor.

Again and again, we took him through the evidence, both actual and circumstantial, that all pointed to the overwhelming conclusion that he and he alone had murdered his wife. As to his suggestion that another man was responsible, we informed him that we had conducted the most intensive house-to-house inquiries around his neighbourhood and found no evidence that there had been strangers in the vicinity at the time, and certainly no one had been seen calling to his house all that evening. Furthermore, we had found no signs of a break-in nor was there any theft from his house, and from our comprehensive investigations, we learned that Anne didn't seem to have an enemy in the world. Despite the mountain of evidence against him, he stubbornly maintained that he was innocent of murder. In several flare-ups, he challenged us again to find the real killer.

As the interview continued, his air of bluster and bravado ebbed away and his protestations of innocence became less convincing. Eventually, after about two hours, he broke down, dropped all the pretence and started sobbing loudly. He put his head in his hands, looked up at me and said, 'What will happen to me? What will happen to my children? I am here because of my temper. I accept full responsibility for my wife's death. If I tell the full truth, what will become of my children? They are all I care about.'

He then made a full written statement describing in graphic detail how he killed his wife in the kitchen of their house by hitting her repeatedly over the head with a hammer. This was a cold, premeditated murder that he had planned down to the last detail. The children had been sent to their granny's house. He had purchased new linoleum for the kitchen floor and lured his wife in to inspect his handiwork. As she was crouching down on her hands and knees to admire the new floor, he had bludgeoned her with a heavy hammer, shattering her skull.

'Afterwards, I lifted her body and wrapped it in a coat, and then I carried her out and put her in the passenger seat of the car. I drove the car out near Coolnafeeragh Bog. When I got there, I got out and placed her body behind the steering wheel and pushed the car down the embankment to make it look like an accident. I then jogged back down the road home, where I cleaned up my mess. I then had a shower and drove back out to my factory in Ballybrittas.'

Before the statement was completed, we could hear the bells in the local church ringing in the New Year. Holmes, in the midst of recounting his murderous tale, stopped for a moment and shook hands with Tom and me. 'Happy New Year, men,' he said. 'It won't be a happy one for me.'

He gave as a motive for the murder of his wife that he was having an affair with a young girl who worked for him. He said his lover had been putting intolerable pressure on him to abandon his wife and children and to go off with her to Australia. He had made promises that he could not keep and he said her constant nagging and threats to expose the affair finally pushed him over the brink. In his desperation, he decided to get rid of his wife.

Holmes was later charged with the murder of his wife and released on bail. He stood trial for the murder of his wife in the Central Criminal Court on 9 March 1983. After a seven-day hearing, the jury could not agree on a verdict and a new trial date was set. His second trial commenced a couple of weeks later. On 20 April, he was found not guilty of murder but guilty of manslaughter and was sentenced to ten years' imprisonment. I was shocked and devastated at the decision of the jury to convict Holmes of manslaughter instead of murder. I had never been involved in a case where the evidence of malice aforethought and premeditation was so incontrovertible. At any rate, I doubt whether Harry Holmes could find any comfort in his conviction for manslaughter. He has to live for ever in the knowledge that he brutally killed his young wife and unborn child. For such a wicked and inhumane crime, there can be no peace this side of the grave.

Over the past number of years, there has been a dramatic increase in the number of incidences of this tragic and appalling crime. Many wife killers are walking around scot-free because of the extreme difficulties encountered by investigators in gathering sufficient admissible evidence to warrant a prosecution. In many incidences, a motive for the murder is unclear or unknown at the time. The perpetrator will have time to prepare a cast-iron alibi with a close friend or more often with one of his own family members to cover his tracks. It has always been my experience in this type of case that the longer it drags on, the more difficult it is to solve.

Trace evidence at the scene, such as blood, semen, saliva, fibres from clothing or carpets, head hair, pubic hair, fingerprints or footprints, which are vital to the solution of every other crime, is virtually useless in these cases. This trace evidence can be legitimately accounted for, as in most of the cases the perpetrator lives in the house.

As the gory details of these horrific murders are splashed across our newspapers, the response from the public is always one of shock, revulsion and disbelief. People find it almost incomprehensible that a man could turn on his own wife or partner and slaughter them in cold blood in the sanctuary of their own home.

The increasing number of unsolved murders in this country is a source of serious concern to our law enforcement agencies and to the public. There is growing evidence that these murderers are becoming increasingly sophisticated and are gleaning information and expertise on how to evade capture from the rash of police shows, such as *Crime Scene Investigation (CSI)* or documentaries like *Forensic Detectives*.

Despite all the advances in forensic science and the skills of experienced detectives, this crime remains, because of its clandestine nature, one of the most challenging to solve.

18

A TEARFUL CONFESSION

IN SEPTEMBER 1982, I WAS INVOLVED IN AN INQUIRY IN ROSCREA, County Tipperary, that resulted in the solving of a brutal murder of an old woman in Glasgow in July that year. On the 19th of that month, the Garda commissioner's office had received a telex message from the chief constable of Strathclyde Police in Glasgow requesting the assistance of An Garda Síochána in an ongoing murder investigation in their jurisdiction. The following day, my unit boss, Inspector Pat Culhane, and I had been briefed on the contents of this message and instructed to investigate it fully. Our Scottish colleagues had requested that we interview Matthew Brannan, a 43-year-old native of Glasgow who they had reason to believe was residing in the Cistercian abbey of Mount St Joseph in Roscrea. They had already interviewed him a number of times in connection with the murder on 22 July of 77-year-old Agnes Stevens, a widow living alone at Havelock Street in Glasgow. During those interviews, Brannan had given various accounts of his movements on the night of the murder, which subsequent investigations had shown to be incorrect. He had also been evasive and uncooperative during these interviews.

When we arrived in Roscrea, we carried out discreet inquiries and established that Brannan was indeed a guest at Mount St Joseph abbey. The detective inspector and I decided we would have to find a way of luring him away from the tranquil haven of the abbey to a location more conducive to our purposes. We decided on a stratagem.

The following morning, we left a message with the bursar of the monastery informing Brannan to go to the post office in the town to collect his mail. He fell for our ploy and one hour later turned up at the post office. We were waiting there and knew we had our man as soon as we heard the Scottish accent. We introduced ourselves to him and asked him to accompany us to the local Garda station.

Brannan was a tall, gaunt, undernourished-looking unfortunate. He was wearing an old brown suit that was two sizes too big for him. His face had a blotchy, florid complexion from years of alcohol abuse and hard living. He had a frightened, furtive look on his long ferret-like face. At only 43 years of age, he had the haggard, worn appearance of a much older man.

In an interview room at Roscrea station, we told him that we had been requested by Strathclyde Police to interview him in connection with the murder of Agnes Stevens. We informed him that the police officers who had interviewed him were not satisfied that he had told the truth about his movements on the night of the murder. In particular, they had not believed him when he said he had not left his lodgings after six o'clock that night.

I told him that they had interviewed a witness who had stated that he had seen Brannan outside the murdered woman's house at ten o'clock. He replied that on the night of the murder he went to his lodgings at six o'clock and sat in for the rest of the night drinking cans of beer, and that the witness must have been mistaken. I also told him that the police didn't believe him when he had said that he hadn't called to the murdered woman's house in two years. Brannan replied that he was an innocent man with nothing to hide and that the police in Glasgow had harassed and hounded him. He said he had come to Ireland to find some peace, as his nerves were at breaking point.

I asked him to tell us about the relationship he'd had with Mrs Stevens. He said he had got to know her after moving into lodgings next door, and he often ran little errands to the shop for her, and that she was almost an invalid from arthritis. He said she would often give him a few shillings when he was down on his luck. He admitted that he was a hopeless alcoholic; Mrs Stevens had been his only friend and had tried to get him help for his addiction. He went on to say that she was a kind and sympathetic person, who never turned him away when he was in trouble.

I said to him that it seemed to me that Mrs Stevens had treated him like her own son and, from his description of her, she must have been a very kind and loving woman. I asked him, what kind of person would brutally strangle a defenceless, harmless old lady? As I was speaking, Brannan began to tremble uncontrollably. It was obvious that he was coming under intense pressure as the questioning proceeded. I pressed ahead and told him that I believed the reason he was hiding out in the abbey was not due to police harassment but because he couldn't live with his conscience on account of the terrible thing he had done. With that, he jumped up and cried out, 'I'm not a murderer! I loved Mrs Stevens like she was my own mother.'

He slumped back into his chair and put his head into his hands, and started to cry softly. I knew what we were saying to him was hitting home, and I expected him at any moment to break down and confess to the murder. I told him that he was a pathetic, hopeless alcoholic who probably did not intend to hurt Mrs Stevens but in a drunken state had panicked and killed her.

Brannan looked up. 'You're right,' he sobbed. 'That's exactly what happened. Oh, Jesus! I didn't mean to hurt her. Oh, poor Mrs Stevens.'

We calmed him down and asked him to tell us the full truth about the night in Havelock Street. He said that he would tell us everything and that he was glad now to have got it off his chest. He said that he had been going insane over the past two months with guilt and shame at what he had done.

Detective Inspector Culhane and I observed the legal requirements and I began to write down his statement. We had only been with him for about 20 minutes when he confessed to the murder. In the course of his statement, he said:

'On that night, I drank about six cans of lager. After they were gone, I went out and bought vodka, Coca-Cola and cigarettes. I stayed drinking with my landlady, Mrs Clarke. Around this time, I got into an argument and left the house. I sat in the park for a wee while. I then made my road back and I mind going in the close. I then rang Mrs Stevens's door and she opened it. She was in her nightie. We stood in the hallway and she closed the storm door. Mrs Stevens then said that I had been taking too much drink lately and that Mrs Gilchrist wouldn't like to see me the way I was going on. Mrs Gilchrist was another friend who lived nearby and had helped me with my alcohol problem.

'I said, "Mrs Stevens, don't preach to me and don't mention Mrs Gilchrist's name to me, as it upsets me." Mrs Stevens said she wasn't preaching to me but that the company I was keeping was no good. She said I was going to rack and ruin, and she said it wasn't in my nature to behave like that. I pushed her into the bathroom to stop her preaching to me, and she fell down. Then she got up and said, "Oh, Matt, Matt, what have you done?"

'I pushed her again. She fell pretty heavy and she hit her head on the toilet pan or on the sink. I tried to lift her then, but I didn't have the power. I knelt down beside her and put my hand around her throat and she was saying, "Oh, Matt, Matt. If Mrs Gilchrist could see you now," and I kept saying, "Oh, Mrs Stevens, stop saying Mrs Gilchrist's name to me." I'm positive blood came from her nose and was running down her lips. I took a handkerchief from my pocket and I'm sure I wiped her nose. I think she was trying to be sick, a kind of "ca-ca" sound. She kept saying, "Oh, Matt, Matt, you're a changed lad." Her words were thick, as I had my hands around her throat.

'I then pushed the handkerchief into her mouth to stop her from talking. At this point, she became very still and she stopped talking and there was no sound from her. I got off my knees and I left the bathroom, pulling the door behind me. I went into the kitchen and got a cup of water. I was as sick as a dog. I was shaking all over. There was a wee table in the kitchen, and I pulled out a drawer in it and I saw a wee dirty, brown purse. I took about £3 out of it and some silver, and I threw the empty purse away. I also pulled out and searched some other drawers in the old-fashioned dresser beside the television. I didn't find any other money.

'I mind coming along the hall and looking into the bathroom again, the lounge door was open. I saw Mrs Stevens lying in the bathroom and she appeared to be dead. The glass door was still open where she had let me in. I went out and locked the door behind me. I threw the key into an empty bin and then went home to bed.

'I am very sorry for killing this old lady. She was like a mother to me. I say the Stations of the Cross for her every day and I pray for her. I came to Ireland because I was so upset about this terrible murder and I wanted to get some peace.'

That day, Brannan was committed to prison on a provisional warrant issued during a special sitting of the District Court in Roscrea. On Thursday, 23 September, DI Culhane charged Brannan with the murder of Agnes Stevens at Roscrea District Court. Brannan replied, 'The charge is correct.'

He was later extradited back to Glasgow where he was tried and convicted of the murder of Agnes Stevens. Like many murderers I have interviewed, Brannan left out some of the more gory details of his heinous crime. He omitted to tell us that he had strangled his victim with a leather belt and that his real motive was to rob the old lady of her meagre few pounds and possessions. Police discovered two gold watches and a diamond engagement ring were missing from her home. The chief constable of Strathclyde Police passed on his congratulations and thanks to us for solving that vicious murder, for which Brannan received a life sentence.

19

THE MAN OF A THOUSAND FACES

THE NEXT MURDER CASE I WAS INVOLVED IN WAS ONE OF THE MOST difficult, protracted and disturbing investigations of my career. The hunt had taken eight long years and stretched halfway across the world when the killer was finally brought to justice.

On Friday night, 23 July 1982, Patricia Furlong, an attractive and vivacious young woman, was at a disco with some of her close friends in a marquee pitched in a field beside Johnnie Fox's Pub in Glencullen, County Dublin. This famous pub, perched on top of the Dublin mountains, lays claim to the title of the highest pub in Dublin. The disco was part of an annual event known as the Frauchan Festival, which takes its name from the berries that grow in abundance in the local hills and are gathered at that time of year. Glencullen is a tiny little village in the foothills of the Dublin mountains. It lies two and a half miles south of Stepaside village and is about twelve miles from the heart of the city.

At 8 a.m. the following morning, two local teenage girls out on an early morning stroll saw what they thought was a person sleeping in Corbett's Field close to the main Glencullen road. They went to

251

investigate but recoiled in horror when they realised it was the lifeless body of a young woman. They ran screaming from the field to raise the alarm. It had been the first time the cold finger of death had touched their young carefree hearts and it was a horrifying experience that would give them many sleepless nights. Within minutes of their placing a call, the Garda from Stepaside arrived at the scene. The body of the young woman was naked from the waist up and a blouse and jacket were knotted around her throat. A local doctor was summoned and pronounced her dead.

Pathologist Dr Declan Gilsenan arrived an hour later and carried out a preliminary examination of the body *in situ*. The scene was cordoned off and preserved for technical examination. At 2 p.m., the body was removed to Loughlinstown Hospital, where a post-mortem was carried out. Dr Gilsenan concluded that death was due to asphyxia caused by strangulation. There was no evidence of sexual assault. At the hospital, the body of the murdered woman was identified by her brother-in-law as Patricia Furlong from Mulvey Park in Dundrum village. She was just 20 years of age. Shortly afterwards, Gardaí from Dundrum and a local curate broke the tragic news to the Furlong family that their beloved child Patricia had been brutally slain.

Later, a conference was held at Stepaside Garda station and a full-scale murder investigation got under way. I attended the conference with a team from the Investigation Section. Detectives were also drafted in from the surrounding districts to assist in the inquiry. We realised from the beginning that we would not have an easy task in solving this murder, as the festivalgoers had travelled to Glencullen from all corners of the city and had included many tourists. The festival and the nearby Johnnie Fox's Pub had always drawn huge crowds. It was estimated that about 1,000 patrons had attended the various attractions at the festival that Friday night.

The subsequent investigation was painstaking, meticulous and massive in scale, involving more than 100 detectives and uniformed personnel. We felt that if there was to be a successful outcome to our endeavours, it was imperative that we attempt to interview every person that attended the festival that night. To that end on Sunday, the 25th, the Garda press office issued appeals in the newspapers, on radio and television, seeking help and cooperation from the public in the hunt for the murderer. In particular they appealed to those who had attended the Frauchan Festival on Friday night to call to Stepaside Garda station for the purposes of being interviewed.

There was an overwhelming response to the appeals and over the next couple of days hundreds of people called to the station. Those who could not be accommodated in the cramped conditions of the little station were interviewed by teams of detectives in the two local pubs. Statements or memos of interview were taken from all callers and, with their consent, they were also photographed in an effort to identify people who might have been in the company of Patricia Furlong that night.

Despite this extensive exercise, very little of any evidential value came to light. From the onset, our investigations were hampered by the hazy and confused recollections of many of the young people who had been present at the festival due to the vast amount of drink consumed that night. However, one vital witness did come forward. He was a 14-year-old schoolboy who lived in Mulvey Park and knew the Furlong family and Patricia particularly well. He remembered speaking to Patricia beside the disco tent at around 1.30 a.m. on Saturday morning for about ten minutes. He said she was slightly tipsy and in the company of a young man whom she was cuddling and kissing. He said the last he saw of her she was walking with that fellow towards the entrance of the field and onto the roadway. They were laughing and joking and linking arms. Despite exhaustive inquiries that was the last time Patricia was seen alive.

This young man described Patricia's companion as being around 19 years of age, slim built, with black hair in a Shakin' Stevens-style tight-at-the-back hairdo, clean shaven and a serious face. He was dressed in a white jacket, white trousers and white shoes. The only words the witness heard him speak were 'We'd better be going,' and that was just before they moved off. This witness also stated that Patricia appeared to know her companion. The description of this man, who came to be known in this investigation as 'the man in white', was circulated in our police gazette *Fogra Tora* and in all the media outlets. Over the following weeks, we also took our young witness on a tour of all the nightclubs of which Patricia was a regular patron in an attempt to locate the man he had seen with her at the festival, but to no avail.

On Saturday, 24 July, Vincent Connell of Neagh Road, Terenure, and his girlfriend, Mary Creedon, drove to Glencullen on hearing the news on the radio about the murder and the Garda appeals for assistance. Vincent, a tall, dark, good-looking man with an athletic build, had the suave, confident air of a man about town. The couple had attended the festival the night before and were on their way to make their statements. They decided to call into Johnnie Fox's Pub on the way to find out the latest developments in the case before going on to the station. They arrived in a village that was numbed with shock and grief by the awful tragedy that had been visited on their close little community. Television crews and reporters mingled with sullen, tight-lipped locals and ghoulish sightseers in the smoke-filled bars. Elsewhere the marquees and tents were being dismantled and taken away since the remainder of the festival had been cancelled. The murder of Patricia Furlong was to sound the death knell of the Frauchan Festival.

As Vincent and Mary were leaving the pub, they encountered one of the festival's organisers, Bobby Gahan, a local man whom they had spoken with the previous night.

'Vinnie, the guards are looking for you,' Gahan jokingly said, 'you're the man in white.' Connell still had on the clothes he had been wearing the night before – a white-lemon top, white trousers and white shoes. Bobby Gahan's words were spoken in jest but would prove prophetic. We were not to know it then, but it was the classic case of the murderer returning to the scene of the crime.

After leaving Glencullen, Connell and his fiancée drove on to Stepaside Garda station. Gahan's words must have struck a chord in Vincent's mind because when he presented himself to the detectives at the station he was aggressive and uncooperative. He gave a verbal account of his movements on the night but at first refused to make a written statement and prevented his fiancée from making one.

Eventually, Mary Creedon and Connell made written statements, although he refused to sign his. He also refused to be photographed or fingerprinted by the detectives. Connell said in his statement that he was with his fiancée all that night in the beer tent except when he went to the toilet on a number of occasions, but he was missing for no more than five minutes at any time. Mary Creedon confirmed Connell's account of his movements in the statement she made on 19 August 1982.

Connell's strange and bizarre behaviour and his hostile attitude aroused the suspicions of my colleagues. He was placed on the list of suspects and detailed inquiries were carried out on his alibi and background. During these inquiries, it emerged that Vincent Connell was the prime suspect for a serious arson attack on the home of his ex-girlfriend, Gillian Kane, at Dangan Park in Kimmage, Dublin, on 15 May 1982. A detailed investigation had been carried out by detectives at Crumlin Garda station but no evidence was found linking Connell to the attack; however, that investigation was still very much ongoing. It was after his break-up with Gillian Kane that he had started going out with Mary Creedon.

Meanwhile the inquiry continued apace. Hundreds of people who attended the festival were interviewed in depth, had written statements taken from them and were photographed and fingerprinted. As a result of the media appeal, information was being received on a daily basis, nominating possible suspects in the case. The description of the killer as 'the man in white', which had been released to the media, had gripped the imagination of the public. All the teams in the case were working up to 16 hours a day in an attempt to process these suspects.

Statements had to be read and re-read and cross-referenced with other statements and memos. Alibis had to be thoroughly checked and re-checked before a decision could be taken to eliminate a person as a suspect. Indeed before the final decision could be taken each suspect elimination team had to have a consultation with a senior officer and explain their reasons in detail backed up with cast-iron alibis.

In the incident room at Stepaside, other teams were burning the midnight oil poring over statements and questionnaire forms and memos, scanning for the crucial clue that might reveal the identity of the killer. Every lead that we had no matter how tenuous was investigated and fully explored. Teams of detectives had even travelled across the border to the north of Ireland to interview possible suspects who had been nominated by members of the public on a confidential telephone line. Officers for the inquiry had also travelled to France to interview a possible suspect who was being detained in a psychiatric hospital there. Former boyfriends of the deceased were tracked down and interviewed, and eliminated from our inquiries. A suspect file was even opened on every lone male who attended the festival in an attempt by a process of elimination to reveal the killer.

The scene of the murder in Corbett's Field was examined minutely and searched thoroughly for any possible clues but with negative results. We found some of Patricia's personal effects in a hedgerow 200 yards from her body, where the killer had presumably discarded them. These were examined by the fingerprint expert but yielded nothing. Despite our intense and sustained investigation, we had run into a brick wall. After a number of months the inquiry was eventually wound down, but a number of detectives were left to man the telephone lines in the incident room and deal with any members of the public who came to the station with information. The case remained open and 'the man in white' was still our only suspect in the case. His failure to come forward despite all our appeals convinced us that he was implicated in the murder.

Vincent Connell was at this time living with his mother and aunt, both elderly ladies, in a modest three-bedroom council house on Neagh Road in Terenure, Dublin. Vincent was born in London on 30 March 1951. He was an only child. He received a very good secondary education and was the holder of a Royal Society of Arts Advanced Certificate in Spoken English. He was an accomplished public speaker and had won a gold medal for oratory. He was also a gifted musician. In 1970, at the age of 19, he returned with his mother to Ireland and went to live at the house in Terenure. Between 1970 and 1976, Vincent worked for a number of insurance companies in Dublin selling insurance policies.

In 1977, he left Ireland and travelled to Liverpool, where he was accepted as a cadet with the Merseyside Constabulary. After six months on the force, he was asked for his resignation 'in the interests of the force'. In 1978, he returned to Dublin and applied for the job of prison officer. He was accepted and attached to Mountjoy Prison.

In 1980, he left the prison service under a cloud amidst charges of improper association with inmates. Prior to this, he had also been a member of the Irish Army Reserve, the FCA, attached to the Military

Police company for a number of years. He also harboured ambitions of joining An Garda Síochána but felt himself to be ineligible as he did not speak Irish.

In 1982, he was holding down a number of jobs that included working as a 'night owl' presenter with the pirate radio stations Big D, Radio Leinster and Ards Radio. He also worked as an assistant manager in the Top Hat Ballroom in Dun Laoghaire, where he coached a roller-skating team called 'Vinnies Wheels and Co.' Towards the end of August 1982, Connell left Dublin to take up a job as a presenter in Liverpool's Radio City.

Around mid-October, Connell returned to Dublin for a weekend. Mary Creedon went back to Liverpool with him and they moved into rented accommodation in the city together. Mary Creedon had only met Connell in January 1982. After a whirlwind romance, they got engaged. A few months later, Mary Creedon was having second thoughts. She had seen flashes of his violent temper and uncontrollable rages. She had already suffered violent assaults at his hand in their short relationship – she had covered up and borne these indignities from her bullying fiancé because she feared causing embarrassment to her family. As a typical bully, Connell preyed on those emotions. During one of his violent outbursts, Connell had grabbed her by the throat and attempted to strangle her. She believes he would have killed her if she had not kicked him in the groin and escaped.

During his visit in October, he had behaved in an aggressive and hostile manner towards her parents. She stated that when she went back to Liverpool with him it was with the sole purpose of breaking off the engagement. In the rented house in Liverpool Connell again showed the Jekyll and Hyde side of his character. When she told him their relationship was over, he went berserk. For days, he forcibly held her in the house against her will and repeatedly assaulted and abused her. She was virtually a prisoner in their house. He told her that he would never allow her to go back to Dublin. He prevented her from contacting her family. He took her money and passport with him every time he left the house.

On one occasion when he was in a drunken stupor, she escaped, but he woke up and followed her. He then dragged her back to the house and gave her a severe beating.

Mary eventually succeeded in contacting her parents, who alerted the Liverpool Police that their daughter was being held captive by Connell. The police made contact with Connell, but he convinced them that it was a lovers' tiff and everything was in order. Mary's parents were fearful for the life of their daughter, so travelled to Liverpool in late October. They managed to rescue her from the house while Connell was out. In their hasty and fearful state, they left behind all Mary's personal belongings – money, credit cards, passport and personal papers. In the early hours of the morning, they left on the Liverpool to North Wall ferry and arrived safely in Dublin.

It had been a terrifying ordeal for the family but at least Mary was back, safe and sound, in the bosom of her family. It had been a nightmarish experience for all concerned. Mary had had a lucky escape from his clutches, but she had not heard the last of Vincent Connell. In the following years, he bombarded her home with malicious telephone calls, in which he threatened to burn the house to the ground and take revenge on the entire family.

In January 1984, the Patricia Furlong case took a dramatic and sudden twist. Vincent Connell was sacked from his £7,700 a year job at Liverpool Radio for poor timekeeping and subsequently took the radio station to an industrial tribunal for unfair dismissal. After he had been dismissed, the radio station examined more closely the written references that Connell had supplied when he had applied for the job. After some initial inquiries, they discovered that some of those references were not genuine. Ciaran Devaney, chief reporter with Radio City, was dispatched to Dublin to investigate the matter more fully. In Dublin, he spoke to ex-colleagues of Connell who had worked with him on Radio Leinster. Devaney was told by one of them that Connell was a suspect in the murder of Patricia Furlong. Devaney decided to investigate the matter further and arranged to meet up with Mary Creedon. He had met her before on a number of occasions and knew she had been engaged to Connell. At that meeting, Mary confessed to him that she had not told the whole truth to the detectives in Stepaside. She told the reporter that she was terrified of Connell at the time but now that she was safe from him she would tell the full truth about what happened on the night of Patricia's murder.

Devaney contacted a senior detective who had worked on the investigation and told him of this important development. On 29 January 1984, Mary Creedon was interviewed by a detective superintendent and made a detailed written statement. She revealed the startling news that her ex-fiancé Connell had left her company on the night of the murder and had been missing for at least three-quarters of an hour. She stated:

'Sometime during the night of the murder while I was in the beer tent with Vincent, I saw a girl at the entrance door to the beer tent. She was with a few other girls and fellows. This girl appeared to be drunk. When Vincent Connell saw this girl, he said to me that he knew her and he had gone out with her on a few occasions. He then said, "I'll go and have a chat with her." He left my company and walked towards the entrance door.

'Vincent returned to the beer tent after he had been absent for about three-quarters of an hour. When he returned, he did not say where he had been and I did not ask him. After he returned and for the remainder of the night, he was in a very bad mood. On the way home in the car, he asked me to go away with him that morning. I refused and he got annoyed at my refusal. I can only describe the girl that Vincent spoke to as having straight, dark hair with a fringe.'

This was the breakthrough that we had been waiting for. Connell had lied in his written statement when he had said that he was with his fiancée Mary Creedon all that night. Mary's statement had demolished his alibi, and now he had serious questions to answer about that vital missing period. He had now become one of the chief suspects in the case. When we went to look for Connell, the bird had already flown the coop. He had embarked on a great new adventure in South Africa, where he would soon be up to his old tricks again.

On two occasions, he came home to Ireland to visit his mother. Once, in 1987, he was interviewed in connection with the case, but he stuck to his original story and no arrest was made. The following day, he flew back to South Africa. However, luck would not stay for ever on his side, and the long arm of the law was already reaching out to snare him.

In 1989, Connell returned to Dublin and auditioned for a job on Capital Radio in Dublin's Stephen's Green Shopping Centre. Though the company had reservations, he landed the job and worked there until January 1990. He was sacked from the company for re-broadcasting a report from a British jail riot which he claimed was from disturbances which had happened that day in Mountjoy Prison. This little deception had cost him dearly.

In early April that year, I was informed by one of my colleagues at Sundrive Road that Vincent Connell was back living with his aunt and mother in Terenure. I informed Chief Superintendent John Courtney, who immediately began preparations to hold a conference to discuss all aspects of the Patricia Furlong murder case.

By coincidence, almost at the same time one of the detectives involved in the inquiry back in 1982, Detective Sergeant Gerard McDonnell, had seen in the police gazette that a Vinnie Connell of Neagh Road, Terenure, was wanted in connection with a serious assault on a young woman named Barbara Rooney. The detective sergeant informed his boss, Detective Superintendent O'Mahony, who was then the Garda officer in charge of the Furlong case. During the latter part of April and early May, Chief Superintendent Courtney and DS O'Mahony joined forces and re-opened the case. Meetings were held and attended by many of the officers who had taken part in the original investigation, including members from the Investigation Section in Garda headquarters.

Inquiries were also carried out by the South African police at our request in relation to Connell's activities during his residence there. We held a final conference on Friday, 18 May 1990. It was decided that I would take a team to arrest Connell at his home the following morning at 7 a.m.

Although the house was under surveillance by local detectives that night, when I arrived there the following morning with a posse of detectives, Connell was nowhere to be found. When I returned to the station empty-handed, there were a lot of red faces, especially amongst the hapless surveillance team who had let their quarry slip through the net. Later on that day, we discovered that Connell was in Ashbourne, County Meath, where he was attending a confirmation ceremony in a local church. He was acting as sponsor for the son of a young woman with whom he had recently struck up a friendship through a dating agency. Before the day was out, she would regret her choice of sponsor for such an important event in her young son's life.

After returning to the house after the confirmation ceremony, Connell went into a bedroom and, to the amazement and shock of his girlfriend, returned sometime later dressed as a priest. He told her that it was just a bit of fun that he had planned for the day and that it would get a laugh when the guests arrived for the celebrations. She said later when interviewed by detectives that she thought it was a bit bizarre but agreed to go along with the pretence at least for a while. She went on to say that Vincent was in great form until he phoned his mother in Terenure a short time before the guests were due to arrive. His mother told him that the police had searched the house under warrant and were looking for him. On hearing that news, he got roaring drunk. He was to have cooked a meal for the 20 guests that had turned up but by that time he was too drunk to even stand up. He then became abusive and assaulted one of the guests. He proceeded to stumble and fall over the barbecue, destroying all the food.

He was eventually forcibly restrained and thrown in a bedroom, where he remained comatose for the rest of the night. He succeeded in completely destroying what should have been a beautiful family occasion. The *Sunday World* newspaper would subsequently publish photographs taken in the house that day of Vincent slumped in a chair in his ecclesiastical garb and as drunk as a lord. On Sunday, when he sobered up, he called Pat Wall, one of the detectives in my unit at Sundrive Road. It was he who had alerted me to Vinnie's presence in Terenure. He had been dealing with him in relation to the outstanding warrant for the assault on Barbara Rooney and also in connection with the arson attack on the home of Gillian Kane.

Detective Wall told Connell to call back at 2 p.m. and he would fill him in on what was going on. After that telephone call, we held a briefing with Chief Superintendent Courtney and the team in Crumlin station. It was decided at this meeting that when Connell telephoned back at two o'clock, Detective Wall would arrange to meet him at 6 p.m. in the Fleet Bar in D'Olier Street, where we would be waiting to make our move. At 5 p.m., Detective Wall and the rest of the team were in place in the Fleet Bar to await the arrival of our elusive prey.

At 5.55 p.m., Connell walked through the door and went straight to the bar, where Pat Wall was sitting having a pint. He was carrying a holdall and a guitar. Minutes later, I approached him at the bar. I identified myself and told him that I was arresting him under the Offences against the State Act for arson on 15 May 1982 at Dangan Park, Kimmage, Dublin 12. I told him that I was taking him to Tallaght Garda station.

We crossed the road from the bar to where the patrol cars were parked. Connell refused to get into the car, and he put up a brief struggle before we got him in it. He turned violent and abusive in the car, and grabbed me around the neck while I was driving, again having to be forcibly restrained. He was screaming at the top of his voice, trying to attract the attention of other drivers. He was shouting, 'Get the Gardaí! I'm being kidnapped!' He struggled and shouted like a man possessed all the way to Tallaght station. I noticed an area of bruising on the back of his left hand and reported same in the custody records. I asked him what had happened to it and he said he had burnt it when he fell into a barbecue in Ashbourne the previous day.

Detective Inspector Canavan and I dealt with him during the first interview. We spent the first two hours trying to get a solicitor for him. It was Sunday evening and we had a great deal of trouble trying to locate one. Connell was adamant that he wanted his own solicitor, but there was no reply from his office number, just an answering machine. Connell took the phone and left a message, giving all his particulars. During this time, we had a general conversation with him about his life in South Africa and Namibia.

We questioned him in depth about the fire we believed he had caused at the home of Gillian Kane on 15 May 1982. He denied all knowledge of the fire and even denied knowing Gillian Kane, a girl to whom he had been engaged and had planned to marry. During this questioning, he became aggressive and excited, and started roaring and screaming. Seconds later, he would sit down and apologise for his behaviour and for losing his temper. Despite prolonged and intensive questioning, he denied all responsibility for the fire at Kane's house and continued to deny that he had ever known Gillian Kane.

We asked him to tell us the truth about the campaign of terror he waged against the Kane family after Gillian broke off the engagement.

Connell just jumped off the chair and started marching about the room shouting abuse. Seconds later, he sat down and started singing a song. At one stage, in a strange move by Connell, he tried to sit on my lap. Despite the gravity of the charges against him, we couldn't help but be privately amused by his outlandish behaviour. We tried several more times to contact his solicitor but to no avail. He was offered food and the statutory rest period in the cell by the custody sergeant but refused both, claiming that he suffered from claustrophobia.

Eventually at 11.20 p.m., we finally made contact with his solicitor. Connell was handed the telephone to speak but became completely irrational and started screaming for help. We had to take the phone from him. In his paranoid state, he became convinced that we had set up the call and that he had not been speaking to his solicitor at all. He then began to recite like a mantra, 'Fuck off for Christ's sake,' over and over again.

At around midnight, we told him we were putting him to bed in a cell for the night. He begged and pleaded with us not to be placed in a cell but that request fell on deaf ears. We were glad to see the back of him that night and eventually the custody sergeant arrived at the room and escorted him to the cell, despite all his protestations. The following day we brought his ex-fiancée to the station to confront him. She had bravely agreed to help in the investigation despite her overwhelming fear and revulsion at the prospect of having to face him again. In his presence and hearing, we asked Miss Kane a number of questions. Connell never spoke while she was there, but when she got up to leave he said, 'I'm sorry for everything, Gillian.'

After she was gone, I spoke to him again about the arson attack at her home. Connell replied this time, 'I cannot deny it any longer, Gerry. I'll tell the truth about the fire.' I then took a detailed statement from Connell in which he admitted carrying out the arson attack. Later that same evening, Chief Superintendent Courtney served an extension order, directing the further detention of Connell for a period of 24 hours. Detective Canavan and I continued to question him and asked him to tell us the truth about the night of the Frauchan Festival, when he went missing from his fiancée, Mary Creedon, for three-quarters of an hour after telling her that he was going to speak to a girl that he had previously dated.

Earlier in the day, Connell had said that when he left the beer tent, he had spoken to a friend called Nella Allen. We told him that we had located and spoken to that woman and that she had not attended the Frauchan Festival on the night of the murder. When he was told that, he changed his story again and said that he had never left the beer tent that night; that Mary Creedon was telling lies. We told him that he was the liar, and that Mary had come across as a very truthful person who had been terrorised into telling lies to cover up for him. I put it straight to him that the reason he was lying about his absence was that he was with Patricia and had crossed over into Corbett's Field with her and had strangled her to death with her own blouse. Shortly after this interview, we took him to the cells for a second night.

The following day, 22 May, I was back at Tallaght station by three o'clock. At this time, I was aware that Connell had confessed to the murder of Patricia Furlong and had made a full inculpatory written statement. I went into the room where Connell was being interviewed. He looked calm and relaxed. When my colleague asked him how he was feeling, Connell replied, 'I feel terrible about it all, but I have it all deep in a cavity in my brain.' Connell then proceeded to tell us the gruesome details of how he snuffed out Patricia Furlong's young life.

'I cannot recall accurately how much I had to drink. At one stage in the evening, I went to the toilet and met a lady that I knew. I can't recall her name now. I spent up to ten minutes talking to her. We were talking about roller skating, probably because she was a customer of mine at the Top Hat in Dun Laoghaire, where I was assistant manager. Actually, I know her name. It was Trish from the Top Hat. She had aspirations to get on my roller-disco dancing team. When she would come to the Top Hat ballroom, she would always come over and acknowledge me. She did not come to me for roller-skating lessons.

'After a few minutes, she and I decided to go for a walk down the road. We walked down the main road. I don't exactly remember the route, but it was down the main road. Somewhere down the road, we saw a gate. It was locked, but we climbed over it. She was very tipsy, so I had to help her over it. I don't really remember what type of gate it was, but it was some form of farm iron gate. The field inside was newly mown, with a slope at the end of it towards the road. I put my arm around her shoulder and then she slapped me in the face. We were a good few yards into the field when this happened. This really incensed me and I hit her back. Then I lost my rag altogether and began to choke her with my hands. She began to scream, but I had to stop her. She fell to the ground.

'During the struggle the clothing from the top half of her body came up around her neck. At this stage, she had stopped shouting. The clothing that came up around her neck was a T-shirt and bra and some type of light jacket. I pulled her clothing up tight around her neck to stop her from shouting. I panicked and tied them around her neck and squeezed around her neck. During the struggle, I . . . actually there was very little struggle. Her handbag fell to the ground and some of the contents fell out of it. There was a little make-up, door keys, perfume and a little diary. I can't recall any money, and there were some women's toiletries. I took the diary and some of the cosmetics away with me . . . I threw the bag down the field from where Trish was lying. Then I got onto the road over a nearby wall and walked back down towards Johnnie Fox's Pub where I threw the diary and cosmetic items into a hedge. I then went back to the beer tent to Mary. There was some kind of fight going on.

'I don't know what I said to Mary when I went back. I was very upset, but I didn't tell Mary what had happened. We stayed on in the beer tent for a short while after that and went home at 3 a.m. I heard the next day she had died. I did not know she was dead when I left her – she was breathing lightly. When I met Trish, I had no intention of killing her. I did not mean to do it.'

After he had signed the statement, Connell asked us if we could take him to the bathroom so he could wash and shave. We duly obliged. We waited as he washed and changed his clothing. He was in great form. He acted as if a huge weight had been lifted from his shoulders but was showing little remorse for his crimes. He then requested his guitar and said he would like to sing us a song. He chose Billy Joel's 'Piano Man'. It was a bizarre display, but we humoured him. He was acting like a condemned man having his last meal. We took him from the station to the court in Chancery Street that evening. There he was formally charged by the judge with the murder of Patricia Furlong. He pleaded not guilty and was remanded in custody in Mountjoy Prison, his former workplace. The following day, along with other detectives and under warrant, I searched his house on Neagh Road. In the shed beside the house, I found threatening letters of the most sickening kind that he was preparing to send to the home of his ex-fiancée, Mary Creedon. Even after eight years, he hadn't forgiven or forgotten her and was still continuing the vendetta, as he had done with his similar hate campaign against the Kane family.

In his bedroom, I took possession of certain items, including a military-style uniform that he had brought back from South Africa. While he was there, he had joined an extreme right-wing militia. His fascination for all organisations that wore a uniform was obviously undiminished.

Connell remained in custody pending his trial for the murder of Patricia Furlong. The trial commenced in October 1991, almost 17 months after his arrest in the Fleet Bar. The trial lasted 42 days and at the time was the longest trial in the history of the state.

It was also the first time that cumulative sum stylometry, also known as the cusum method, was introduced into an Irish court of law. I have dealt with the system already in this book and my contemptuous opinions on it have been well elucidated. There was a good deal of consternation amongst our legal team that this unproved theory was to be introduced as part of Connell's defence, but it was ultimately the decision of the trial judge to allow it as evidence. The defence called on Dr Farrington to attempt to discredit the written confession of the accused. He tried to persuade the jury that his method of cumulative sum stylometry would prove that Connell's statement was a fake and had been concocted by the interrogating police officers.

Our prosecuting barrister, the late Eamon Leahy, who possessed an awesome legal mind, completely demolished Dr Farrington's far-fetched and unproven theories. He exposed the cusum method as nonsensical gobbledygook that would never be accepted in an Irish court. In a 1993 article in the Forensic Science Society journal my opinions were backed up on the issue. The author wrote that the system should not be accepted in court proceedings as providing trustworthy evidence unless and until the system is refined and properly validated.

This lengthy trial was not without its moments of high drama. On one occasion midway through the process, Connell's legal counsel alleged that his client was denied legal representation on the first night of his detention in Tallaght Garda station. In fact, nothing could have been further from the truth because, as previously mentioned, we had spent half the night trying to get in contact with his solicitor. By a most incredible coincidence, a member of the public who was following the proceedings at the Central Criminal Court read in the newspapers of Connell's allegations. He contacted us and handed us an audio tape which he had been handed as a sample tape when purchasing a tape recorder in an electronics shop on Capel Street. He said that the transaction took place sometime during the summer of 1990. When he got home, he played the tape and there was a message on it that he thought we would be interested in. It turned out to be a vital piece of evidence and completely contradicted the allegation of Connell regarding his denial of legal representation. This is the transcript of that tape:

'Hello, my name is Vincent Andrew Connell.

'I am here in Tallaght Garda station. I have been arrested in connection with some fires. I would like you to contact me as soon as possible.

'My name again is Vincent Andrew Connell.'

We listened to the tape and recognised beyond any doubt the voice of Vincent Connell. It was one of the voice messages he had left on the answering machine of his solicitor on 20 May 1990. How the tape ended up in a shop on Capel Street remains a mystery, but it was a fortuitous occurrence that helped us prove Connell to be a blatant liar.

On another occasion during the trial when Connell was giving evidence on his own behalf, he made an allegation claiming that the statement he made admitting to the murder was a tissue of lies that he had been forced to sign because of the rough treatment he had received. He said that he had signed the statement 'V. Connell' so that when his case came to trial it would indicate to the judge and the jury the falsity of his statement. He told the jury that he had never in all his life in all the thousands of documents that he had signed used the signature 'V. Connell'.

Detective Sergeant Gerard McDonnell was sitting in the court. He had prepared the Garda report and was involved in the original inquiry in Stepaside in 1982. In the run-up to the trial, he had answered hundreds of queries from Connell's defence team. He knew more about the Patricia Furlong murder and about Vincent Connell than any other detective on the case. He was certain that Connell was lying through his teeth. When the case resumed after lunch, Sergeant McDonnell produced for the court not one but two letters that Connell had written from South Africa to the Garda commissioner's office in the Phoenix Park applying for a police certificate of character. He had signed both documents 'V. Connell'. He had told the judge and jury a brazen lie that totally undermined his defence and credibility.

The trial also had its lighter moments. One day, the defence team submitted a 95-page document to the judge in which they made the application that the beer tent should be re-erected on the site near Johnnie Fox's Pub in Glencullen, and that Vincent Connell with his defence team and the judge and jury should visit the scene but without the presence of any Gardaí. The judge, Mr Justice Richard Johnson, an extremely wise and experienced man, leaned forward on the Bench, as if he could not believe what he was hearing. The judge dismissed the application without hesitation.

There was yet another dramatic development before the proceedings came to a close. The intrinsic weakness in the prosecution case was our failure to find anybody who had been at the festival on the night of the murder who personally knew Connell and witnessed him leaving the marquee area with Patricia Furlong. The redoubtable Sergeant McDonnell in his trawl through almost 1,000 statements came up with a witness who would redress this situation. There was tremendous excitement in the court at the prospect of hearing this witness. Statements of additional evidence were served on Connell's defence team that morning. This witness took the stand and was sworn in. He told a hushed and expectant court that he had known Vincent Andrew Connell and Mary Creedon personally; he had, in fact, introduced them to each other. He told the court that on the night of the murder he saw Vincent Connell leaving the marquee area sometime after midnight with a young woman who was 'definitely' not Mary Creedon.

Connell, who was shaking his head, slumped forward in the dock and buried his face in his hands. He appeared to be on the point of collapse. He knew this evidence would put the final nail in his coffin. During the course of his testimony, Connell made serious and unsubstantiated allegations of ill-treatment and assault against certain members of An Garda Síochána who had interviewed him, myself included. I was able to rebut those baseless charges during my evidence to the jury, as he had made some outrageous suggestions to me on 29 May 1990. On that occasion, Detective Inspector Canavan and I were taking him from Mountjoy Prison to a court appearance. He turned to me and said, 'Gerry, if I get bail, will you consider coming to live with me, and will you protect me?' I told him not to be talking nonsense. It put paid to the scurrilous allegations he had made against me. The jury would hardly believe that if I had assaulted him he would have sought my protection.

The trial ended on 19 December. The jury went out and after seven hours of deliberation, they returned a unanimous verdict that he was guilty of the murder of Patricia Furlong. Judge Johnson sentenced him to life imprisonment, the only sentence that can be imposed for those convicted of murder in this jurisdiction. Connell was still protesting his innocence and screaming, 'I didn't kill her, I didn't murder her!', as he was dragged away in handcuffs to begin his sentence.

The marathon trial had been a gruelling ordeal for everyone involved, not least for the Furlong family who had attended every minute of the trial. The family, who had maintained a dignified presence throughout, became very emotional, and embraced and hugged one another and thanked us for our support and encouragement to them over the past eight years. Even hardened detectives were emotional. I know I was. I was particularly happy for the victim's family, who had endured that long nightmare but now, at last, the search for justice for their beloved Patricia had ended.

Vincent Connell subsequently appealed against his conviction, and on 3 April 1995 the Court of Criminal Appeal delivered its judgment. Mr Justice Egan, who was one of the Appellate Court, said that the appeal had succeeded on very narrow grounds. The judgment states that Connell had been deprived of legal advice, and there had been technical breaches of the Garda custody regulations. On those grounds, the court quashed his conviction for murder. He was released on bail with the most stringent conditions attached to it. One of the conditions was that he had to reside with Franciscan monks in a centre for peace and reconciliation in Rossnowlagh in County Donegal, and had to sign on each day at the local Garda station at Ballyshannon.

There were still ten very serious charges outstanding against him, which included three attempted murders and serious assaults on four women, as well as the arson charges. I had charged him with these offences in June or July 1990 while he was still in custody. On 17 April 1996, Connell again appeared for his trial on the outstanding charges at the Central Criminal Court in Dublin. That day, on the direction of the DPP, the charges for the attempted murder of three women were withdrawn, as were the two outstanding arson charges. Connell pleaded guilty to four remaining charges of assault occasioning actual bodily harm against Gillian Kane, Mary Creedon, Agnes Long and Barbara Rooney. He had seriously assaulted his fiancée, Gillian Kane, in the Kelly's hotel in South Great Georges Street in Dublin in 1978. Gillian and Vincent were celebrating their engagement, which had taken place a couple of days earlier. At 1 a.m. that night, Gillian was pushed into a toilet by a drink-crazed Connell. He gave her a vicious beating, knocking her unconscious. When confronted, he told the hotel owner that Gillian had suicidal tendencies and had deliberately injured herself by banging her head against a wash-hand basin. It would take months before she recovered from the resulting bruising and swelling. Gillian was lucky to have escaped with her life that night.

When she broke off their engagement, he instigated a campaign of terror against her and her parents, Ned and Phyllis. He burgled their house, and stole clothing and other articles. On two occasions, he poured petrol through the letter box and almost burned the house to the ground. On the second attempt, Gillian and her parents only just escaped with their lives.

Connell also paid two criminals almost £3,000 to break into the house, and rape and torture Gillian's mother. He even gave instructions on the methods that they were to use to carry out his diabolical plan.

The two criminals did call to the house, intending to carry out his instructions, but when they saw Mrs Kane, a beautiful and kindly woman, they had a change of heart and left. I interviewed one of those thugs, a hardened criminal with a string of previous convictions. He told me that when they realised what a vile monster Connell was, he and his accomplice had intended to lure him up to the high-rise flats in Ballymun and hurl him over the balcony to his death. They said they made several attempts, but Connell smelt a rat. They never gave him back the three grand. This criminal, who is himself serving a long prison sentence, had christened Connell 'the man of a thousand faces'. Connell had met him when he was working as a prison officer in Mountjoy.

Another of the four remaining charges against Connell was an assault on Mary Creedon, to whom he had also been engaged. This happened at a party in the city centre when Connell, who was drunk at the time, saw her talking to another man and went insane with jealousy. He grabbed her around the neck and tried to strangle her. She only escaped his clutches by kicking him in the groin. Mary believes to this day that he would have choked her to death that night. As it was, she ended up with severe bruising and black eyes from the beating.

The third charge was for an assault that took place in May 1981. He was going out with a new girlfriend, a nurse called Agnes Long. Towards the end of that month, they were out together at a nightclub in Dun Laoghaire. Connell again was drunk and because he saw her talking to another man he attacked her, punching her in the face and throttling her to the point where she thought she was going to be killed. He also inflicted several burns on her neck and shoulders with a cigarette.

The fourth charge related to an assault on Barbara Rooney, who had the misfortune to meet and fall in love with Connell. He moved into her apartment in Melrose Avenue in Clontarf in November 1989, after he had come back from South Africa. Later that same month, they went out for a drink. When they returned to her apartment, Connell accused her of flirting with another man in the pub before flying into one of his insane, jealous rages. He grabbed a knife and threatened to slit her throat, saying that anyone who interfered would get the same treatment. Connell then dropped the knife and grabbed her around her throat. She felt sure he was going to kill her and passed out with sheer terror. When she woke, she was in bed beside a sleeping Connell.

I gave evidence to the court that all four women were severely traumatised, and had a primeval, unnatural fear that could not be assuaged. I told the judge that the four victims regarded Connell as the incarnation of all evil, and lived in mortal dread of him. I told him that I had never seen people so terrified of another human being as these four young women were. After hearing my evidence and that of Detective Sergeant McDonnell, Judge Budd handed down sentences to Connell totalling twelve years but suspended the sentences on the condition that Connell 'enter into a bond to keep the peace and be of good behaviour for twelve years and keep away from the four victims and their families'.

He walked free from the court and I never saw him again. He had spent five years and one month in custody. On leaving the court, the unrepentant, remorseless Connell made a last defiant speech to waiting reporters.

He announced with breathtaking hypocrisy and a brass neck that he had pleaded guilty to crimes that he did not commit. He stated:

'I pleaded guilty to four crimes I did not commit under threat from the state of having to undergo a lengthy trial on further serious charges, including arson, which I firmly believe never took place, and was a device used to arrest me and hold me for forty-eight hours under the Offences against the State Act. None of these incidents took place and I pleaded guilty to one incident at Peekers Hotel in Dun Laoghaire, a place I have never been in my life.'

Connell further stated that it was his intention to go abroad, saying, 'What would you do after going through what I have been through?' For the Furlong family, he added further insult to injury when he said, 'They, the family, have been brainwashed by the police into believing that I was responsible for her murder.'

Along with the other detectives who were involved in the case and who had spent so much time and effort over the past eight years, I was bitterly disappointed at the trial judge's decision to suspend the twelve-year sentence. The lenient sentence also enraged many women's groups. In a hard-hitting statement published in the *Irish Independent* newspaper on 19 April, one group called Women's Aid stated:

> We ask how in 1996, a year in which we are witnessing the rape, murder and disappearance of women in ever increasing numbers, the judiciary and the courts of this country refuse to send out a clear message that violence against women will not be tolerated in any civilised society.

In this case, as in so many other serious cases I was involved in, the punishment certainly did not fit the crime. The scales of justice had inexorably tilted, once again in favour of the criminal.

Connell was acquitted by the Court of Criminal Appeal on the flimsiest of technical grounds, namely minor breaches of the Garda custody regulations. He had been found guilty of murder by a jury of his peers. I firmly believe, as do the Furlong family and colleagues involved in the investigation, that Vincent Connell murdered Patricia Furlong. The case is closed and will never be re-opened.

We were complimented in the most glowing terms possible for our handling of the case by the top law officer in the state, the Director of Public Prosecutions. In a letter written to one of the officers in the case, he states as follows:

> However, the real credit in this case goes to the investigating Gardaí. This is not a polite response to your letter. At the time of my original directions in this case, I formed and expressed the view that it was one of the most skilful and painstaking investigations which I had encountered in 17 years' experience of Garda investigation files. I remain of that view.

The letter was signed by the Director, Eamon Barnes, and was dated 3 March 1992.

In my long career as a policeman, I never met another criminal who had so intrigued and fascinated me as much as Vinnie Connell. He was described by all who knew him as a 'Jekyll and Hyde' character: he could be charming, courteous and a perfect gentleman one moment and the next he would turn into a raging homicidal maniac.

When he lived in South Africa, he had been the Gay Byrne of the airwaves on his Sunday morning radio show 'Sunday Braii'. He was extremely popular and raised thousands of pounds for animal welfare organisations and other charities. On one occasion, he helped to raise over £500,000 to fund liver transplants for two girls, Samantha Bunce and Nikky Hobowsky, who knew him as 'Uncle Vince', their saviour. In 1987, after a whirlwind romance, he married Felicity Louw. When she threatened to break it off with him, he said he would harm her parents. She married him and endured six months of hell before the marriage broke up. Her daughter, Sally, whom he also viciously assaulted, called him 'a brutal man with an uncontrollable temper. Twice he beat me up for trying to get Mum to leave. He hit her with anything he could lay his hands on.'

On one occasion during the trial, I met a couple from South Africa who were touring Ireland. They had seen the publicity surrounding the trial and called to see me at Sundrive Road Garda station. They told me their names were Denis and Lorraine Raine from Port Elizabeth. They told me that Connell, the man on trial for murder, had had a brief relationship with their daughter, Denise. One night after coming back from a party an argument broke out between them and he attacked her with a hammer, leaving her permanently paralysed down one side of her body. Despite their pleadings, she refused to report him to the police because she believed that he would burn down her parents' home. I sympathised with the Raines but told them that I was powerless to bring him to justice for that terrible crime.

During a search of his house on 23 May 1990, I found a letter from St Paul's Retreat, Mount Argus, Dublin, dated 6 April 1970. It stated:

> To whom it concerns,
> Vincent Connell of Neagh Road, Dublin 6, has been known to me for some five years. I have always found him to be of upright character and can positively recommend him for any position involving honesty and responsibility.
> Yours sincerely,
> Father X

In typical Vinnie Connell fashion, he had conned the trusting priest into believing that he was a paragon of virtue. Another item I found amongst his personal papers was a handwritten book of poetry that went some way to explain the disturbed psychopath that was Vincent Connell. There was a dedication to his mother on the front page. In the most poignant and tender words, he asked for her forgiveness for all the hurt, suffering and misery he had caused her. In a searing flash of self-revelation he confided to her that 'he was driven by demons he could not control, to the very gates of hell'. I sat on the side of the bed enthralled and read his poems, which I can only describe as truly original. I marvelled at how such a sick and twisted mind could produce such sensitive, perceptive writings.

On 21 March 1998, police officers from the Hampshire Constabulary broke down the door of a house on Eastern Road, Portsmouth, in the south of England, and found the body of Vincent Connell. He had last been seen alive on 11 March. When they found him he was in a kneeling position, face down in the corner of the room. A subsequent post-mortem revealed that he had died from a massive heart attack.

It is difficult to have sympathy for this evil man who caused so much pain, suffering and fear to the very human beings who loved him. He died alone and unloved without anybody to hold his hand or whisper him an act of contrition in his ear. Perhaps only in death would Vincent Connell finally find peace from the demons that had pursued him all his short and troubled life.

20

DEATH OF A PRIEST

IN THE SUMMER OF 1986, I WAS IN THE COMPUTER SECTION OF GARDA headquarters in the Phoenix Park. As I was computer illiterate, I found my time there the most unrewarding and frustrating period in my entire career. However, at that time, I became embroiled in the investigation into the killing of Father Niall Molloy after receiving confidential information surrounding the mysterious circumstances of his violent death. In June that year, Richard Flynn, a businessman from Clara in County Offaly, had gone on trial in the Circuit Criminal Court in Dublin for the manslaughter of the Roscommon-born parish priest. On the Sunday morning, 6 July 1985, Father Molloy's body had been found in a bedroom at Richard and Theresa Flynn's home at Kilcoursey House, Clara, County Offaly. There was some confusion as to the time of death, but it may have occurred sometime between one o'clock and three o'clock in the morning. The real truth of what happened that night will never be known. All that we do know comes from the limited evidence given by Richard Flynn and other witnesses, and from the medical evidence that emerged during the trial.

In brief, these are the events leading to the tragic death of the priest. That Saturday, Maureen, the daughter of Richard and Theresa, married

Ralph Parkes, the son of a well-known local businessman. The wedding reception was held in a marquee in the grounds of the Flynn mansion. Father Molloy attended the reception but left after a couple of hours to celebrate Mass with his parishioners in his church in Castlecoote, County Roscommon. He returned to Kilcoursey House for a buffet lunch later that afternoon. In the evening, when almost all the guests had left, Father Molloy and Richard and Theresa Flynn drove to a friend's house for drinks. The three then returned to Kilcoursey House at around half-nine. When they got home, the newly married Maureen and her sister were still there. Shortly afterwards, they left to join their other sister Zandra and their brother David, his wife Anne, and Maureen's new husband for celebratory drinks in White's pub in Clara. Afterwards, they returned to David and Anne's house to round off the evening.

Meanwhile back at Kilcoursey House, Father Molloy and Richard Flynn had a nightcap. It would appear that Theresa said her goodnights and went to her bedroom, feeling tired after the long day. Very little is known of the exact sequence of events that followed, but it would appear that at some stage, Father Molloy went up to speak to Richard and Theresa in their bedroom.

At around one o'clock that morning, Richard Flynn telephoned Father James Deignan, the local parish priest, and told him that there had been a terrible tragedy and to come quickly to the house. Father Deignan was only a few minutes' drive away. When he got there, Richard Flynn met him at the hall door and escorted him to the bedroom, where he saw a man lying down on the floor. He started to administer the last rites to him, not knowing at this time that the man was a fellow priest.

From Father Deignan's evidence it would appear that Father Molloy was still alive at this stage. However, incredible as it may seem, it was one whole hour before either Richard Flynn or Father Deignan summoned medical help for the dying man. This delay was explained by both men in the most unconvincing manner. Their efforts were at best bungling and inept. Father Deignan said that he tried to look up the telephone numbers of some local doctors but couldn't read the pages of the phonebook because he had forgotten his reading glasses. It is unbelievable that neither of them thought of dialling the emergency services for an ambulance, which just might have saved the priest's life. In fact, it was around two o'clock when Dr O'Sullivan finally arrived at the house, examined Father Molloy and pronounced him dead. He said he saw Theresa Flynn lying on the bedroom floor in a highly distressed and agitated state, sobbing uncontrollably. Dr O'Sullivan said he made several attempts to calm her down and had in the end administered a sedative to her.

By this time, David Flynn and his wife, along with Ralph Parkes, Maureen and the other Flynn sisters, Anita and Zandra, had arrived at the house. According to what Dr O'Sullivan later told the Gardaí, Richard Flynn told him that there had been an argument downstairs and Father Molloy had come into his bedroom later, where a row broke out. Richard Flynn told him that Father Molloy and his wife had attacked him, and he had retaliated and knocked both of them out.

At around three o'clock, Theresa Flynn was taken to Tullamore General Hospital by Dr O'Sullivan. She had suffered bruising to her left cheek and the doctor stated later that he was also worried that she might be suffering from concussion. Maureen and Anita accompanied them by car to the hospital.

Father Deignan then drove to Clara Garda station, where he spoke to Sergeant Kevin Forde. He told Sergeant Forde that there was a dead priest in Richard and Theresa Flynn's bedroom in Kilcoursey House. He told the sergeant that Father Molloy had hit his head off the bedroom wall. He asked him if the whole thing could be hushed up, as it would create a dreadful scandal in the parish.

Sergeant Forde told him that there would have to be a full Garda investigation into the death. The sergeant then drove to Kilcoursey House, arriving at about 3.30 a.m. Richard Flynn spoke to him and told him that there had been a stupid row over drink and that he had been attacked by Father Molloy and his wife, and he had retaliated in self-defence by striking both of them with his fists. He mentioned that he had struck Father Molloy a number of times. Richard Flynn appeared to have bruising on his hands. Sergeant Forde was then joined by a senior colleague. Richard Flynn was asked but refused to make a written statement about what happened that night.

The following day, Theresa Flynn was interviewed at the hospital but said she had no recollection of what had happened except waking up and seeing Father Molloy lying on the floor. That day a team of detectives were dispatched from the Investigation Section in Garda headquarters to assist in what was now a possible murder inquiry.

The scene in the bedroom, which had been preserved, was examined by experts from the Garda Technical Bureau. They found blood on the outside and the inside of the bedroom door, and minute quantities in a number of other locations in the bedroom, including the headboard and on the clothes of Richard, Theresa and Father Molloy. They found an eight-foot-long and nine-inch-wide bloody drag mark on the white bedroom carpet leading from the bed to the bedroom door.

Dr John Harbison performed a post-mortem on the body of Father Molloy on Sunday evening at Tullamore General Hospital. His examination found no evidence of heart attack, thrombosis or hypertension to the liver. He concluded that Father Molloy died of pulmonary oedema as a result of sustaining head injuries.

During the course of the investigation, it emerged that Father Molloy and Theresa Flynn were involved in a business deal to purchase some of the land at Kilcoursey House from Richard Flynn for £35,000. Father Molloy and Theresa hoped to put down a deposit of £24,000 between them. We know that this business was conducted in 1984 at the offices of Mr Egan, Father Molloy's solicitor. It was well known at the time that Richard Flynn was having financial difficulties. There was nothing unusual about their dealings – they had known each other for over 28 years and had mutual business interests and a love of horses. However, shortly afterwards, this particular deal fell through, and Father Molloy was very concerned when his deposit of £11,000 was not returned to him. It also emerged that Father Molloy had sold a horse around that time for £6,000 and lodged the money in his personal account instead of the joint account he shared with Theresa Flynn. Apparently, this action on his part had become a source of friction between them.

After the investigation file was examined by the DPP, the direction was given to charge Richard Flynn with the manslaughter of Father Molloy. His trial took place in the Circuit Criminal Court in Dublin in June 1986 before Judge Frank Roe, a very experienced trial judge. From beginning to premature end, it was a strange and unsettling trial. The Molloy family observed in disbelief and growing unease as witness after witness was excused from cross-examination, the prerogative of the defence team. The trial was moving at breakneck speed. Dr Harbison was called to the witness stand and gave evidence that Father Molloy had died from head injuries due to pulmonary oedema and not from any underlying heart disease or other medical condition.

Richard and Theresa Flynn never took the witness stand. At the end of the prosecution case, Richard Flynn's defence counsel addressed the judge in the absence of the jury. In his inimitable way the defence barrister outlined to the judge his own version of the likely scenario that occurred in the Flynns' bedroom that night, which led to the priest's death. He postulated that the injuries to Father Molloy could have been sustained as his head struck against the bedpost, then the bedboard and finally the floor, following the assault by Richard Flynn. The forensic evidence in this case did not support that dubious theory.

Despite Richard Flynn's own admission that he was responsible for Father Molloy's death and the clear-cut medical evidence of the cause of death, Judge Roe instructed that the jury bring in a verdict of not guilty. It was a surprising and controversial decision that shocked and angered the Molloy family. They watched in abject disbelief as Richard Flynn walked out of the court a free man.

Following his acquittal, there was widespread public disquiet. The Molloy family called for a public inquiry into the whole affair and were supported in their call by a number of leading politicians, including Liam Skelly TD. Skelly had been one of the most vociferous and strident opponents of Judge Lynch and the tribunal report into the Kerry Babies case. He has subsequently become an ally and a close friend of mine, and was one of the few public representatives who supported our campaign for justice.

A week after that trial, I received confidential information from a highly respected medical source concerning the death of Father Molloy. For obvious legal reasons I am constrained from making public those startling revelations; however, I submitted detailed reports of same to the assistant commissioner in the Crime Branch in Garda headquarters.

By June that year, I was meeting Liam Skelly on a regular basis to discuss tactics in my ongoing confrontation with the Garda authorities. Skelly told me that he had been approached by Ian Maher, a nephew of Father Molloy, who had asked for his support in their efforts to have a public inquiry into the death of their loved one. Skelly told me that the Molloy family were totally devastated at the conduct and outcome of the recent trial and believed that the truth about the death of their relative had not been properly examined. The family, having been refused a public inquiry, were now pinning their hopes on the public inquest that was due to be held shortly. Skelly told me that he had been apprised by the family of certain aspects in the case that they found disturbing. He told me he was making discreet inquiries into these allegations to establish if there was any truth in them. I told him that by a strange coincidence I was also checking out new quite dramatic revelations that had recently come to my attention. Liam Skelly was aware at the time that I was 'grounded' in the Computer Section, but I assured him that if he shared with me whatever information he had from the family, I would investigate it fully in conjunction with the information that had come into my possession. We agreed that day that we would work closely together in the interests of the Molloy family.

During the conversation I had with my informant, he spoke about the bloody eight-foot drag mark on the white carpet in the Flynn bedroom that had never been explained. He suggested that if I examined the post-mortem photographs of Father Molloy, I might find the answer to that mystery. Later that month, I spoke to the detective inspector from the Investigation Section who had been in charge of the Molloy case. I told him about the information I had on the case, and I asked him for the post-mortem photographs of Father Molloy to check out certain aspects of the report I had received. He agreed to hand them over to me later that day. When he didn't show up at my office, I went directly to the Photographic Section and spoke to the detective who had taken the photos of the body. I told him that I needed to examine the pictures to check out the veracity of certain information I had received about Father Molloy's death. Later that day, I received the images in question.

Towards the end of June, I travelled to Castlereagh in County Roscommon accompanied by Deputy Liam Skelly to carry out further inquiries. I spoke to Mona Molloy, Father Molloy's sister-in-law, at the family home in Carraghroe House. I identified myself and told her that I was making inquiries about the death of Father Niall because of certain information that had come into my possession. She then confided in me that a couple of weeks before his death, he told her that his parish house in Castlecoote had been burgled and that personal papers and important legal documents had been stolen. She said he had been extremely upset at the loss of those valuable documents and papers but did not report the matter to the Gardaí. He told her that nothing else had been stolen, even though there was a considerable sum of money and valuable silver trophies in plain view on the sideboard. She said that, following the theft, he said he was sick to the heart of the greed and materialism of an increasingly Godless world.

Father Molloy then informed her that he was going to sell all his property, everything he owned, and request a posting from the bishop to the mission fields of South America. Father Molloy's stated intentions would appear to completely contradict Theresa Flynn's statement that he wanted to purchase land at Kilcoursey to build a house and retire there.

Later that day, we drove to Castlecoote to say a prayer at Father Molloy's grave. He is buried in the little graveyard beside the parish church. She told us that the family had been distraught following the recent trial, that there had been malicious gossip circulating of some sort of sexual impropriety surrounding his death, which had further increased the anguish and hurt of the family. She told us she was certain that he had never broken his priestly vows. He had always been a kind, gentle and peace-loving man, and had never raised his hand in anger to another human being. Before we said our farewells that evening, she handed me Father Molloy's wristwatch, which I had requested. The glass face was shattered and it had stopped at 10.40. She assured me that she had received it from the Gardaí in that condition, along with other items of his property.

I had the watch examined later by a professional watchmaker. He identified it as an expensive Favre-Leuba watch with a gold bracelet. He confirmed that the face was made from specially toughened glass and was almost indestructible. He concluded that it could not have been broken by merely falling to the ground, but was probably broken by being struck by another object with great force. Father Molloy was wearing that watch on his left wrist the night he died.

Following my visit to Castereagh, I spoke to Father Deignan and Dr O'Sullivan, who had rendered both spiritual and medical attention to Father Molloy at Kilcoursey House, to clear up some other matters about the case.

283

During the course of making further inquiries, I spoke to a local who mentioned to me that Cardinal Tomas O'Fiach had telephoned the station a number of times that Sunday in June 1985 inquiring about the circumstances surrounding Father Molloy's death.

In early July, my inquiries were complete. I passed on all the information I had in my possession to the assistant commissioner in the Crime Branch in headquarters. One week later, two detective superintendents paid an official visit to my office and demanded the return of the post-mortem photographs. My investigation into this murky affair must have set alarm bells ringing around Garda headquarters. I protested that I deeply resented their actions, which inferred that I was acting outside my authority by pursuing my own investigations into Father Molloy's death. It would appear that I had got myself into hot water in my efforts to shed some light into the darker corners of this tragic affair. With reluctance, I handed back the photographs and they left. The two superintendents then interrogated the detective who had handed over the photographs to me.

I stated that I felt it was my duty, despite my current restrictions, to investigate any information that came to my attention in relation to the death of Father Molloy. I further stated that, as a member of An Garda Síochána, I was concerned that every scrap of information I had learned that could throw some light on the murky events surrounding the night of the priest's killing be available to the coroner.

The following day, I received a personal letter from the commissioner in which he stated: 'Of course, I agree with you when you rightly state that you, in addition to all members of the force, have a responsibility to assist in the investigation of crime. The case in question is an important one and any item of information coming to our notice must be fully explored.'

The inquest took place a week later and had been eagerly awaited by the Molloy family, as well as the public in the wake of the recent media publicity. During the inquest, Richard Flynn was called to the witness stand to give evidence to the coroner and jury. It was the first time he had spoken in public about the events that took place in Kilcoursey House on the night Father Molloy died. He did not deviate or elaborate on the extremely limited account he had given to the Gardaí about the incident. He gave evidence that his wife, Theresa,

Father Molloy and himself were in the bedroom enjoying a drink and discussing a holiday to France. At some point, his wife suggested that he go downstairs and get more drinks. Richard Flynn then stated that he told his wife that Father Molloy already had a drink and if she wanted one, she should get it herself. He then said that Molloy and his wife suddenly attacked him, and Father Molloy attempted to punch him in a vicious fashion. He went on to tell the court that he punched Father Molloy a couple of times, and he punched his wife and knocked her unconscious. When questioned, he couldn't explain why the priest's body was dragged across the bedroom floor. He said he couldn't remember anything else that happened.

Theresa Flynn had even less recollection of the night's events. She only remembered waking up and seeing the body of Father Molloy on the bedroom floor. She had no memory of a row having taken place and was unable to shed light on any other aspects of the case.

Dr Harbison was then called to the stand. He gave clear, concise and unambiguous evidence that during his examination of the body of Father Molloy he found no evidence of hypertension to the liver, heart attack or thrombosis. He again said that Father Molloy had suffered head injuries that were the cause of his death.

On the second day of the inquest, after all the evidence had been heard, the jury retired to consider their verdict. Within 15 minutes, they returned. Their decision was that Father Molloy had died as a result of head injuries. The Molloy family was overwhelmed with relief. Outside the court, they hugged and embraced one another. Now at least they could console themselves that the truth had finally emerged: their beloved relation had died from head injuries and not through natural courses, which the trial judge had accepted and which had led to the acquittal of Richard Flynn.

Despite a criminal trial and inquest, the death of Father Molloy remains a mystery. It leaves a question mark hanging over the administration of justice in this country. One of the great imponderables of this case is why, despite the overwhelming evidence of Dr Harbison that Father Molloy had died from head injuries, the trial judge did not allow the case to proceed for the jury to decide the issue? One of the imperative maxims of our law is that 'not only must justice be done, but it must be seen to be done'. It was not seen to be done in this instance.

The Molloy family, almost 20 years on, continues its campaign for justice for Father Niall. Billy Maher, Father Molloy's nephew, only recently confirmed to me that the family is renewing its call for a full public inquiry into the death. Below is an excerpt from a statement on behalf of the Molloy family given to me by Billy Maher in April 2004:

> The effect of Fr. Niall's death 19 years ago was not only to rob his family of a kind and gentle pastor and friend but to place them under a dark cloud, which still hangs over us all to this day. Some family members, particularly his nephew Ian Maher, fought with all their strength for justice to be done, lost their jobs and sometimes their health and their family in the process, and perhaps died before their time. There were sometimes temporary breaks in the cloud, when it looked like the truth might somehow be revealed, but which were only to be thwarted by further setbacks.
>
> The greatest of the many injustices done to Father Molloy and his family, apart from the taking of his life, was the damage done to his good name by the calculated and vicious leaking of false innuendo to sully his reputation.
>
> The family may have lost faith in the country's institutions, but they have never lost faith in the intrinsic goodness of the Irish people and their belief that one day someone would look to their conscience, and once and for all reveal the truth.
>
> To facilitate this, the members of Father Niall's family call for a full public inquiry into ALL aspects of this matter, including the roles played by the institutions of the state in preventing the truth from being revealed. Only when this has been done will the family find closure and the cloud will finally be lifted.

The Molloy family has never recovered from the loss of Father Niall, a beloved brother and uncle, and a good shepherd to his flock. He was about to dedicate the rest of his life to the care of the poor and oppressed in the developing world when his life was cruelly ended. Justice has surely failed this family, but their quest for the truth of what happened that fateful night carries on.

21
·······

MASSACRE AT TIBNIN BRIDGE

ON WEDNESDAY, 27 OCTOBER 1982, THREE IRISH UNITED NATIONS
soldiers were shot dead at Tibnin Bridge at checkpoint 6.23A in the
guard area of the Irish Battalion within the UN forces in South
Lebanon. The checkpoint where the incident took place was situated at
a four-way crossing connected to a wide bridge and consisted of a
bunker close to the road with a machine-gun post. The area behind the
concrete bunkers was very hilly. Little valleys known locally as wadis
ran between these hills. That day four soldiers of the 52nd Infantry
Battalion were on duty at the checkpoint. They were Corporal Gregory
Morrow, who was 19 years of age and was the detachment leader,
Private Thomas Murphy, also 19 years old, Private Peter Bourke, who
was 20, and finally Private Michael McAleavy, aged 21 years. They
were all members of A Company.

Corporal Morrow was armed with a sub-machine gun and the
requisite number of rounds of ammunition. The three other soldiers
were armed with the standard Irish Army issue FN rifle and 40 rounds
of ammunition per soldier. The four had taken up duty there at around
two o'clock that day.

The Israeli Army had invaded Lebanon earlier that year, and armed factions of every persuasion were active in the Irish Battalion-controlled area. The most bellicose of these warring elements was the 'South Lebanon Army' commanded by Major Haddad, who was supplied and armed by the Israeli Defence Forces (IDF). His army was little more than a puppet in the hands of Israel but posed a considerable danger to the Irish soldiers trying to keep the peace in the region. The Irish soldiers lived under the constant threat of being injured or killed on their patrols by roadside bombs or indiscriminate shell fire from all factions. In a country torn apart by invasions and civil war, the blue helmets of the UN soldiers were seen as a beacon of hope by the beleaguered and war-weary people. The four Irish soldiers on duty at Tibnin checkpoint that day were fully aware of the perilous nature of their mission. Before the day was out, three of them would be cut down in a hail of bullets, not by the guns of any warring faction but at the hands of a trusted friend and comrade.

The 50th anniversary of Ireland's membership of the United Nations was marked on 14 December 2005. Since our accession, the Irish Defence Forces have had a proud and honourable record of service with the UN in over 30 countries around the world. Indeed, as a young boy I remember well reading and hearing about the bravery and courage of our soldiers in places like Elizabethville, Jadotville and Niemba in the Congo. I can vividly recall the sense of shock and the outpouring of grief in Ireland when the bodies of soldiers who were killed there were brought home for burial.

Irish peacekeepers have earned a well-deserved reputation worldwide for their professionalism, humanity and discipline, and the sensible and even-handed way they have carried out their duties in the face of the most difficult and dangerous front-line situations. One of the longest, and certainly one of the most complex, operations ever undertaken by our defence forces was the UN mission in the Lebanon, or to afford it its official designation, the United Nations Interim Force in Lebanon (UNIFIL).

After Lebanon was invaded, the country was plunged into anarchy and civil war. Bombings, shootings and kidnappings became an everyday occurrence as the various surrogate militias of Syria and Israel waged an unrelenting terrorist campaign for control of different regions of the country. The Irish Battalion was stationed in the southern part of the country and their sphere of influence was known as 'Irish Batt'.

The first indication of any trouble at the checkpoint was an unreadable radio message that was received at 8.40 p.m. at the signal post in neighbouring As Sultaniyah.

'They came in, they came in!' said a garbled and panic-stricken voice. There was a period of heavy breathing and then the words, 'We've been hit, Number 1. Jesus, there's blood all over the place.'

The corporal at the signal post asked, 'What happened?'

'This is Private McAleavy at Checkpoint 6.23A, Tibnin Bridge,' came the reply. 'We've been hit, we've been hit! They're still out there, Number 1.'

The alarm was raised, and Lieutenant Brian Sweeney and Corporal Paul Clarke were dispatched to the scene with a squad of men. When they arrived there, they saw Private McAleavy holding two civilians at gunpoint. There was a BMW car parked alongside with the engine still running. Private McAleavy was in a highly excited and agitated state.

He told Lieutenant Sweeney that he had stopped the BMW because he believed its occupants had opened fire on his unit. It was a scene of utter devastation and confusion. Lieutenant Sweeney and Corporal Clarke found the lifeless body of Private Peter Bourke lying on his back. Close beside him, they found the body of Private Thomas Murphy, also lying on his back, in front of the bunker. At its side was the body of Corporal Gregory Morrow. It was obvious from their injuries that all three soldiers had been shot dead. Private McAleavy told Lieutenant Sweeney that he had gone up to the toilet and was halfway there when he heard shooting. He said that he 'hit the deck' but that he hadn't seen any persons or vehicles prior to the shooting. He had his rifle with him and he returned to the road and fired shots in the direction of the waterhole, where he thought he saw movement, but he couldn't remember how many shots he had fired. He said that moments prior to going to the toilet, one of his colleagues had remarked that he heard a noise near the waterhole. When he saw a car approaching, and suspecting that the occupants had opened fire on his colleagues, he stopped the car and held them at gunpoint, pending the arrival of reinforcements.

McAleavy had been disarmed when Lieutenant Sweeney arrived at the scene because he seemed to be distressed. As the Private was recounting what happened, he suddenly tried to grab a rifle from one of the soldiers. He then lunged at a civilian and punched him, shouting, 'You bastard! You did it!' He was forcibly restrained by his colleagues and taken off to the hospital in nearby Tibnin village, suffering from apparent shock. The civilians were questioned and released. They were unarmed and completely innocent of any involvement in the shooting.

The scene of the carnage was examined by Lieutenant Sweeney and shortly afterwards the three bodies were removed to Tibnin Hospital. They were later taken to the American Hospital in Beirut for further examination. The subsequent post-mortems revealed that Corporal Morrow had been shot four times. The report went on to note, 'It

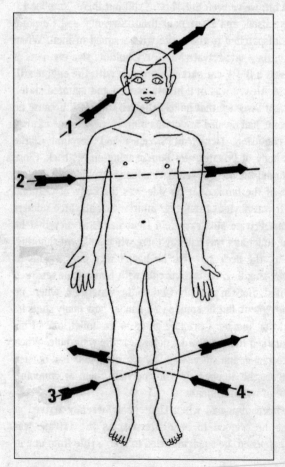

As indicated in the post-mortem, the four shots that killed Corporal Gregory Morrow

would appear that the shot in the head occurred much closer to the moment of death. Perhaps this was the last wound and was inflicted at very close range.'

The post-mortem on Private Murphy revealed that he had been shot eight times and that one of the bullet wounds to the head had been inflicted at point-blank range.

The examination of Private Bourke revealed that he had been shot six times and that one of the bullet wounds was inflicted at point-blank range.

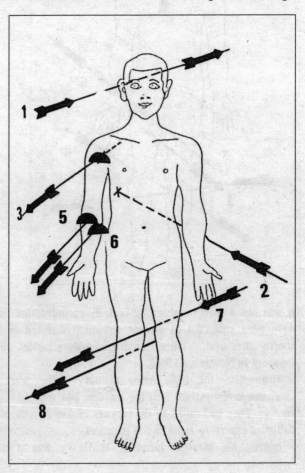

As indicated in the post-mortem, the eight shots that killed Private Thomas Murphy (reproduced as in original)

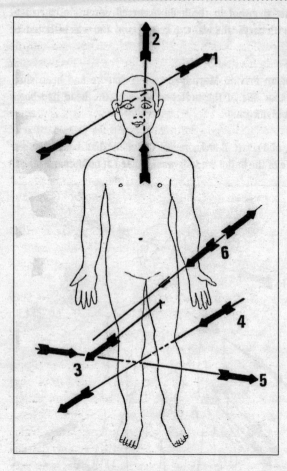

As indicated in the post-mortem, the six shots that killed Private Peter Bourke

It was noted that 'It cannot be entirely excluded that the head may have been subjected to violent treatment directed at the left-half shortly after death.' These examinations were carried out by Dr Jan Lindberg in November 1982.

Meanwhile, the Irish Army Military Police were conducting extensive investigations into the murders but were having very little success. They had called in the services of Ake Abrink, a UN forensic ballistics expert, to assist in the inquiries.

During his stay in hospital, McAleavy was a difficult and

troublesome patient, and never once discussed the events of the night of the killings with medical staff or the chaplain. He was interviewed on a number of occasions by Military Police personnel but was hostile and uncooperative in his dealings with them. He stuck to his story that his three comrades had been shot dead by hostile forces.

In early January 1983, following a top-level discussion between high-ranking army officers and the Minister for Defence, it was decided to call on An Garda Síochána to assist in the murder investigation of the three soldiers. I was one of the detectives selected for the operation. On 19 January 1983, I headed off to the Lebanon with Detective Chief Superintendent Dan Murphy, Detective Inspector Pat Culhane and Detective Sergeant Thomas Connolly from the Investigation Section in Garda headquarters.

When we landed at Beirut airport, I remember noticing the bus that took us from the aircraft to the terminal building had bullet holes in the windscreen. I pointed them out to Chief Superintendent Murphy. 'We're a long way from Dublin now, boss!' I commented.

The atmosphere in the arrivals hall was strangely eerie. Indeed, later that year, on 23 October 1983, 241 US soldiers would be killed in a horrific bomb attack on the airport compound after a truck packed with explosives was detonated there.

Apart from the passengers who had come off our flight, the airport was empty of civilians. Heavily armed soldiers and police on full alert patrolled all areas. War planes from a United States aircraft carrier anchored in the harbour patrolled the skies overhead to protect aircraft landing and taking off from attacks by surface-to-air missiles, which were used extensively by combatants on all sides. It suddenly dawned on us that we were in the middle of a war zone, and we were very relieved when our Irish Army escort arrived to collect us. We were taken by a convoy of Irish UN soldiers of the 52nd Infantry Battalion to the headquarters of the UNIFIL mission in Naquora in South Lebanon.

During the journey south, I was shocked by the devastation all around me. The road was littered with the debris of war: burnt military vehicles, spent bullet cartridges and shell casings were littered along the highway; almost every building we passed was pockmarked by shell fire or had been reduced to a blackened ruin. We passed close to the shattered remains of the Shatila and Sabra refugee camps. It was there that the Phalangist militia had run amok and slaughtered hundreds of defenceless men, women and children, whose charred and broken bodies still lay buried in the ruins.

We reached Naquora on the morning of 20 January, and later that day a conference was held with senior Irish Army personnel, the two Swedish experts, the forensic pathologist Dr Lindberg and Ake Abrink, a UN forensic ballistics expert. The conference lasted most of the day, during which time we were briefed on all aspects of the case. That evening, we were shown to our accommodation in Camp Shamrock, the headquarters of the Irish Battalion. I shared my prefabricated hut with Detective Sergeant Connolly. There were no toilet or washing facilities in them. On our first night there, the temperature fell to well below freezing and no amount of blankets could keep us warm. I took a few slugs from my duty-free whiskey during the night to restore my circulation, but my colleague, a teetotaller, had no such remedy.

The next morning, we went to wash and shave in the communal bathroom. The water had frozen solid in the taps, so we had to use bottled water. I have to admit that over the following nights I was well fortified after my visits to the Officers' Mess and the cold conditions never troubled me again. During our stay with the 52nd Battalion, my colleagues and I were afforded the utmost courtesy, friendship and cooperation, and made to feel so welcome by the officers and their men that the harsh climate and spartan conditions were soon forgotten.

The following day, we travelled by army convoy from Naquora to Tibnin. The next morning, further briefings were held with key military personnel that included the Military Police (MP) at Camp Shamrock. We visited Tibnin Bridge and checkpoint 6.23A, close by the scene of the killings. On the Saturday morning, my colleagues and I were escorted to the headquarters of the Military Police Irish Battalion, known locally as 'Gallows Green'. Like most of the other buildings in the area, it had been severely damaged by shellfire during the recent invasion. The perimeter walls were riddled with holes like Swiss cheese. Blankets suspended from the ceiling separated the different rooms, as most of the internal walls had collapsed. Conditions were little short of primitive. Michael McAleavy had been taken there earlier by the MPs to await our arrival.

Chief Superintendant Murphy and Inspector Culhane began the first interview with McAleavy. Tom and I sat outside the building in the glorious morning sunshine but were warned by one of the MPs to be careful as a nest of poisonous snakes had made their home close to where I sat. From time to time, I heard an angry voice in an unmistakeable Belfast accent coming from the adjoining room. It was obvious that Private McAleavy was not too pleased at the visit from members of An Garda Síochána. After about an hour, Inspector Culhane came out of the interview room and spoke to Tom and me. He looked as pleased as punch and I knew he had good news for us.

He told us that McAleavy had confessed to killing the three soldiers, and that Chief Superintendant Murphy and he were now going to take a detailed statement from him. There was widespread relief and a sense of quiet jubilation felt by all in Gallows Green on hearing the dramatic breakthrough in the case. It had been an intolerable strain on the officers and the men and women of the 52nd Battalion to have watched McAleavy strut around the camp day after day, knowing that he was the prime and only suspect in the merciless killing of their three comrades. One of the senior army officers told me that some of his men had been close to breaking point, especially close friends of the murdered soldiers. He felt that if the matter wasn't resolved, there was a real risk that one of them might have taken the law into his own hands. The shocking events at Tibnin Bridge coming so soon after the start of their tour of duty had dealt a terrible blow to the morale of the battalion.

On hearing that Private McAleavy had admitted to the killings, Commandant Eamon Moriarty of the Military Police was highly optimistic that morale would be restored and things would return to normal once McAleavy was taken back to Ireland. Around midday, Tom and I took over from our colleagues. They had taken a full written statement from McAleavy, and when we entered the room he was sitting quietly, and looked calm and relaxed. We introduced ourselves and after the usual legal formalities began to question him about what had happened that night at the checkpoint at Tibnin Bridge. He first asked us to contact his father in Belfast and to explain to him what had happened. Tom agreed to look after that matter. He then looked up and in a steady, unemotional voice he said:

'The situation built up because of stubbornness. When the jeep left, the aggro started between Corporal Morrow and me. I am sorry now that I didn't tell the truth that first day. Morrow made me get up off the chair and sent me to the sandbags on the bridge. I was fucking annoyed by him. I told him to fuck off or I would burst him. I started to go to the sandbag position and he started to act the cunt just to show he was giving the orders. I was at the sandbag position for roughly half an hour and I could hear the lads laughing. I got fed up and after a while I went back over to them and told Corporal Morrow that I wasn't going to stand there like a bloody idiot. That's when the real aggro started.

'I slagged him about his weapon. He told me he would fucking see to it that I would be going home on the next chalk. I started to walk away, as I was getting fed up with them. I turned away and cocked my rifle. Turned again and started to fire automatic at them, starting with Morrow and then to my left. They were all sitting down on chairs. They fell to the ground. I went up to them and finished them off. The spare magazine I had I got from one of the lads going back out of the 51st Battalion and I got rounds of ammunition from other lads going back.'

As he was relating this account, he did not display the remotest sign of remorse. I realised that I was in the company of one of the most ruthless, cold-blooded, psychopathic killers I had ever met or would be likely to meet again. Detective Sergeant Connolly and I took notes.

Then, with a sigh of relief, he said, 'Boys, I feel a lot better now that I have told ye what happened and I'm glad ye came.' When I told him that I was still a little confused about certain aspects of what he had told us in relation to locations and directions, he drew us a remarkably detailed plan of the murder scene. As he was drawing this plan, he gave us a running commentary on the events as they happened.

In fact, McAleavy was quite the artist. A pencil sketch he had drawn and signed 'Mike '82' is a chilling depiction of a soldier holding a rifle with rivulets of blood dripping over his head (see picture section). Lying on the ground behind this soldier is the prostrate body of someone with blood flowing from a head wound. There is a circle drawn to show the point where the bullet entered the head. This drawing is disturbingly prophetic of the dreadful scene enacted by McAleavy within the year.

Late in the afternoon, members of the Military Police took charge of Private McAleavy, as he was now their prisoner. After I left the interview room, I spoke to Inspector Culhane and Chief Superintendant Murphy about McAleavy, and repeated to them what he had told us. He had made the same confession to them, but in even greater detail. Inspector Culhane said that when they had entered the interview room that morning, McAleavy had been aggressive and abusive to them, saying, 'Did you not know I am a fucking werewolf? I shoot everybody. I go around and shoot up this fucking world.'

I later learned that the catalyst for the killing had been an altercation between McAleavy and a member of the IDF at the checkpoint earlier in the day. Private McAleavy had demanded identification from the occupant of an IDF vehicle at the checkpoint and had been overruled by Corporal Morrow, who had let them pass through. McAleavy, in his warped mind, had perceived it as a humiliation and was seething with anger that had eventually exploded into an orgy of killing.

Late on the Saturday evening of 22 January, McAleavy was in custody and plans were already in progress to fly him back to Ireland. Colonel Anthony McCarthy, the battalion commander, had informed him that evening that he was being repatriated to Ireland, where legal aid would be made available to him. That night, we relaxed in the Officers' Mess and were treated to the legendary hospitality of the 52nd Battalion.

We spent the next couple of weeks carrying out further inquiries in the area. When the locals found out we were with the Irish Army, we were greeted with smiles and handshakes everywhere we went. We were invited into many homes for tea and coffee, and our attention was drawn to the Irish Flag and photographs of our president hanging proudly alongside their nation's flag and photographs of their president. The little children who followed us around could even speak to us the cupla focal that they had picked up from the Irish lads. It was obvious that they loved and respected the Irish peacekeepers and saw them as their saviours.

For our return journey, the UN authorities had decided to fly us by helicopter from Naquora to Beirut, but on the day we were due to depart they had to cancel the arrangements because of a prohibition on all UN flights by the Israeli Army. After a couple of days' delay, it was agreed that we would be escorted to the airport in Beirut by a contingent of French Army UN peacekeepers. We had an Irish Army driver assigned to us for the journey. The distance from Naquora to Beirut is approximately 60 miles. About halfway through our journey, which was painfully slow due to potholes and craters on the road, we saw a huge plume of black smoke suddenly billow into the sky ahead of us. The escort stopped and the captain informed us in impeccable English that he was not proceeding any further because of the bombs that had exploded ahead. He was returning with his men to Naquora. We had to drive on to Beirut airport in a single unescorted vehicle along a road where there had been numerous hijackings of UN vehicles.

For the remainder of the nerve-racking journey, I was up front with the driver, riding shotgun with a Gustav machine gun, which the corporal had handed me with a wry smile, cradled in my arms. He didn't relish the prospect of driving four civilians through that bandit country and I didn't blame him. Luckily, we made our way to the airport without any further mishaps. We said our farewells to our friend and wished him a safe journey back to the base. I must say, my three colleagues and I were extremely relieved when we eventually lifted off from Beirut airport. We had been in the Lebanon for about three weeks and although it had been a fascinating and unique experience for us all, we were happy to get home to our wives and children.

Once back in Dublin, we carried out further investigations in preparation for the forthcoming court martial, which was convened in a special building in the Curragh Military Complex in County Kildare in July 1983. The charges McAleavy was facing were: 'When on active service he murdered Private Peter Bourke, Private Thomas Murphy and Corporal Gregory Morrow at Tibnin Bridge, Lebanon, on the 27th day of October 1982, contrary to common law.' Private Michael McAleavy pleaded not guilty. He was defended by the eminent senior counsel Paddy McEntee. The current Minister for Justice, Michael McDowell, was a member of the prosecuting team.

The court consisted of five senior army officers in full uniform and was a most impressive affair, totally unlike any other court I had ever stood before to give evidence. Every morning, McAleavy was ceremoniously marched into the court flanked by two Military Police officers. The court, although faultlessly fair and businesslike, showed little tolerance for any form of repetitious questioning or perceived time-wasting by either side.

The legendary advocacy skills of Paddy McEntee did not prevail on this occasion and Private McAleavy was found guilty as charged. He was sentenced by the court in September 1983 to the mandatory sentence of life imprisonment.

The first day we attended the court martial we were invited to lunch in the Officers' Mess in Ceannt Barracks; however, because of some outlandish and arcane military tradition, non-commissioned officers were not welcome in the mess, and the invite was withdrawn the following day. For the rest of the proceedings, we decided to dine alfresco on the Curragh Plains.

Michael McAleavy was one of the most callous and vicious killers I have ever come across in my career. The murder of his comrades while on active service was an act of gross treachery and a crime unparalleled in the long history of our defence forces. One of the most poignant aspects of this case was that Private McAleavy should not have been on duty that night – he had swapped a shift with one of the other soldiers. Life for Irish peacekeepers in South Lebanon in 1983 was fraught with enough danger and hardship without having to cope with the added grief and corrosive anger in the aftermath of the murders.

Since the foundation of this state, there has been a long and proud tradition of friendship and cooperation between the defence forces and An Garda Síochána. During the Troubles in our own country, we stood shoulder-to-shoulder to defend our people from the deadly menace of the Provisional IRA and other subversive groups whose sole aim was to destroy our democracy and our way of life. My colleagues and I considered it an honour and a privilege to have been of service to our army colleagues in their darkest days.

This is part of a little poem that I composed and recited in Camp Shamrock a couple of nights before returning to Ireland:

The stars they shone and the moon was bright
When gunfire filled that silent night
As comrades rushed to where they lay
They cried aloud in wild dismay
And soldiers' tears, they fell like rain
To find Morrow, Bourke and Murphy slain.

22

MISSING PRESUMED DEAD

AFTER THE KERRY BABIES CONTROVERSY, I WAS TRANSFERRED AS detective sergeant to Sundrive Road 'G' District Southern Division in August 1986. I soon realised that there were many adjustments that I would have to make in this new phase of my career. I would miss the excitement and challenges that I had been accustomed to in my old job in the Murder Squad; however, I soon adapted to the less high profile but equally essential duties of a district detective. Although I hadn't applied for the posting, it turned out to be one of the most enjoyable periods of my service.

Around the time I arrived at Sundrive Road, the district was being plagued by a spate of armed robberies. Hardly a week went by without a raid being carried out on a building society or jewellery shop. I remember one particular day I was out with my men and we captured two separate gangs that had carried out armed robberies on two post offices in our district. We arrested them without firing a shot and seized their money and guns. At least three times a week, we would carry out early morning raids on the homes of suspected armed robbers. We recovered many firearms and a lot of stolen property, and gained valuable intelligence on the most persistent of the gangs.

Eventually, we gained the upper hand and succeeded in arresting and convicting their most active members.

Drugs were another major problem in the area. The trail of destruction left behind in the wake of that evil trade was everywhere to be seen. In the adjoining inner-city flat complexes of Fatima Mansions, Dolphin House and St Theresa's Gardens, and in our own district, hard drugs, heroin especially, were wreaking devastation on hundreds of families. Sons and daughters were dying of overdoses, contaminated heroin, hepatitis and AIDS- or HIV-related illness from the sharing of infected needles. On an almost weekly basis I led raids into those flat complexes to arrest drug addicts who had carried out crimes in my district mostly to feed their habits. On many occasions, we were met at the door by grief-stricken parents telling us that the son or daughter whom we had come to take away was dead and buried. All we could do was leave them in peace to mourn their loss and walk away mumbling condolences.

Aside from the human misery, we also had to deal with the emergence of organised drug gangs made up of young thugs who carried firearms as the tools of their trade and were prepared to use them in their turf wars.

I would learn in the most bizarre way that I and two of my men could have become casualties during a feud that developed between two of these gangs. One Saturday afternoon as I was working in my office, I was informed that an anonymous call had been received which stated that armed men had been seen going into a house near to the station. I got a search order from the district officer immediately. With these two other officers, I headed to the address armed with the warrant. We were admitted by the owner, who was a criminal himself but whom I knew as he had helped me out in the past. We found four notorious local gangsters sitting around the living room. They were nervous, edgy and aggressive and were obviously agitated by our arrival. We searched them for weapons but found none; however, under the cushions they were sitting on we found machetes, samurai-style swords, hatchets and hammers. It was evident that they had been expecting company, but not ours.

We carried out a full search of the ground floor, back garden and shed but found nothing else. We were about to search the upstairs bedrooms when the owner called me aside and swore that there was no one else in the house and not to bother searching upstairs. Ninety-nine times out of a hundred, I would have insisted on carrying on with the search, but this time, for some unknown reason, I decided not to. We seized the weapons we had found, then escorted the four villains from the house and watched them go their separate ways. There was no point in arresting such seasoned thugs, as I'm sure they would not have opened their mouths about what they had been planning to do with their array of deadly weapons. It was obvious to me that they were expecting a serious assault on the house by a rival faction, and they were fully prepared for action. For the rest of that day, uniformed patrols kept a watchful eye around the area but nothing else happened and I thought no more of the incident.

A couple of months later, we arrested Seamus 'Shavo' Hogan, an inveterate and incorrigible armed robber. Shavo had been one of Martin Cahill's most trusted henchmen. We had nailed him during Operation Tango and he had been sentenced to seven years' imprisonment for shooting at the police. In the course of questioning, he asked to speak to me alone. He reminded me of the incident a couple of months previously when I had surprised some of his associates in a nearby house and seized their stash of weapons. He told me that I and my two colleagues, whom he named, were very lucky to have escaped with our lives that Saturday. He went on to say that one of the gang had been hiding behind the shower curtain in the upstairs bathroom armed with a loaded pump-action shotgun and would have shot us dead had we confronted him. When he told me the name of the gunman, a shiver ran down my spine. He was a violent, sadistic psychopath who was loathed and feared even by his own kind. He was used as an enforcer by all the gangs: on one occasion, he had attacked another villain in his bed and chopped off most of his toes with a machete almost crippling him for life. When I told the two men who had accompanied me on that search, they were equally shocked at our close encounter with the grim reaper. Shavo himself was not so fortunate. In July 2001, he was shot in a gangland-style execution in Clogher Road in Crumlim.

I also investigated one of the most unusual cases in my entire career while stationed at Sundrive Road after meeting Graham Curtis-Hall, an undercover reporter with the British tabloid *News of the World*. He had been given my name by Inspector Mike Butcher of the Royal Society for the Prevention of Cruelty to Animals, whom I had previously had dealings with.

Graham informed me that he was working on a story investigating dog-fighting rings in the UK and Ireland. He told me that a vanload of criminals with pit bull terriers had travelled across to Dublin on the ferry from Liverpool on the night of 30 January. He said that the Liverpool boys had arranged to fight their dogs against Irish dogs for cups and trophies, and that huge wagers would be placed on the outcome of these contests. He told me the Liverpool gang were involved in organised crime and were highly dangerous men. The reporter felt he was risking his life in order to expose the awful savagery of dog fighting.

He then showed me several photographs of dog fights he had filmed secretly in a disused warehouse in Ballymount industrial estate close to the Crumlin area of Dublin. He told me that he had been taken to the warehouse by four young Dublin men early one morning. He pointed out a number of men in the photographs who had been fighting their dogs, including some of the Liverpool thugs. He also showed me some of the photographs of the dogs that had been fighting. Many had suffered horrendous injuries, including one poor animal that was missing a part of its jaw.

With the help of Graham, we later identified the warehouse where the dog fights had taken place and I had it examined by experts from the Garda Technical Bureau. The ring where the poor animals had been forced to tear each other to bits was swamped in blood. It was truly a disgusting and shocking sight. Graham stayed at my house that night for his own safety, and I escorted him to the airport the following day. We continued our investigations and finally succeeded in identifying at least ten of the people who were in the warehouse that day, including three of the sadists who were fighting their own dogs in these so-called contests. We subsequently interviewed these three individuals.

During a search of their homes, one of the culprits proudly pointed out a silver cup on the mantelpiece that he had 'won'. I took prosecutions against all three men and in September 1989 they were convicted in the Dublin District Court, where each man was sentenced to three months' imprisonment. The prosecution had been the first of its kind under the Prevention of Cruelty to Animals Act in almost 80 years.

Graham Curtis-Hall, who had given evidence at the trial, was some weeks later wounded in a gun attack in England by persons who were believed to have been involved in the dog-fighting business there. This was an indication of how far these cruel brutes were willing to go to conceal their 'pastime'. In January 1990, Detective Garda John Harrington and I were awarded the Irish Society for the Prevention of Cruelty to Animals (ISPCA) plaque, one of the highest honours the society gives, by the president of the Dublin District Court.

However, life wasn't always so fraught with danger or filled with glamour. I don't want to give the impression that it was all *Starsky and Hutch!* Most of our time was taken up in dealing with more mundane day-to-day activities, such as visiting and examining crime scenes, and carrying out investigations into everyday crimes such as car thefts, minor assaults and shoplifting. Statements had to be taken and file reports completed on each and every incident. When not engaged in such duties, we spent the day patrolling the district and meeting and speaking with the locals.

One of the detectives in Sundrive Road, Pat Munnelly, a kind and warm-hearted man, used to bring me on visits during our duty to the homes of many of our elderly residents. They deeply appreciated our courtesy calls. Pat and some of our colleagues in the Detective Branch also delivered Christmas hampers to some of the more needy senior citizens during the festive season. Pat showed me what real community policing was all about.

As well as looking after our own district, we were also called, from time to time, to assist in the investigation of serious crimes such as murders, rapes and shootings in adjoining districts within our division.

In October 1986, shortly after my transfer to Sundrive Road, I was called to assist with the investigation into the disappearance of a 13-year-old Rathfarnham schoolboy named Philip Cairns. His disappearance sparked one of the biggest search operations ever mounted for a missing person in this country. Philip left his home on Ballyroan Road, Rathfarnham, at around 1.30 p.m. on Thursday, 23 October 1986, to return to his school, Colaiste Eanna, a 15-minute walk from his house. Philip had only started secondary school that September. Before he left the house, he said goodbye to his grandmother. Although other members of the family were present, no one else saw him leave. He never turned up at school that afternoon.

Philip's mother came home from the city that evening and one of her daughters told her that Philip hadn't come home from school. She later checked with the school and one of the teachers told her that Philip hadn't returned there after lunch. By now, the whole family was beginning to get really worried. Philip was a sensible boy who had kept very much to the same daily routine and was not the type to go wandering off without telling his family.

His mother next went to check with Philip's best friend. It was about half past six and worry was giving way to panic. His friend's father telephoned Rathfarnham Garda station with details of the missing boy and an investigation got under way immediately. The next morning, I turned up at the first conference in Rathfarnham station. It was attended by at least 60 detectives and uniformed Gardaí. Many of us present had boys the same age as Philip attending Colaiste Eanna and other schools in the same area. The prospect of a similar fate befalling one of our children gave a grave sense of urgency to the inquiry. From the outset, we believed we were dealing with abduction or worse and I feared, almost from the very beginning, we would never find him alive.

It was hardly credible that he could have disappeared without a trace on one of the busiest roads in South Dublin in broad daylight without somebody noticing something unusual. Yet there had been no reports of a child being dragged into a car, or of any struggle or altercation involving a young boy, or of any shouts and screams being heard in the vicinity. We had no crime scene, which was going to make our job all the more difficult and seriously diminish our chances of bringing the case to a successful conclusion.

The usual questionnaire teams had been sent out to do house-to-house inquiries along Ballyroan Road and adjoining streets. Checkpoints were set up at all the major junctions and motorists were questioned. Appeals were made through all the media outlets for any information that might lead to Philip's whereabouts. A massive search operation was commenced that day involving hundreds of volunteers, specially trained Gardaí search teams with sniffer dogs, and members of the civil defence forces. For days and weeks, these extensive and exhaustive searches went on unabated. We combed through every piece of waste ground and parkland, and along every riverbank and laneway. Garda underwater units examined ponds, lakes and quarry holes. Garda and civilian teams searched the local Featherbed mountains, but these all proved fruitless. Meanwhile, many other detectives, myself included, were searching every house within a half-mile radius of Ballyroan Road. Each room in each house and every garage, outhouse and shed were entered and examined. On the very few occasions where we met with opposition to our request, a guard was kept on the house until a warrant could be obtained and the dwelling searched. All known sex offenders in the country were questioned regarding their movements between 1 p.m. and 2 p.m. on the day Philip disappeared.

A week after Philip's disappearance, in a dramatic development that brought about a ray of hope, his schoolbag was found in a laneway off Ballyroan Road close to his home. When it was examined, a number of his school books were missing. The bag was bone dry when it was found even though it had been raining heavily that night, so it was obvious that it had been placed there only a short time before it was found; and besides, those laneways had been thoroughly searched already. The bag was subsequently taken to Rathfarnham Garda station and was examined by experts from the Technical Bureau but nothing of evidential value was uncovered.

The finding of the schoolbag led to much speculation, conjecture and theorising amongst us all. Had Philip's abductor brought it back to the laneway, and if so, for what purpose? Why would the culprit, after carrying out such a serious crime, risk being seen and possibly identified as he dropped the bag in the laneway? There was also the innocent explanation that other school children had found the bag after it had been discarded by Philip's abductor and had stolen some books out of it and thrown it away in the laneway. Even so, the person or persons who left it there might have provided vital information if they had come forward and told us how the schoolbag had come into their possession.

The finding of the schoolbag did not in the end bring us any closer to solving the case and it still remains a baffling mystery to this day.

Because of the widespread publicity surrounding the case, we received hundred of calls on the special telephone lines in the incident room. Many were genuine and helpful, but a small percentage of them were malicious and evil hoaxes.

We also had a number of calls from psychics, who let us know that they knew where Philip Cairns was being held captive. A couple of these people called in person to the station and pinpointed certain locations on maps using the pendulum method. This is a technique used by psychics, which involves dangling an object on a piece of string over a map to pinpoint locations. We searched every place they had indicated, no matter how far-fetched or outlandish the information seemed. One of these alleged psychics, an elderly lady, told us that Philip had been abducted by a satanic cult who intended to make a human sacrifice of him on Hallowe'en inside the 'Hellfire Club' in the nearby Dublin mountains. The Hellfire Club is situated on Montpelier Hill and is one of Dublin's best-known landmarks. It was originally built as a hunting lodge but was later used by members of this secret society, which was associated with occult practices such as the Black Mass.

Yet another of them told us that Philip was being held prisoner by a religious cult in an empty warehouse on the Dock Road in Limerick city, and they were also going to make a human sacrifice of him on Hallowe'en. We took no chances, no matter how bizarre the information was, and contacted our colleagues in Limerick city, who carried out a thorough search but found nothing.

I myself spent Hallowe'en sitting in a car with a group of armed detectives keeping the Hellfire Club under observation. We had moved into position at about eleven o'clock and remained there until dawn the following morning. We neither heard nor saw any black-robed satanists during that long, cold night. The only visitors were the occasional deer foraging in the woods.

In the weeks and months that followed, we pursued every lead and investigated every scrap of information but went down one blind alley after another. The flood of information then flowed to a trickle and the investigation slowly wound down. Eighteen years on, Philip Cairns's disappearance remains as much a mystery as ever. I am convinced that Philip was inveigled into a vehicle by a friend of the family or somebody he knew and trusted. He would not have taken a lift from a stranger and the seeming absence of any struggle or resistance on his part would lend credence to those assumptions. Various detective sergeants in Rathfarnham have kept the file on this crime open, and we are all still hopeful that a breakthrough will eventually come in this intriguing, tragic case.

I, like many of my colleagues who worked on the case, have a deep and lasting regret that we failed to find Philip, or arrest the person who abducted or murdered him. Almost every day as I drive along Ballyroan Road past his house, I am reminded of the ongoing agony of his family. I remember the smiling, trusting face of little Philip and curse the perverted monster who blighted his young life all those years ago.

The Cairns family are, unfortunately, only one of a growing number of families who have been consigned to a life of perpetual despair by the disappearance without trace of a loved one. Over 1,000 people go missing every year in Ireland. Almost all show up unharmed within 24 hours; however, a small number of them are never seen again.

Many explanations for this have been put forward by various experts, and missing-person support groups and organisations. Some people decide to disappear for ever because of domestic or monetary pressures, and move abroad and never contact family or friends again. Others, who suffer from various psychiatric illnesses and are in and out of various mental institutions all their lives, eventually decide to end their lives in such a manner that their bodies are never found. There remains a small percentage, how small I cannot say, who I believe are murdered and their bodies disposed of probably, and most likely, by secret burial.

One such person who, we believe, fitted into the latter category was a young Dutch woman called Leidy Kaspersma. During the early '70s, Leidy was living in a hippy commune near Kenmare, County Kerry. She left one morning in a car with her boyfriend, a long-haired university dropout, to collect their dole in the town. Leidy never arrived there. When questioned later about her disappearance, her boyfriend seemed evasive and aggressive, and gave contradictory accounts of what had happened. He basically said that they had a blazing row on the way and, at her request, he stopped the car and she got out and ran away. He continued into the town on his own never to see her again. In fact, he never reported her missing to the police and told the others in the commune that she had gone back to Holland.

In 1982, the case was reopened but it was still only a missing persons inquiry as her body had not been found. I was assigned to the case, along with another detective sergeant from the bureau. We did our best, but it was a pretty hopeless task, as most of the people who could help us were living a nomadic lifestyle and couldn't be traced. After we had exhausted all our leads in that area our inquiries led us to England in a bid to track down the main suspect. After intensive investigations with the help of several local police forces, we finally traced him to another hippy commune in Penzance in Cornwall. We contacted his common-law wife who told us that our suspect had long since disappeared. She said she remembered that the last time she had spoken to him was after he had returned from Ireland. The dates that she gave us roughly coincided with the date that Leidy Kaspersma had vanished. We spent a couple of days with her and finally gained her confidence. She then told us that around the time he came back from Ireland he got drunk with her one night and broke down and cried. She asked what was wrong and all he said was, 'I've done a terrible thing.' He seemed so remorseful that she had pressed him time and time again to tell her what he had done, but he had said no more. He left the following morning and she never heard from him again.

She learned afterwards that he had gone to Beirut to teach English and was killed in a bomb explosion. He had taken to his grave the tragic secrets of what really happened to that young woman, as her body was never found. Leidy is just another statistic in a growing number of missing women.

Between 1993 and 1998, eight young women in the province of Leinster vanished into thin air without explanation. During a recent radio interview I gave my considered opinion, as an experienced detective who has been involved in many murder investigations, that I believe most, if not all, of the missing women were the victims of a serial killer. I told the interviewer that only in the context of a serial killer being responsible could one find any rational explanation for the disappearance of so many women often in broad daylight and all within a specific area of the country. I postulated that the killer was male with limited social skills, was under 40 years of age, and targeted an area of the country where he worked or lived. From my knowledge of the profiling of serial killers, I believe that he is a cunning, cold-blooded and organised murderer who is improving his modus operandi with every crime.

In all eight disappearances, he left not one iota of evidence behind. In all eight cases, there was no crime scene, no screams for help, no sightings of suspicious strangers or vehicles in the area, no items of personal property, such as handbags or cosmetics, left behind by the victims, and, most tragic of all, none of their bodies has ever been found. Concealment of a victim's body is one of the hallmarks of a serial killer. Criminologists, police forces and law enforcement agencies around the world, who study and deal with this ever-growing menace, have proven that this type of murderer kills, and kills repeatedly, until he is caught and imprisoned or dies.

Thankfully, there have been no other reports of disappearances which fit this particular pattern since 1998. I can only surmise that the killer of these missing women has been arrested and imprisoned for other serious crimes, has left the jurisdiction or is dead. The fact that John Crerar was convicted and imprisoned for murder, and Laurence Murphy was convicted of kidnapping and rape, both since 1998, may also be highly significant. In July 1999, John Crerar, an ex-Irish Army sergeant from Woodside Park, County Kildare, was arrested for the murder of a young woman, Phyllis Murphy, who had been abducted in Newbridge in December 1979. Her body was discovered four weeks later in the Wicklow Gap. A blood sample he had given almost 19 years previously was matched by the process of DNA profiling to a sample of semen found in the murdered woman's body, and was instrumental in securing a conviction. He is now serving life imprisonment for the murder of Phyllis Murphy.

Larry Murphy, a carpenter from Baltinglass, County Wicklow, who was convicted in May 2002 of the kidnapping, rape and attempted murder of a young woman, is now serving 15 years. Murphy abducted the young girl from Carlow town in February 2000. He then brought her on a terrifying journey across country while bound and gagged in the boot of his car. Having driven about twenty miles, he finally stopped his car in a forest clearing about three miles from his own home in Baltinglass, County Wicklow, in the foothills of the Wicklow

Mountains. There he subjected his victim to a series of ferocious sexual assaults. He was about to suffocate her to death with a plastic bag when he was interrupted by the arrival on the scene of two men who were out shooting foxes.

All the evidence would suggest that Murphy had fully intended to kill her and conceal her body somewhere in the forest. This young woman's escape from the clutches of that madman was little short of miraculous. The efficiency, brutality and daring with which he had carried out the abduction of his victim, the violent sexual assaults he inflicted on her and his deadly intent to murder her must surely indicate that she was not Murphy's first victim.

His previous predatory sexual behaviour and the opportunity he had as he drove about on his business to target and abduct a suitable victim must surely mark him out as a prime suspect in the abduction and murder of at least some of the missing women. He has already been interviewed on a number of occasions by detectives investigating these disappearances but has refused to cooperate and shown no signs of remorse or regret for his heinous crimes.

In the future we will inevitably face the prospect that other sick psychopaths will emerge in our society, who will abduct and murder women. We should be prepared to meet this challenge by having skilled police officers trained in the art of psychological profiling to identify likely suspects. The Behavioural Science Unit at the FBI's headquarters in Quantico, Virginia, leads in this field and through this method has solved hundreds of serial-type murders across the United States.

The FBI estimates that at any time upwards of 50 or 60 serial killers are operating across the United States. These are chilling figures and we cannot afford to be complacent in Ireland. We should also consider amending the law to force suspects in all crimes of murder, abduction, unlawful imprisonment and rape to provide blood samples. If these samples were held on a national DNA database, they might one day prove to be vital evidence in identifying the killer of the missing women should the bodies ever be found.

Equally vital to the efficacy of the justice system is that such a database could prove the innocence of a suspected murderer. Indeed, in recent years, DNA evidence has resulted in the acquittal of convicted murderers in the US who were on death row awaiting execution.

Evil men like Crerar and Murphy, and other killers who have not yet been brought to justice, have robbed the grieving families of these missing women of any hope of happiness or peace this side of the grave. They have been condemned to a living hell of intolerable pain and endless suffering that no balm can soothe or heal.

Mary Phelan, a sister of the missing woman Jo-Jo Dollard, and her husband, both dignified and courageous people, have been calling over the last number of years for a missing persons unit to be set up in An Garda Síochána. Along with John McGuinness, a Dáil deputy, they have campaigned tirelessly, even travelling to the United States to further their knowledge by meeting with members of the FBI who work in the missing persons bureau there.

In light of recent events, I believe that it is now time that a properly staffed and funded missing persons unit be established in An Garda Síochána. Knowing that the cases on the missing persons were open and active and being dealt with by highly trained, specialised staff would be a source of tremendous encouragement, hope and consolation to those grieving families.

23

IN COLD BLOOD

IN MARCH 1992, I WAS INVOLVED IN AN INVESTIGATION INTO THE knifing of a young man on Balfe Road in Walkinstown in Dublin. It was the first murder in the area for some years and it shocked the people of the community. Keith Wall, a 19-year-old apprentice mechanic attached to the Irish Army Corps at Baldonnell aerodrome and barracks, and his friend, Robert Banks, were attacked by a number of youths at the junction of Balfe Road and Bunting Road as they were returning home one night. Keith was a handsome, outgoing young man who was widely respected in the area because of his involvement in the local youth club and other youth groups. In the mêlée, one of the assailants stabbed Keith through the heart. He died shortly afterwards in hospital. Later that evening, a 15-year-old local youth, who cannot be named for legal reasons, was arrested for the murder. I was part of a team that interviewed him at Crumlin Garda station. The following day, I charged him with assault occasioning actual bodily harm on Keith Wall and brought him before the Dublin District Court, where he was formally charged and remanded in custody.

In April, I further charged the youth with the murder of Keith Wall and he later stood trial at the Central Criminal Court. That day, on the instructions of the DPP, the charge of murder was withdrawn. The youth pleaded guilty to manslaughter. He was sentenced to four years' detention in Trinity House School in County Dublin, a secure unit for young offenders with a liberal and relaxed regime, run much like a boarding school with cells. Later that day, I escorted him in handcuffs to begin his education in that institution. On the way there in the car he showed neither remorse nor any real understanding of the suffering and heartbreak he had inflicted on the Wall family. A few months later he would be back at home enjoying the festive period with his family.

That Christmas, I had a visit at the station from Keith's angry and distraught parents, Eric and Annette Wall. Their young son was dead, yet because of the abject failure of the judicial system their son's killer was back home after spending a total of just five months at Trinity House. They also could not comprehend how, having been sentenced to two months' detention at the Children's Court in February that year, the young killer had been released by the judge because no suitable place could be found for him.

The following year, I was involved in an investigation into another tragic death that was almost a carbon copy of the killing of Keith Wall. In August 1993, Glen Ward, a 16-year-old youth, was stabbed to death in Cooley Road in Drimnagh. He was an enterprising, responsible young man with his own fuel-delivery business and was a mainstay in supporting the family despite his youth.

After a brief investigation, I charged a local teenager with the killing. He pleaded guilty to the manslaughter of Glen Ward and was sentenced to four years' imprisonment, which were suspended. He walked free from the court, as if he hadn't a care in the world, again seemingly oblivious to the desolation he had caused to the Ward family. Once again, I had the unenviable task of having to deal with the heartbroken parents of the murdered boy. Like the Walls, Theresa and Eddie Ward were angry and confused, and could not understand or accept the decision of the court, which had released their son's killer back onto the streets without any punishment whatsoever. I tried to comfort and console them, but no amount of soothing words and platitudes could hide the truth. The justice system had utterly failed them, as it had Eric and Annette Wall. Both families were left to cope not only with the unbearable grief and devastating loss of their loved

316

ones but also to endure the humiliation and injustice of witnessing the young killers walk away from their crimes without penalties or sanctions.

The cold-blooded killings of the two young men in separate knife attacks deeply upset me. I had witnessed at first-hand the horrific destruction that knives could cause in the hands of young thugs and I was determined to make some real effort to highlight the problem. I met up with some like-minded people and we formed a committee to lobby the government for a change in the 1990 Firearms and Offensive Weapons Act. We campaigned to have the Act amended to include the ban of sales of all combat-type knives and other martial-art-type weapons to anybody under 18 years of age, and the registration to be kept in all outlets where these weapons were sold to record the verified name, address and age of all persons purchasing such weapons. We also called on the government to announce an amnesty on a specified date or dates, so that knives could be deposited in special steel bins outside Garda stations or other suitable venues.

Similar amnesties had been held by the Liverpool, Manchester and London Metropolitan Police forces with enormous success and thousands of knives had been taken off the streets. We held a highly successful press conference at Buswells Hotel on Molesworth Street in September 1996 to highlight our campaign. It was attended by many people in public life and the CEOs of various youth organisations. A prominent Fianna Fáil TD in his address called for the legislative changes that we had been campaigning for.

Government minister Willie O'Dea in his response said that he would discuss the matter of tightening up the legislation governing the sale and availability of such knives with the Minister for Justice. At the press conference, a selection of deadly blades that were being sold across the counter in certain city-centre shops were put on display to highlight the availability of such weapons.

A spokesman for the Association of Garda Sergeants and Inspectors addressed the meeting. He stated, 'The number of youths carrying knives has greatly increased the serious threat to Gardaí on the streets. It is frightening to think that in spite of all the concerns that have been expressed over the years on this issue it is still possible for a young person to purchase a deadly army combat knife across the counter in this city.' Eric and Annette Wall and Eddie and Theresa Ward, the parents of the two murdered young men, also attended the conference. Their courage and strength were an inspiration to us all. Both sets of parents addressed the conference and spoke of the circumstances surrounding the deaths of their sons at the hands of knife-wielding thugs. They made a heart-rending and tearful appeal to the young men of the country not to carry knives on their person or to become involved in the culture of knives.

Despite the overwhelming support we received at the time and the blaze of media publicity, the government has not responded to date to our calls for a knife amnesty.

Hardly a month goes by without hearing reports of savage murders in which knives have been used. I am now calling on the Minister for Justice to order an amnesty along the lines of our 'Bin the Blade' campaign in every large town and city in the country. If only one life were saved by such an amnesty, it would be worthwhile: there would be one less family grieving the loss of a loved one.

Two years later, in October 1994, I was brought in to join a team investigating another cold-blooded killing, this time the shooting of Patrick Shanahan outside Sphere's health club on Drimnagh Road in Crumlin. Shanahan was a big, burly bear of a man, skilled in martial arts, with a volatile temper and a formidable reputation for violence. Even amongst the hard men in Dublin's criminal underworld, he inspired fear and respect. Unlike most criminals, who are born on the wrong side of the tracks, Shanahan came from a respectable, middle-class family from Kill, County Kildare. He was a well-educated man and had attended university for two years. He had drifted into crime when he had gone to work in England in his early 20s.

In 1981, he was caught red-handed during an armed raid on the home of a retired doctor who was also a well-known antique dealer. In 1985, he returned to Ireland having served a prison term for his part in this crime. In the intervening years, on the surface at least, Shanahan had seen the error of his ways and had reinvented himself as a successful, legitimate businessman. He still associated with the biggest gangsters in the city but had never been convicted of any crime in Ireland. He had just completed the refurbishment of 80 tenement flats in a run-down part of the north inner city and was engaged in the construction of a retail development in Stephen's Street, close to the prestigious Grafton Street shopping district.

When he drove into the health club that night for his weekly karate session in his brand-new Pajero jeep, death was lurking in the shadows. He was accompanied by a friend, and as the two of them arrived in the car park they were joined almost immediately by another. They chatted for a few minutes, then all three of them started to walk the short distance to the main entrance. Just as the first man had entered the doorway, a lone gunman, who was hiding in dense shrubbery nearby, walked up and shot Shanahan in the face at point-blank range. Only one shot was fired. The bullet entered his face beside his nose and lodged in his skull.

The gunman then exited through the adjacent pedestrian gate onto Drimnagh Road and made his escape on foot. I was at the scene with other officers from Sundrive Road within minutes of the shooting. We immediately began an investigation and cordoned off the scene. The victim was removed in a critical condition by ambulance to St James' Hospital close by. He died of his wounds two days later.

A full-scale murder investigation got under way immediately. The usual questionnaire and house-to-house teams called to every home and business premises in the vicinity. As a result of confidential information, a number of suspects were arrested and detained in Sundrive Road and Crumlin stations. One of those I arrested was Patrick 'Dutchie' Holland, who would later figure prominently in the Veronica Guerin murder inquiry. Holland was later released, as the investigation uncovered no evidence that he had any part in Shanahan's shooting.

Despite an intensive and protracted investigation, we made little progress in finding those responsible for the crime. We did, however, have one eyewitness, who had seen the gunman leave through the pedestrian gate after the shooting. He was one of the two men who had accompanied Shanahan when he was killed, and was also a close friend and an employee. He had been interviewed time and time again about the shooting, but he always insisted that he did not know and could not identify the killer. But finally, in early December, we got the breakthrough we had been hoping for: this witness at last decided to tell the truth.

I met him with a colleague of mine and he told us that he had known the identity of the gunman all along but had been terrified to make a statement to that effect. He said he now feared for his life. He told us that he could not live with himself any longer, as he felt that by keeping silent and allowing Paddy's murderer to walk free he was betraying the memory of his friend. He agreed to make a further statement in which he would name the killer. Later that evening, he and his girlfriend, along with my colleague and me, met in the offices of a local solicitor. With everyone present, he made a full written statement naming the killer and fully explaining why he had held back from identifying him on previous occasions when we had interviewed him.

The man he named had been a long-time associate and friend of Shanahan and had previous convictions for violent crime. When the statement was completed, he signed it and all the others in the room, including the solicitor, witnessed his signature. We had made a vital breakthrough and had solved the murder, and were quietly pleased that our persistence had paid off.

I immediately informed the officer in charge of the case of this dramatic development. He was as satisfied as I that once the Garda report, together with our recommendations, was received and examined by the DPP, directions to charge the suspect named in the statement with the murder of Paddy Shanahan would be given. In the Garda report, we had pointed out that our witness was prepared to testify in any further court proceedings despite real fears for his life in so doing. We also pointed out he had previous criminal convictions. The penultimate paragraph of the report stated: 'This file is forwarded for your information and for favour of transmission to the Director of Public Prosecutions for directions to have [Mr X] charged with the murder of Mr Patrick Shanahan.'

Between taking this crucial statement and receiving the response from the DPP, I had initiated an unofficial 'witness protection scheme' for this individual. With a colleague, I moved him into a secret location. We paid for his accommodation and, through our contacts with officials in the Department of Social Welfare, secured for him an ad-hoc weekly allowance towards his living expenses. It would take the murder of the journalist Veronica Guerin two years later for such a programme to be officially implemented by the Department of Justice.

The superintendent who was the officer in charge of the case had a number of meetings with the DPP in the weeks following the submission of the Garda report. The report and recommendation to charge Mr X with the murder was very forcibly put to him by my boss but to no avail. Needless to say, my colleagues and I, who had put so much effort into solving the case, were angry and bitterly disappointed by the refusal to charge our main suspect. The Director never even proffered a reason or explanation as to why he refused to sanction the prosecution of Mr X. We felt that the interests of justice would have been better served if the case had gone to trial and the jury had been allowed to decide on the guilt or innocence of Mr X. To this day, nobody has been charged with the murder of Patrick Shanahan, although the case was officially listed on the Garda crime figures in 1995 as 'detected'.

* * *

On 26 June 1996 at around 1 p.m., Veronica Guerin, a journalist with Independent Newspapers, was shot dead in her car on the Naas dual carriageway. When I heard the report of the shooting over the Garda radio, I was driving out of the car park of the Red Cow Inn. I was at the scene within a minute or two. The traffic was already piling up behind her car, a red Opel sports car, which was stopped at the lights near the junction of Boot Road with the engine still running. Shocked and frightened motorists had abandoned their cars and were standing around in a daze. Veronica was lying back in the driver's seat. I could see that she had been shot a number of times in the chest and the right side of her upper body. Her features were contorted in terror and her lifeless eyes were open and staring into eternity.

I identified myself as a policeman to those who had witnessed the shooting. They told me that they had seen a large motorbike pull up on the driver's side of the red car. The pillion passenger had aimed a handgun and fired several shots at the driver of the car, then headed off in a screech of tyres in the direction of the city. Both the driver and the pillion passenger were wearing full-face helmets. Within minutes of my arrival, dozens of uniformed Gardaí and detectives had gathered at the scene.

Veronica Guerin, a young wife and mother, had been murdered in cold blood. In the coming weeks and months, the biggest murder investigation in recent history got under way led by Assistant Commissioner Tony Hickey. He and I had been colleagues and friends in the old Investigation Section in Garda headquarters. Veronica, who was 37 years of age, was a pretty, vivacious blonde and a likeable, highly intelligent woman. She had been a superb athlete in her day and had represented her country in a number of sports.

She had joined the staff at the *Sunday Independent* in 1994 as their crime correspondent. Within months, she was showing the mettle that over the next two years would gain her the reputation as one of the country's finest crime journalists. Veronica had all the attributes required for her challenging and dangerous occupation. She was brave, resourceful and dedicated, and displayed a dogged determination to surmount any and every obstacle in the pursuit of a good story. In her crusade to expose the kingpins of organised crime in Dublin's murky underbelly, she put herself in danger time and time again. Colleagues and friends had advised her of the many real risks she was taking, advice she did not readily dismiss; however, Veronica was not the type of person to allow concerns for her personal safety to stand in the way of her chosen profession. It was those same virtues of zeal and passion for the truth, and her extraordinary personal courage, that would eventually lead to her death.

In January 1995, a notorious north city criminal and his gang pulled off a major robbery at the headquarters of Brinks Allied cash-holding depot in north County Dublin netting almost £3 million. In her column in the *Sunday Independent*, Veronica named the main suspect and wrote about how he had already been availed of a tax amnesty for money he had stolen in previous armed robberies. The following evening, Veronica was shot when she answered her front door.

The lone gunman fired one bullet from a handgun that struck her in the thigh, narrowly missing a vital artery. She later recovered from her injuries and, undeterred, carried on with her job. Nobody was ever charged with her shooting, but a notorious Dublin criminal, John 'the Coach' Traynor, was suspected of being behind the attack. He was taken in for interview by the Gardaí but released due to lack of evidence.

When she recovered from her injuries, Veronica turned her attention to the activities of John Gilligan. Although diminutive in stature, he was a vicious criminal who had specialised in the past in targeting warehouses and factories throughout Ireland. He was a prolific and daring armed robber who, despite his dwarf-like, pudgy appearance, had a malevolent presence that instilled terror in his accomplices and underlings.

By 1995, Gilligan was emerging as one of the new breed of top drug barons in the city. His new-found wealth and extravagant lifestyle was attracting the attention of the Garda serious crime and drug squads. He was at the time living in a lavish mansion in Enfield, County Kildare. He had built one of the biggest equestrian centres in the country close to his house and enjoyed all the trappings of a country gentleman.

Veronica was determined, as were other journalists, to uncover the real source of his riches. In September that year, she drove to his home, 30 miles from Dublin, to confront him about how he had acquired such enormous and instant wealth. When she arrived at the house, Gilligan opened the door. She had barely introduced herself when he launched an unprovoked and vicious assault on her. He punched her black and blue, and tore at her clothes like a madman. In his insane rage, he inflicted severe bruising to her arms, chest and face. The attack was so ferocious that she thought he was going to beat her to death there and then. She managed to escape in her car but was traumatised by her horrendous experience. Gilligan later phoned her and told her that if she reported this incident to the police, he would kill her and her husband and son.

Despite these threats, Veronica went ahead and reported the assault to the police. The *Sunday Independent* carried details of the assault later in the month. In November, Gilligan was interviewed by detectives in connection with the attack. He denied any involvement. On the directions of the DPP, he was subsequently summonsed to appear in the District Court charged with assault and criminal damage.

Gilligan had vowed to friends and foes alike that he was never going back to prison, least of all for an assault on Veronica Guerin. Her fate was sealed and the countdown to her murder had begun.

I was one of over a hundred detectives involved in the case. The cold-blooded, cowardly murder of a young wife and mother, and a journalist, sent shock waves around the country and beyond. There was a massive outpouring of public anger and grief over the atrocity. The government was outraged and saw the murder as an attack on one of the democratic institutions of the state. The investigation was one of the most wide-ranging, complex and demanding that I have ever worked on.

The two evil killers who had carried out the execution left the jurisdiction shortly afterwards. Gilligan flew out to Amsterdam on the day of the murder. The motorcycle that was used for the job was recovered from the Liffey shortly afterwards near the Strawberry Beds and provided the first big break in the investigation. One by one, various members of the gang were arrested and questioned, and confessed to their part in the conspiracy. A number of them turned state witness and testified in the subsequent trials against their former criminal associates. A witness protection scheme, the first of its kind in the country, was established to protect the so-called 'supergrasses' from fatal retribution from their erstwhile friends after they had been dealt with by the courts.

One member of the gang I was dealing with in Lucan told me that he knew where the .357 magnum revolver used in the killing was buried and he was prepared to help us recover it. This prisoner was a habitual armed robber and drug dealer. But he was prepared to help us despite the danger to his own life if his actions were ever discovered because even he was totally disgusted and sickened by the murder. Around three o'clock in the morning, we took him from the cells, handcuffed him and drove him in my private car to a location on the Old County Road in Crumlin. When we got there, he pointed out an entrance into a large private residence and told us that one of the gang had taken the murder weapon after the shooting and buried it inside the gates on the left-hand side. I removed his handcuffs and he immediately went down onto his knees and started digging frantically in the earth with his hands. He poked about in the ground for about ten minutes with no success. The gun was gone. He swore to us that it had been there, that it must have been dug up and moved somewhere else in the meantime. He appeared to be genuinely upset and disappointed about this failure. We shared his feelings but were satisfied that he had been telling us the truth that night. The following day, he was released as we had concluded he had no involvement in the crime.

The same day at our daily conference, it was decided to call in a specialist search unit from the army to carry out a detailed examination of the grounds we had been in earlier that morning. Despite a week-long search there, using specialist equipment and sophisticated metal detectors, the weapon was not found.

A week later this informant contacted me and asked me to meet him at the Papal Cross in the Phoenix Park. I met him at midnight, and he handed me a .357 magnum revolver wrapped in a tea towel. He told me that he thought it might be the gun used to kill Veronica. The news that I might have recovered the gun was greeted in the incident room with great excitement; unfortunately, we were to be disappointed once again, as ballistics tests ruled it out as the murder weapon.

Meanwhile, the investigation was going from success to success in Lucan. Two of the gang, Russell Warren, the bagman for Gilligan, and Charlie Bowden, who had supplied and prepared the weapon and ammunition, had turned state witness and were granted immunity from prosecution in connection with the murder from the DPP. They were, however, charged and convicted of other offences and sentenced to terms of five and six years respectively. They later gave evidence in the Special Criminal Court against other members of the gang, including Gilligan, and were accepted into the witness protection programme.

Patrick 'Dutchie' Holland, another member of the gang, was arrested in November 1997 in Dun Laoghaire after he arrived back in the country from England. I was directed back to Lucan to question him during his detention there under the Offences against the State Act. When he was being processed there by the custody sergeant, sophisticated bugging equipment was found in his clothing and shoes. During subsequent searches, further electronic transmitting and receiving devices were found in a house close to the station. I found similar equipment in a hotel room near Tallaght Garda station that had been reserved by Holland. He had intended somehow to sabotage the investigation by having all the details of his interrogation transmitted to a select audience, who would have assembled in either of the two locations. Perhaps he was hoping he might have recorded some breach of his constitutional rights or custody regulations that would have invalidated any admissions he might have made during his questioning there.

While in Lucan station, Holland admitted to being part of Gilligan's drug operation but denied that he was the hit man in Veronica's murder, although he was, in fact, the main suspect for the actual shooting. After the expiry of his period of detention, Holland was charged and remanded in custody on drugs charges.

A couple of days later, with a member of the Lucan team, I travelled to London to track down the source of the bugging equipment that Holland had set up. For over a week, we carried out extensive inquiries in most of the specialist security shops, wholesalers and manufacturers in the city. We had with us a photo album featuring some of our most high-profile drug dealers, including one of Dutchie Holland, which we showed in the various premises. Eventually, in a shop in north London an employee identified Holland as the man to whom he had sold the bugging equipment. He remembered that one of the items was a specially constructed shoe into the false heel of which they had fitted a powerful transmitter and receiver. Holland had paid £25,000 for the equipment.

I gave evidence at Holland's trial in the Special Criminal Court in November 1997. He was convicted on all the drugs charges and was sentenced to 20 years' imprisonment, which was later reduced to 12 years by the Court of Criminal Appeal. Holland was 58 years of age at the time and cut a pathetic figure as he was escorted from the dock to begin his sentence. Bald and slightly stooped, he had the ruined features of an ageing prizefighter. He was released in 2006, having served nine years.

He had had a privileged upbringing and a decent education, and on an earlier occasion, when I had asked him how he had fallen into his criminal ways, he had confided in me that he had never been in trouble with the law in his life until he was framed by police officers and jailed for a petty theft, a crime that he had never committed. The burning injustice that he suffered led to a hatred and resentment of the police and all authority, and condemned him to his life of lawlessness. In the intervening years, he had chalked up a string of convictions for firearms and explosives offences and had been released from prison in 1994 having served seven years.

In November 1998, Paul Ward was convicted of being an accessory before the fact to the murder of Veronica Guerin and sentenced in the Special Criminal Court to life imprisonment. Ward was the member of the gang who had disposed of the motorcycle and the murder weapon after the assassination. His sentence was subsequently quashed by the Court of Criminal Appeal. Brian Meehan, who was the driver of the motorcycle, was convicted in the Special Criminal Court in July 1999 of the murder of Veronica Guerin and sentenced to life imprisonment. He was a heartless monster who had celebrated Veronica's murder by throwing a party for his friends and associates, and who had boasted of the prowess and professionalism of the hit man.

Gilligan, the leader of the gang, was acquitted of the murder of Veronica Guerin at the Special Criminal Court in March 2001 but was sentenced to 28 years for drugs charges, the longest sentence ever handed down by the court in Ireland for drug offences. Gilligan appealed, however, and this sentence was reduced to 20 years.

The murder of Veronica Guerin marked a watershed in the violent, bloody but fairly recent phenomenon of organised crime in this country. It was seen by a shocked and outraged public as an affront to every norm of civilised society. Such was the universal furore that even a complacent and lethargic government was galvanised into taking action when confronted with the reality that the murder of a journalist was an attack on the very institutions of the state.

The Proceeds of Crime Act and the Criminal Assets Bureau Act became law in October 1996. The Criminal Assets Bureau, a multi-agency task force, is staffed by officers from Customs, revenue, social welfare and the Gardaí. The bureau has become one of the most potent weapons in the state's armoury in the fight against organised crime. The success of the unit has attracted the interest of law enforcement agencies from all over Europe.

I was a vociferous and passionate advocate for the introduction of such an agency. In the spring of 1996, I spoke at a number of political meetings to highlight the necessity for action on this issue. I warned again and again that unless we tackled head-on the godfathers of the burgeoning drug trade, the flood of dirty money into the country would in time become a major corrupting influence in public life and threaten the very integrity of our democratic institutions.

As a direct result of one such meeting, Michael Donnelly, a long-standing Fianna Fáil councillor and ex-Lord Mayor of Dublin, moved a resolution at a meeting of Dublin City Council for a debate on the issue. Subsequently, the Prevention of Crimes Committee of the council met to discuss how those same drug barons could be stripped of their ill-gotten gains. The seminar was attended by two senior officials from the revenue commissioner's office.

In May 1996, I spoke about the same topic at a public meeting with the Kildare Fianna Fáil Women's Forum, which was attended by over 500 delegates, including some high-profile politicians. My comments subsequently received widespread publicity in the media. The Criminal Assets Bureau remains a lasting legacy and monument of Veronica's tragic and heroic sacrifice.

Two films have since been made based on the events surrounding the brutal murder of Veronica. One of them, *When the Sky Falls*, was adapted from the book *A Letter to Veronica* written by journalist and author Michael Sheridan. Made in Dublin in 1999, the film starred Irish actor Patrick Bergin and twice Oscar-nominated actress Joan Allen, who played the role of Veronica. I was introduced to Ms Allen on the set. She was a beautiful woman with a gentle manner and a warm, friendly personality, without any airs or graces whatsoever. I met her on many occasions both on and off the set during the shooting of the film, and she also visited my home for Sunday dinner. During my conversations with her, I helped her to better understand the circumstances that led to that awful tragedy.

24

INTO THE SUNSET

IN 1997, I WAS PROMOTED TO UNIFORMED INSPECTOR. ON ONE LEVEL, I was highly pleased that I had finally made the breakthrough after having spent nearly 19 years as a detective sergeant. On the other hand, I was sad to say farewell to my friends and colleagues at Sundrive Road and Crumlin stations where I had spent 11 happy, successful and rewarding years.

I spent the next two years at Store Street Garda station in Dublin's city centre. It was the first time I had worn a uniform in 24 years. At first, I felt a little self-conscious, but after a few short weeks, I was relishing my new role as patrol officer. I was back on the beat again, pounding the pavements in hail, rain and sunshine, working the regular alongside my men.

In early 1999, I was transferred to Bray in County Wicklow as detective inspector, and in May, I was involved in the investigation into the murder of Keith Fortune, a young man who had been stabbed to death in the hallway of a pub on Quinsboro Road in Bray. Within hours of the killing, we had arrested the culprit, Richard O'Carroll, a local who worked as a builder. He was known as a hard man and looked the part, being almost six feet tall with a muscular physique. He made a statement admitting to the killing, and was later charged with murder and remanded in custody.

There was a christening party of a friend's child on the day Fortune was stabbed. A lot of alcohol was being consumed and towards the end of the night, O'Carroll accused Fortune of passing a derogatory remark about his little daughter, who had been born with Down's syndrome. He waited for Fortune to come out from the pub and then, without any warning, walked up to him and stabbed him in the chest several times. Keith didn't stand a chance. As he lay dying in the hallway, he cried out 'I don't deserve this! I did nothing!'

In all the statements taken from those present that night, no one recalled Keith Fortune ever passing any insulting remark about O'Carroll's little daughter or indeed anyone else. Keith was regarded as a good-natured lad, who had no violent tendencies whatsoever and wouldn't hurt a fly. It was a brutal, senseless murder and a shocking waste of a young life.

Almost two years into my retirement, I gave evidence at the Central Criminal Court in this murder case. During cross-examination, the defence counsel for O'Carroll attempted to besmirch my reputation, asking me if I had been forced to resign from An Garda Síochána. I told him that I had retired of my own volition. At this, the presiding judge, Mr Justice Paul Carney, asked him if he was making specific allegations against me of any wrongdoing in the case or in any other case I had ever been involved in. He said he was not and retracted his statement. He was pressed again by the judge to state clearly if he had any allegations of wrongdoing to make against me. The defence counsel replied that he had not and sat down. Judge Carney then stared at him and said, 'You have the will to wound, but fear to strike.'

I was excused from the witness stand and O'Carroll was later found guilty of the murder of Keith Fortune. He was sentenced to life imprisonment. O'Carroll's supporters caused uproar in the courtroom. One of them, who was wrestled to the ground, had a knife in his possession. O'Carroll verbally abused and threatened the judge and had to be forcibly restrained by the prison officers. He appealed against his conviction on the grounds that the trial judge had not instructed the jury that they could have brought in the verdict of manslaughter. At the subsequent retrial, the jury could not agree on a verdict and another retrial was ordered. The second trial was marred with widespread intimidation of witnesses, some of whom, fearful for their own lives, left the jurisdiction. The DPP, not wishing to proceed with another trial and with limited hope of success, accepted O'Carroll's plea of manslaughter and he was sentenced to six years' imprisonment, a small price to pay for his crime.

Four months after the killing of Keith Fortune, I was called in on the investigation into the murder of Raonaid Murray, a 17-year-old schoolgirl from Gleangeary. Raonaid was a beautiful, bright young girl. She was on her way home one night around eleven o'clock to pick up some cash before heading out for the night with her friends. As she was making her way through a laneway only a couple of hundred yards from her home, she was attacked by a knife-wielding maniac and suffered horrific stab wounds. She staggered out onto the pavement, where she collapsed and died.

Weeks later, we interviewed a witness who had been reluctant to come forward initially for personal reasons. This witness told us that she had identified the murdered girl from photographs in the media and had seen her on the night of her death close to the scene of the crime arguing with a young man, who had been dressed in a beige jacket and trousers. She described him as looking similar to Liam Gallagher from the band Oasis. We never established the identity of this man and were unable to back up this sighting with any other witness.

Despite the scale of the investigation and the taking of thousands of statements, we failed to find the person responsible for this brutal murder. At the time of writing, the investigation is still very much alive, but the murderer remains at large.

With my posting to Bray as a detective inspector, I had fulfilled my modest ambitions of promotion within the force. The position of DI allowed me an operational role that I would not have in any higher rank. It was my intention when I went to Bray that I would see out the rest of my service there. Bray is a bustling, prosperous place, and although cheek by jowl with the city, still retains the friendly, neighbourly atmosphere of a country town. However, an event forced me to question my continued service and commitment to the job.

James O'Connor, a 35-year-old married man, was shot dead at his home in Bray in 1983. A number of men were subsequently arrested and charged with his murder. O'Connor had been murdered as a result of a row that occurred in a local pub between himself and his so-called friends. Three of the men involved drove to his house and one of them, John Maloney, who was a member of the INLA, shot dead O'Connor as he stuck his head out of an upstairs window. Two of the gang were convicted on charges in connection with the murder and sentenced to terms of imprisonment. Maloney absconded before his trial and disappeared. He was not heard of again.

In February 1999, I was informed that Maloney had been arrested in Spain and extradition proceedings were under way to bring him home. In early March, I flew to Madrid with a colleague from the Extradition Section. We returned with our prisoner to Dublin and took him before the Special Criminal Court, where he was remanded in custody. Maloney, who was then 52 years of age, did not look like the cold-hearted killer I was expecting to see. On our way back on the plane, he spoke freely of his life in Spain during the years he had been on the run. He asked me to convey to the authorities and the DPP that he would plead guilty to the manslaughter of James O'Connor; however, he warned that if that plea was not accepted he would open a can of worms at his trial that would have implications for the administration of justice in the country.

As the case was 17 years old, I had great difficulty in locating witnesses. Indeed one vital eyewitness to the shooting told me that she would refuse to give evidence in court. In early January 2000, I visited Maloney in Portlaoise prison to serve an additional book of evidence on him in connection with his trial, which was due to commence on the 11th of that month. When I spoke to him, he was extremely agitated and angry and asked why his plea to manslaughter had not been accepted. I told him that it was the DPP's decision that he would be tried for murder. He again said that if his plea was not accepted he would make disclosures in open court that would be extremely damaging. He gave me a very detailed account of these allegations, which seemed to come straight out of the pages of a John le Carré spy novel. He told me that he was determined to tell his extraordinary story, even though he would be signing his own death warrant – he would be branded a tout and an informer, and would face retribution from his former comrades in the INLA.

As officer in charge of the case, I recommended to the DPP that the manslaughter plea be accepted not because of the threats this man had made but because in this case there was much difficulty with witnesses due to the large amount of time that had elapsed. I feared the case might be thrown out altogether if the murder plea was not changed.

Shortly afterwards, I was interviewed at divisional headquarters by two very senior officers, where I was questioned at length about my meeting with Maloney at Portlaoise prison. The interview was almost confrontational and somehow I was given the impression that my actions in the affair were entirely misconstrued, in that my insistence to accept the plea of manslaughter amounted to some form of impropriety on my behalf.

As the meeting progressed, I realised with growing anger and indignation that I was being interrogated like a suspect. As a seasoned old hand, I recognised in their demeanour, body language and barely concealed hostility that I had become their adversary. From their intense and penetrative questioning and the sly innuendos, I was left in no doubt that they suspected me of entering into some unsavoury pact with Maloney regarding his forthcoming trial.

John Maloney's plea to manslaughter was accepted. He was convicted and sentenced to a couple of years' imprisonment and afterwards left the country. Although this sentence was a totally unfitting punishment for a cold-blooded shooting, it brought some closure to the bereaved family of his victim, who had waited so long for the killer to stand trial. This whole affair left me with a sour taste in my mouth. It was the last straw for me. I decided to call it a day and retire as soon as the first suitable opportunity presented.

Later that year, I saw a notice in one of the Garda magazines advertising the post of head of security in Ireland of a major logistics company. I was successful in my application and the following day I submitted my retirement report. It was the briefest report I have ever submitted. It read, 'I wish to give notice that I wish to retire on the 21st of August 2000.' I retired after serving 33½ years on the force.

During my career, I had the privilege and honour to work alongside some of the most decent and honourable men and women that a man could ever hope to meet during life's travels. Some of those people I have mentioned already in my telling of the various investigations and incidents I was involved in. Although it is invidious to single out one name, I hope that I will be forgiven for giving a special mention to the late Detective Chief Superintendent Dan Murphy.

Dan was the officer in charge of the Investigation Section in Garda headquarters in the late '70s and early '80s. He became my mentor and friend. He was an extremely kind and humane man and an extraordinarily gifted detective who all of us in the Investigation Section admired and respected. Following the Kerry Babies case and shortly after Dan passed away in 1984, the unit that he commanded with such success and distinction was disbanded. In my opinion, it was a truly short-sighted and disastrous decision. I believe it was politically motivated because of the constant negative media blitz it received following the publication of the tribunal report.

For years, the Investigation Section, or the Murder Squad, was by far one of the most powerful weapons in the fight against organised crime and the rampage of murder and robbery being carried out by the Provisional IRA and other subversive organisations. Over the last few years, the value of human life seems to have been debased in Ireland. There has been a dramatic increase in the murder rate – in 2005, it was up by 47 per cent – and what is now of growing concern is the number of unsolved murders that are mounting up. The alarming increase in gangland-style executions caused by turf wars and fuelled by the ever-growing menace of the drugs trade in major cities is redolent of Al Capone's Chicago in the '30s. Only a tiny percentage of these murders have been solved. The ferocious hit men have been acting with impunity, carrying out bloody executions in broad daylight with little fear of the forces of law and order. We have to stem the tide of lawlessness otherwise the most vulnerable sections of our society will fall prey to homicidal drug barons and ruthless gang bosses.

Over the past couple of years, a number of high-profile murder-related drug trials have collapsed because of the flagrant intimidation of witnesses by the accused and their cohorts. Cold-blooded killers have walked free from the courts, and television footage of them giving the two-fingered salute of contempt to the laws of the land is a truly sickening and demoralising spectacle to behold in a democracy like ours. As a matter of urgency, the Minister for Justice should give serious consideration to changing the law so that vital witnesses in murder cases and other serious crimes would be brought before the courts to swear a deposition of their evidence before a judge. At the subsequent trials, if a witness became hostile because of threats or intimidation, the original deposition would be allowed before the jury to help decide the innocence or guilt of the accused. I believe that this one measure alone will go a long way in combating the insidious menace of witness intimidation that has blighted the administration of justice in this country in recent times.

The Minister for Justice should also explore a system that would allow witnesses, who have reported being threatened or intimidated, to give their evidence to the court via video link. I further call on the Minister to urgently examine the ludicrous and farcical procedures that have been forced on investigating Gardaí when interrogating suspects in cases of serious crime. When in custody, murder suspects in many of these drug-related gangland killings stare at a spot on the wall and never open their mouths, availing themselves of the right to silence – an archaic and outmoded practice, which should no longer be tolerated by our legal system, its having been originally enacted in a bygone era to protect the innocent. In addition, every four hours, under the custody regulations, every suspect must be taken to their cell for a little nap in case they get fatigued. Each interview is recorded on audio and video. The Garda interviewer must write down every question he intends to ask the suspect. If he asks the same question more than three times, it is regarded as oppressive questioning; any subsequent admission is deemed inadmissible by the courts. Having to operate with these rigid and unrealistic constraints, the interviewing detectives have no scope to utilise interrogation skills in eliciting any worthwhile information or to break an alibi, or try to convince the suspect to confess to his crime.

In my time, the legal requirement for a lawful interrogation was that the suspect would not be subjected to any inducement, threat or bribe that would make him confess to a crime. The current system imposed on interviewing Gardaí by senior management is unworkable, ineffective and a joke, and is having a profoundly demoralising effect even on experienced and dedicated detectives, and is a major obstacle on the fight against organised crime.

In many murder trials down through the years in response to defence cross-examination, I readily admitted that I had engaged in hard but fair interrogation of suspects and that it was no tea party. I also admitted to being an interviewer who would use every emotional, psychological and intellectual skill I had acquired to rattle a suspect in order to get at the truth. As a result of the current asinine regulations, the Gardaí are operating with one hand tied behind their backs. Confessions have slowed to a trickle and killers are walking free. To further compound this ridiculous situation, suspects at the termination of their period of custody are entitled to copies of their interview tapes. In many instances, these same tapes are played back in the local pub to the amusement of criminal buddies and to show insolence and defiance towards the Garda interrogators. In more sinister circumstances, gang bosses have insisted on listening to these tapes to ensure that their associates did not tout or inform on them while in Garda custody.

The threat of a bullet to the back of the head is a powerful incentive for any suspect to keep his mouth shut in these circumstances and again highlights the gross and unbelievable inadequacies of the current system.

I am calling for the re-introduction of a properly structured and fully resourced unit staffed by highly trained personnel, who are totally dedicated to the fight against crime. They must also be supplied with the tools to win the fight. The current period of detention for those suspected of most categories of crimes under Section 4 of the Criminal Justice Act, 1984, including murder where firearms have not been used, is a derisory 12 hours. It is a woefully inadequate period of time in which to process any person suspected of having committed such a serious crime. I believe that the law should be amended without delay to increase the detention period to 72 hours to bring it in line with the detention period currently permitted under the Offences against the State Act, 1939. It is a ludicrous anomaly that somebody suspected of the importation of illegal drugs can be held for up to seven days whilst a suspected murderer must be released after twelve hours. In a civilised and just society, the crime of murder is rightly regarded as the most reprehensible of all crimes; society shows its revulsion by imposing the most severe punishment on the offender including, until quite recently, the ultimate sanction of the death penalty. Despite reservations, I was glad to see the passing of that barbaric practice; however, the punishments handed down in our courts for this most heinous of crimes are nothing short of a national disgrace. They have made in many instances a mockery of justice and, I feel, have been offensive and insulting to the friends and relatives left to mourn their murdered loved ones.

When persons are convicted of murder in our courts, judges have no discretion but to hand down the mandatory sentence of imprisonment for life. However, a life sentence can vary from as little as seven and ten years to twenty-seven years' incarceration, as in the case of serial killers Shaw and Evans, who are now the longest-serving prisoners in the state.

I firmly believe that any person convicted of murder in the course of committing a felony such as rape, armed robbery or a drug-related crime, kidnapping or abduction should receive a mandatory 25 years' imprisonment without parole. I have been outspoken in the past, both in the print media and public airways, that this is my absolute belief. I have no doubt that if this proposal were enacted into law, it would prove to be a powerful deterrent and would dramatically reduce the spiralling murder rate.

I also believe that in a modern democracy like ours, the Dickensian practice of putting people in prison for non-payment of fines and other civil debts is an appalling waste of tax-payers' money and a ludicrous and outdated punishment. Surely it is not beyond the bounds of the Law Reform Commission or one of the many select committees of the legislature to come up with a more humane and cost-effective system. If this practice was to end, it would free up prison places for the real law breakers.

I welcome the proposed introduction of the new police inspectorate, which will act as a totally independent watchdog in monitoring the activities of the force. Because of the enormous power that is wielded by police officers, it is imperative that the guards should also be guarded. The vast majority of my ex-colleagues will accept and welcome the new inspectorate. Many years ago at an Association of

Garda Sergeants and Inspectors Conference, I expressed publicly that I had a wish that one day An Garda Síochána would get out from under the dead hand of the Department of Justice. I would still like to see the department sever that umbilical cord and allow the force to breathe the pure air of a separate and independent existence.

I believe that in a modern, mature democracy it is very unhealthy for the police force to be under the direct control of a political department. In such an incestuous relationship, there is always the danger that the political masters bend the will of a compliant police force to their own ends. History is littered with such examples – one has only to look northwards in our land to see the dire results of that collusion. We police this country with the consent and support of the people and must always be seen as their servants and never a tool of the government.

In the course of my career, I may not have always abided by the letter of the law, but I always tried to carry out my duties without fear, favour, malice or ill will, and with justice and fair play. From the very foundations of the state, we have been extremely fortunate that the people of this country have admired and respected the men and women of An Garda Síochána. We must always remember that we continue to earn that respect and admiration by carrying out our duties with humanity and humility. At our peril we forget that we are servants to the people and not their masters.

In the An Garda Síochána Act now going through the Dáil, provision has been made for the recruitment of reserve Gardaí. The move is bitterly opposed by Garda staff associations, which have vowed to use every means at their disposal to prevent their deployment on the streets of this country. The idea that these part-timers after one week in Templemore and a couple of hourly training sessions should be given the same powers as the regular Gardaí is almost beyond belief. It's a charter for cranks, busybodies and power-trippers. The concept of bringing these untrained individuals into the force, who might undo the work and reputation that has taken 80 years to build, is a risk not worth contemplating.

We are still waiting for the 2,000 extra Gardaí who have been promised for the past number of years. In view of the increased population, this figure should now be doubled and should include the recruitment of officers from the different ethnic groups that are now an integral part of our society.

Following my retirement in August 2000, I appeared as a guest on the RTÉ *Liveline* programme hosted by Joe Duffy. Such was the reaction to that and subsequent programmes I appeared on that I received a number of offers from various publishing companies to write a book about my life and times as a member of An Garda Síochána.

This book has been a voyage of discovery for me. It is not, nor do I claim it to be, a concise history of the past 30 years of life in An Garda Síochána. It is my subjective recollection of events and how they affected my life and the lives of the people around me. It is an account of my own personal odyssey. It has been a highly enjoyable and rewarding journey for me. As in all jobs, I have known success and failure, triumphs and defeats, but all in all I am without regrets. Most importantly of all, I have known the loyalty and true friendship of decent comrades down the years in good times and bad. I am proud that I have made some small contribution in the fight against crime.

> To laugh often and love much; to win the respect of intelligent persons and the affection of children;
>
> To earn the approbation of honest citizens and endure the betrayal of false friends;
>
> To appreciate beauty; to find the best in others; to give of one's self; to leave the world a bit better,
>
> Whether by a healthy child, a garden patch or a redeemed social condition;
>
> To have played and laughed with enthusiasm and sung with exaltation;
>
> To know even one life has breathed easier because you have lived –
>
> This is to have succeeded.
>
> Ralph Waldo Emerson (1803–82)

APPENDICES

Para 452: 'From the statements that are attached to the report the following sequence of events appear to be the exact facts of this bizarre, unprecedented case.'

Para 453: 'At about 12 midnight on Thursday, April 12th 1984, Joanne Hayes felt flushed and hot. She went out of the door into the farmyard. There, without assistance, she gave birth to a baby boy. She says she pulled the baby from her vagina and pulled the umbilical cord to sever its connection from her.'

Para 454: 'She states quite openly that the child cried and she held its neck tightly until it stopped crying. She placed it on some hay and returned to the house revealing nothing to her family.'

Para 455: 'She went to the bathroom, stayed there for some time, changed her nightdress, discarding the bloodstained one and disposed of it in a rubbish container outside the back door.'

Para 456: 'Her sister, Kathleen, who was around the kitchen, certainly became suspicious as she saw bloodstains on the kitchen floor after Joanne walked through.'

Para 457: 'Kathleen asked Joanne if she was all right, receiving the reply that she was after having a heavy period and also a request for some sanitary towels.'

Para 458: 'Joanne went to bed weak and weary thinking all was now past, and her secret for ever hidden.'

Para 459: 'At about 2.30 a.m. on Friday, the 13th Joanne again experienced the pains of labour, but she could not hide this fact and sought the assistance of her family.'

Para 460: 'When this baby was born, it breathed and cried . . . the scene was set for its imminent death and disposal by one caustic, though infinitely significant, remark by the baby's grandmother, Mary Hayes, when she said "one of his children is enough to have".'

Para 461: 'The child was then murdered and the conspiracy began to effect its secret concealment from the public at large; all except Joanne Hayes were unaware of the existence of the first-born baby.'

Para 462: 'There are ambiguities throughout the cautioned statements of the entire group.'

Para 463: 'How many of them were actually present at the death of the second-born child?'

Para 464: 'How did Joanne get the carving knife? Did she get it herself? Unlikely, more probable that Kathleen, as she freely admits, supplied it.'

Para 465: 'How many of them actually went to the west of Kerry to throw it into the sea?'

Para 466: 'These are points that can only be answered by the Hayes family or Miss Bridie Fuller.'

Para 467: 'Whether they were all party to the entire episode, or to specific parts of it, matters little.'

Para 468: a) 'Did Joanne Hayes have a baby outside the house at Drumcunnig, Abbeydorney, County Kerry, around midnight on the 12th April 1984? The answer is "Yes" because we have located the infant's body.

b) 'Did Joanne Hayes kill this baby? "Yes." She held her hand tight on its neck until it stopped crying. Even if she did not kill the baby by the free use of her own hands, she certainly committed a callous act by omitting to take proper care of the baby to prevent its death. The assertion in this case was basically that Joanne did not take care of the new-born infant in a manner in which she was required to. It does not matter whether that requirement was legal or moral. The legal definition is quoted on page 360 of the Dictionary of Law, L.B. Curzon, 2nd Edition, "Failure to take action where it is required."

'Surely a person would be required to protect and take care of a new-born baby.

c) 'Did Joanne conceal the child from her family and from the public at large? "Yes" – she told her sister Kathleen that she was having a heavy period outside.

d) 'Did Joanne give birth to a second baby in her bedroom at about 2.30 a.m. on Friday, the 13th April 1984? "Yes" – she and five of her family said she did.

e) 'Did Joanne kill this child? "Yes" – she and the rest of the family said she did.

f) 'Did Joanne and the rest of her family, with her Aunt Bridie, secretly conceal this body? "Yes." They all said they did.

g) 'Did Joanne and her family all cooperate in the child's disposal so that it would never be found? "Yes." They all said they did.

h) 'Did the family of Joanne Hayes, which for the purposes of the report and file includes her aunt Bridie Fuller, know of the existence of the first born child prior to being interviewed on 1 May 1984? "Certainly not." Why not? Because Joanne did not tell them. Kathleen approached Garda Liam Moloney on 2 May and said that Joanne had only told her and the family subsequent to their being charged the previous night.'

The conclusion to the Garda report reads as follows:

Para 498: 'Within the covers of this report and file is told a sad tale.'

Para 499: 'All the Hayes family was interviewed separately, all after a short period of time told the same basic story.'

Para 500: 'It may be said that inconsistencies appear in their statements, this point had certainly been accepted but while investigators are desirous of the whole truth, they have to settle for a part thereof on many occasions.'

Para 501: 'Throughout this comprehensive file the Gardaí totally accept that the Hayes family, with the exception of Joanne, knew nothing about the existence of the baby that was found on their farm at Drumcunnig, Abbeydorney, until after Joanne had informed Kathleen subsequent to their interview at Tralee Garda station on 1 May 1984.'

Para 502: 'There is no doubt that the Hayes family and Miss Bridie Fuller are telling as much of the truth as they desire about the baby born inside the confines of Joanne's bedroom in the old farmhouse.'

Para 503: 'They all knew that Joanne was in an advanced state of pregnancy and near due to be delivered of a child.'

Para 504: 'If they at some time submit that their statements are a tissue of lies manufactured at the whims of various experienced Gardaí, the burning question that they can never escape from is: "Where is the baby that Joanne was delivered of?"'

'They cannot now say that it was the baby in the pool beside the stream, they had their chance to do that but could not, because they did not know of its existence, but they did know that she had had a baby and they could not deliver it for inspection because they had witnessed its destruction and eventual disposition.'

APPENDIX II
Affidavit of Sgt G.P. O'Carroll

With regard to my recent notification of redeployment to computer section and reversion to uniformed sergeant, I wish to point out the following:

Since 11 October 1984, when the charges against the Hayes family were dropped, until Wednesday, 23 October 1985, when I was notified of my move, and with the exception of the days on which I was in attendance at the tribunal, I was precluded from functioning in any meaningful capacity with An Garda Síochána.

Prior to the commencement and subsequent to the ending of the tribunal I can see no reason why, and was given no reason why, I was not permitted to be employed in my normal investigative duties. Repeated requests for resumption of duties were refused without satisfactory explanation. The only explanation given was that this was the decision of the commissioner of An Garda Síochána.

I would point out that in addition to the frustration of enforced idleness, this also placed severe financial strain on my family, with all the consequent emotional strain and worry.

This period of enforced idleness, in addition to its devastating effect on my own morale, could not have been seen by my colleagues as anything other than an indication that Sergeant Shelly and myself were considered by the commissioner of An Garda Síochána as unfit for duties. During this period, it was repeatedly indicated to me by senior officers that their 'hands were tied in the matter'. It was also commented on in the media on several occasions that Sergeant Shelly and myself were being denied the right to perform our normal duties under such euphemistic terms as 'deskbound' and 'on low-profile duties'.

Having waited so long for the report of the tribunal, I was deeply gratified by the explicit exoneration of Garda behaviour made in the report. Although the judge had pointed to some deficiencies in the investigation, I felt that my part in the investigation had been fully satisfactory.

With the removal of these grievous allegations, I felt that public statements of support would be issued from the commissioner's office and that we could look forward to an immediate resumption of normal duties to which effect a written submission was made. It was precisely at this critical juncture that I became aware through articles in the media of an intention to transfer me. It was particularly distressing for my wife and my family to read in a newspaper that I had been transferred, and this before any official communication had been conveyed to me.

Because the intention of a transfer at this time, immediately following the publication of the tribunal report, could be easily interpreted as disciplinary in nature, and had in fact, already been described by the media as 'demotion', and because I knew of no reason and was given no reason for any action which could be construed as disciplinary to be taken in regard to me, I felt under the circumstances I had no option but to oppose a transfer even if the transfer was one that on another occasion and in other circumstances, I would have regarded as favourable, or at least not undesirable, such as transfer to a detective division in the city or suburbs. I had indicated therefore that I would oppose any transfer through internal review procedures. It was then with incredulity and resentment that I learned of my reversion and allocation against which I was entitled to no appeal before the Review Body. I have the following observations to make in relation to this.

Whereas a transfer to a detective division within the city or elsewhere could have been interpreted as a non-disciplinary action which in no way reflected on my competency or integrity, and which in fact could be in the best interests of the force, my allocation to a highly specialised, technical and non-investigative branch and my subsequent reversion to uniformed sergeant was interpreted by myself, my family, my colleagues without exception and the media as punitive. Attempts by the Minister for Justice in the Dáil to deny the disciplinary intent of this move were hollow and unconvincing. Considering the widespread public acceptance that this treatment of me was disciplinary in nature it was particularly frustrating to have been denied access to internal Garda appeal structures. The summary dismissal of my appeal for reconsideration of this action was a further source of frustration.

The manner in which I was informed of this allocation was most extraordinary. To be addressed by an assistant commissioner, who made no reference to any reason for this happening but who informed me that as and of that precise moment in time I was transferred and reverted to uniform must be without precedent in the history of An Garda Síochána.

The immediate implications to me of this move were obvious: a) I would be perceived in the eyes of the country as being effectively demoted and disciplined. I would point out that this was in direct contradiction of the tribunal's findings; b) I was to be denied any meaningful appeal internally within the force; c) I was to be placed in a situation of employment for which I possessed no technical qualifications, no known aptitude and no known aspirations and which was in direct contrast with all my previous proven areas of expertise; d) I was to accept that the disastrous financial repercussions which the Kerry Babies case had so far caused me and my family were to be continued indefinitely by the loss of my detective allowance, plainclothes allowance, overtime possibilities, public holiday allowance, and also night-duty and Sunday allowances, in connection with overtime, drastically reducing the salary to which I had been accustomed for the last five years and upon which my financial commitments and family responsibilities were based; e) I have been involved in the investigation of serious and subversive crimes which have resulted in potential danger to myself and even possibly to my family. In being reverted to uniform, I would now be expected to surrender my firearm, thus leaving me defenceless. At another time, I would not consider this relevant, but in view of the serious allegations made by Miss Joanne Hayes in her book *My Story* relating to the existence of a Garda unit under the command of Superintendent John Courtney and known as the 'heavy gang' and allegations of extraction by force of false confessions by the 'heavy gang', I now feel particularly vulnerable. I also feel that these scurrilous allegations have been given official credence by the disciplinary nature of the moves against me and the other members involved. Added to this is the failure of the commissioner of An Garda Síochána to issue any public statement of support for the findings of the tribunal and the exoneration of his own men amounts to a tacit endorsement of the claims made against my colleagues and myself by the Hayes family.

The intolerable position created for me by this effective demotion as well as the denial of the internal appeal mechanism has forced me to contemplate embarking on costly legal proceedings in search of natural justice and basic human rights for me and my family. In embarking on this procedure, I will be seeking to show that discriminatory treatment of Sergeant Joseph Shelly and myself, to wit the arbitrary denial of the right to perform our investigative duties or indeed any other duties except court appearances, the substantial loss of income suffered and the lack of support from the commissioner through our period of trial by the media constitutes a breach of basic rules of fair play and natural justice.

I will also be seeking to show that, far from being in the best interests of the force, this discriminatory treatment meted out to Sergeant Shelly and myself was seriously damaging to the morale of the force. I will be seeking to show in these proceedings that we have had the support of all the senior officers in the Technical Bureau up to and including deputy commissioner. They have variously described our treatment by the commissioner of An Garda Síochána as 'disgraceful', 'unprecedented' and 'completely unjust'. I will be seeking to show that remarks by the Minister for Justice in Dáil Éireann and widely reported in the media were pre-emptory and prejudicial to the interests of fair play, and contributed to the ongoing trial by public opinion and the media to which we have been subjected. All this was in stark contrast to the judicial findings of the tribunal, which exonerated myself and my colleagues of any improper behaviour.

Central to the action will be my desire to show that Sergeant Shelly and myself have been singled out from the 28 officers involved in the Kerry Babies case and have been forced into unwelcome idleness during this period. I have considered the possibility that the Minister for Justice's widely reported remarks concerning 'bad apples', 'one or more members found wanting' and 'no mercy being shown' have been taken by the commissioner of An Garda Síochána to refer specifically to Sergeant Shelly and myself. In view of how widely reported these remarks were at the time and in view of the action that has been taken in respect of Sergeant Shelly and myself since the publication of the report of the tribunal, I feel that the general public now have no option but to assume that the Minister for Justice's remarks referred to

Sergeant Shelly and myself. If these remarks were intended to refer to me, it is my opinion that they are intemperate, vindictive and a gross defamation of my character.

I would like to refer here to headlines in the *Sunday Tribune* of 27/10/85, page seven, 'Were the confessions rigged?' I would further point out an editorial in the same paper which calls for a 'hard line against the Gardaí who induced the confessions of the Hayes family in Tralee Garda station in May 1984'. In spite of the exoneration of Garda behaviour by Judge Lynch in the tribunal report, there has been no move by the commissioner's office or the Garda press office to issue any rebuttal of these malicious, unfounded allegations, which are a discredit to the entire Garda force. Rather there has been direct and widely publicised action taken by the commissioner against members of the investigation team, which cannot but by their implications give overt credence to the allegations. At this point, I do not think it inappropriate to make reference to my record of service, to my special promotion on meritorious grounds, to my repeated commendations in the discharge of my duties and to my involvement in many of the major crime investigations in this country and overseas (Lebanon) in the past decade. I would like to refer also to the fact that I lecture to classes of trainee detectives in the Detective Training School in the Technical Bureau on the subject of sexual crime. It is noteworthy that during my period of enforced idleness, when I was considered unfit to carry out my normal duties, I was still deemed fit to carry out this function which involved the training of young detectives, and also that during this period I delivered to the Irish Medical Organisation a lecture that received wide and favourable publicity, including radio and television coverage.

During my career, I have never been the subject of any disciplinary proceedings within An Garda Síochána or the courts. I consider that my career, which could have been fairly promising, has suffered grievously as a result of allegations made against me which were totally groundless, over which I had no control, and of which I have been completely exonerated.

I will exhaust every financial and emotional resource available to me in my attempt to redress this victimisation, to clear my name and to satisfy myself that the tenets of fair play and natural justice are applied to each and every member of An Garda Síochána. I hope that the result of this will be that I will once more be able to carry out my duties with the pride and pleasure I formerly embraced and which has lately been denied to me.

APPENDIX III

Internal memo re: leak to the media of Kerry Babies file

RE: Joanna [*sic*] Mary Hayes, Kathleen Hayes, Edmund Hayes, Bridie Fuller, Mary Hayes: Murder of unnamed infant, concealment of birth

1. To quote Frank Aylmer's minute to the Commissioner in the Private Bowe case, 'the prosecution of crime could be seriously and adversely affected if witness confidentiality were breached outside the area of criminal proceedings'.

2. Apart from its being a breach of the Official Secrets Act, the *Sunday Independent* article of 14th October 1984 on the Kerry Babies case was a flagrant breach of the above principal [*sic*].

3. We are frequently hung up on the fact that this Office is a prosecuting and not a 'complaining' agency. Nevertheless, I am surprised the Commissioner has not investigated that publication.

4. However, in this Report, Kevin Lynch has 'found' that the Kerry Babies file was leaked either from the Gardaí or from this Office. This 'finding' did not exactly flow naturally from his terms of reference. He need not have mentioned any source. He has specifically mentioned this Office. This is very serious.

5. To make matters worse, one of the rash of books on the Babies, 'Lost Innocence' by Barry O'Halloran, contains the passage which I showed you which, if true or substantially true, describes a source which does not read like a Garda source.

6. Leaving aside, yet again, the unfortunate deceased infants, when the dust settles on the Kerry case and report, the integrity of the Garda and this Office must survive. To that end, there should be some form of inquiry or investigation into the leak.

7. I suggest you have a statutory consultation with the Attorney General about the matter. It would be better if the initiative came from within than from without.

APPENDIX IV
The wives' statement to the media

We are the wives of Sergeant Joseph Shelly, Sergeant Gerard O'Carroll and Sergeant P.J. Browne, two of whom were moved from the Technical Bureau and one from Finea, County Cavan, following the Report of the Tribunal of Enquiry into the Kerry Babies Affair.

This action by the Commissioner of An Garda Síochána, which was given full national and even international headlines and television coverage, and which was described in several front-page articles as 'demotion', has been interpreted by the media as a clearly punitive action, despite a statement to the contrary by the Minister for Justice in Dáil Éireann. This, added to the fact the Commissioner of An Garda Síochána has issued neither a public statement in support of the findings of the tribunal nor comment on the exoneration of the Gardaí involved in the allegations of the Hayes family, has been the cause of great distress and public humiliation for our husbands, our families and ourselves.

We now feel that a very large section of the population has been led, or misled, into believing that our husbands were responsible for injustices to the Hayes family, guilty of negligence in their work and, as a result, responsible for the costly tribunal which followed.

Our husbands do not feel that they were in any way, by action or neglect, responsible for any of these things. Judge Lynch totally exonerated them of all the allegations and he did not point them out as being guilty of any of the 'deficiencies'.

They have been given no reason or explanation for their transfers. In fact, they have been offered no opportunity of any communication with the people involved in the decision to 'transfer' them. The method in which they have been moved, in the cases of Sergeants Shelly and O'Carroll, had deliberately and effectively denied them access to any form of appeal through normal Garda procedures. In the case of Sergeant Browne, a second transfer in less than a year would appear to be needless since it was his wish to remain in Finea, and he was about to move his family there.

The public nature of the announcement of their transfers immediately following the report has been the cause of great suffering to our families and that after the long ordeal of the tribunal and 12 months during which we had to put up with daily press and television reports, which treated the malicious allegations with total credibility, sympathising with those who made the allegations and castigating our husbands against whom they were made. We feel that the time chosen for this announcement was a deliberate appeasement by the Minister for Justice to the media and to minority public opinion, making scapegoats of our husbands and having no consideration for the feelings of the Gardaí and the families involved. We consider it to be a cruel and unjust act, which has cast on our husbands' characters a slur that will not easily be erased.

Our husbands all have excellent records of service with An Garda Síochána. They had great dedication, pride and pleasure in their work. In the years they spent in the Technical Bureau, their work caused personal sacrifice for them and us in that they had to be away from home for long periods, often when it would have been preferable to have been with their families.

This did not deter them from doing their work well, and we feel that their previous good records have been ignored in the way they have now been treated.

We appeal to you to consider if there is anything you can do to redress this unjust action, which has been the cause of a devastating blow to their integrity, to their personal reputations, to their morale and to the morale of the whole Garda force. We would like to see our husbands carry out their duties with the enthusiasm and satisfaction they formerly had.